Food Security in Asia: Challenges, Policies and Implications

Monika Barthwal-Datta

Food Security in Asia: Challenges, Policies and Implications

Monika Barthwal-Datta

The International Institute for Strategic Studies
Arundel House | 13–15 Arundel Street | Temple Place | London | WC2R 3DX | UK

First published February 2014 by **Routledge**
4 Park Square, Milton Park, Abingdon, Oxon, OX14 4RN

for **The International Institute for Strategic Studies**
Arundel House, 13–15 Arundel Street, Temple Place, London, WC2R 3DX, UK
www.iiss.org

Simultaneously published in the USA and Canada by **Routledge**
270 Madison Ave., New York, NY 10016

Routledge is an imprint of Taylor & Francis, an Informa Business

DIRECTOR-GENERAL AND CHIEF EXECUTIVE Dr John Chipman
EDITOR Dr Nicholas Redman
ASSISTANT EDITOR Mona Moussavi
EDITORIAL Nicholas Payne, Zoe Rutherford
COVER/PRODUCTION John Buck, Kelly Verity

The International Institute for Strategic Studies is an independent centre for research, information and debate on the problems of conflict, however caused, that have, or potentially have, an important military content. The Council and Staff of the Institute are international and its membership is drawn from almost 100 countries. The Institute is independent and it alone decides what activities to conduct. It owes no allegiance to any government, any group of governments or any political or other organisation. The IISS stresses rigorous research with a forward-looking policy orientation and places particular emphasis on bringing new perspectives to the strategic debate.

The Institute's publications are designed to meet the needs of a wider audience than its own membership and are available on subscription, by mail order and in good bookshops. Further details at www.iiss.org.

Printed and bound in Great Britain by Bell & Bain Ltd, Thornliebank, Glasgow

British Library Cataloguing in Publication Data
A catalogue record for this book is available from the British Library

Library of Congress Cataloging in Publication Data

ADELPHI series
ISSN 1944-5571

ADELPHI 441–442
ISBN 978-1-138-79247-0

Contents

ACKNOWLEDGEMENTS

This book is an outcome of a research project on 'Food Security in Asia: Strategic Challenges and Risk Mitigation' funded by the MacArthur Foundation, under its Asia Security Initiative, between January 2011 and March 2013. The project was located at the Centre for International Security Studies (CISS), University of Sydney where I worked as a postdoctoral research fellow between December 2010 and June 2012. I am grateful to the MacArthur Foundation for making this research possible, and to other members of the research team and former colleagues at CISS for providing an intellectually stimulating and supportive research environment for the project until my departure in mid-2012. I would particularly like to thank Professor Alan Dupont, former Director of CISS; Vivian Puccini-Scuderi, former CISS Centre Manager; Gemma Ashton and Erin Hurley who expertly managed the research project; and Christopher Baker for his research assistance in the later stages of the project.

In July 2012, I joined the School of Social Sciences, University of New South Wales (UNSW) in Sydney as a lecturer. I am grateful to my colleagues in the School for graciously supporting my efforts to fulfil my commitments under the research project and write this book.

As part of my fieldwork, I conducted interviews with stakeholders in the Philippines, Vietnam, Cambodia and India. I remain indebted to all those who gave me their time, contacts and invaluable insights on food security. I am also thankful to the editorial team at IISS for their time and support in helping to bring this project to fruition. I would particularly like to thank Nick Redman, Nigel Inkster and Sarah Johnstone for their inputs. Finally, I am grateful to Puneet Kumar Datta who is my pillar and a constant source of encouragement, support and inspiration.

GLOSSARY

ADB – Asian Development Bank

agflation – Price increases across a broad range of agricultural commodities brought about by increased consumption demand and the use of such commodities in biofuels production.

agribusiness – Large-scale commercial farming, including the production, processing and distribution of agricultural products and the manufacture of farm equipment.

agricultural extension services – Training and advisory services offered to farmers.

ASEAN – Association of Southeast Asian Nations

CPO – crude palm oil

FAO – United Nations' Food and Agriculture Organization

ha – hectare

IFAD – International Fund for Agricultural Development

IFPRI – International Food Policy Research Institute

monocropping – The practice of growing only one crop on the same area of land, year after year. This is undertaken to increase agricultural productivity and allows for specialisation of farming equipment.

SAARC – South Asian Association for Regional Cooperation

salinisation – The build-up of salts (such as sodium chloride) in soil which can damage soil fertility. This build-up can occur both naturally, as in arid or semi-arid regions where the rate of evaporation exceeds precipitation, and artificially through irrigation with water with high salt content.

UNESCAP – UN Economic and Social Commission for Asia and the Pacific

value-added agriculture – Agricultural business models that raise the value of primary agricultural commodities through production processes which transform raw commodities into higher-value products demanded by consumers.

waterlogging – The saturation of soil with water, such that land can become infertile.

water table – The upper boundary of the zone in which rock or soil is saturated with groundwater.

WDI – World Development Indicators

INTRODUCTION

Asia sits at the heart of global food security, with more than half the world's population and around two-thirds of global hungry and poor. How countries in the region, particularly China and India, feed their citizens in coming decades is vital to the wider security of Asia and the rest of the world.

The continent mainly comprises developing and low- or lower-middle income countries that are struggling to cope with the forces creating global food-security challenges: rising populations; shifts in consumption as the growing middle classes switch to more meat-based and resource-intensive diets; the 'exhaustion of the Green Revolution' as the gains in crop yields in the latter half of the twentieth century begin to fade; the loss of farmland to urban development; the depletion of groundwater resources for irrigation; the increasing interconnectedness of global food-supply chains; and the diversion of edible crops to produce biofuels.[1]

Left unchecked, these and other complex forces – from poverty and small farmers' lack of adequate land rights to the unpredictable effects of climate change – threaten the well-being of hundreds of millions of Asians. Yet developing countries with weak government institutions are particularly vulnerable to, and are ill-equipped to deal with, such difficulties.

Food insecurity has the potential to undermine political stability and to strain relations between states. Throughout history, civil unrest has broken out in the wake of widespread hunger and food inflation. During the protests that sparked the French Revolution, for example, rioters 'cried for both bread and blood',[2] and in Russia famine and poverty played a clear role in fuelling peasant violence in the revolutions of 1905 and 1917.[3]

More recently, as global prices spiked in 2007–08, there were food-related riots in countries such as Bahrain, Yemen, Jordan, Egypt and Morocco. All of these countries witnessed political upheaval in 2011 and long-standing regimes fell in Tunisia, Libya and Egypt. The increasingly unaffordable cost of basic staples was seen by many as an aggravating factor in precipitating the unrest – 'the final nail in the coffin for regimes that were failing to deliver on their side of the social contract'.[4]

In Asia too, governments in Bangladesh, Pakistan, India, Indonesia and the Philippines have faced the wrath of those most affected by rising food prices. Developing Asian nations have generally poor records when it comes to inclusive growth or socio-economic and political equality. Research indicates that these are the sort of countries where sudden jumps in food prices are likely to have the most damaging impact.[5] In 1998, for example, rising onion prices in India played a major role in the ousting of the ruling

Bharatiya Janata Party in Delhi state elections.[6] In 2007–08, violent protests against corruption and food shortages took place in several districts in the states of West Bengal and Bihar. Thousands took to the streets to protest against food-price inflation in New Delhi in early 2011.[7] Some 20,000 textile workers also took to the streets in Bangladesh in 2008, demanding higher wages to cover increased food prices.[8] Clashes – sometimes deadly – have occurred in China, Cambodia, Indonesia, the Philippines and Vietnam over the appropriation of farmland and forced land acquisitions (see Chapter Four).

The effects of a food crisis can transcend national borders. Indeed, in their efforts to blunt shocks to domestic food supply and to curb rising prices at home, governments often resort to policies that may hurt political stability and food prices in other countries. Asia is home to both major food-exporting countries (such as India, Thailand and Vietnam) and food-importing countries (such as Indonesia and the Philippines). The policies adopted by the former can affect domestic food security not just in the latter, but also in food-importing countries around the globe. For instance, when Vietnam, India and Cambodia imposed restrictions on rice exports during the 2007–08 crisis, there were fewer supplies on the world market for other countries to buy and global food prices rose, worsening the plight of poor people not only in Asia but also in Africa and the Middle East.

China and India are two of the world's largest food producers and consumers. Advances in agricultural productivity since the late 1970s have meant that both have managed to stay largely self-sufficient in the production of staple food grains, such as wheat, maize and rice, in the face of rising demand. However, overall agricultural imports have been rising, as each country has turned increasingly to international markets for certain food items. India, for example, now relies heavily on imports of vegetable oils and pulses to meet domestic demand, while China has been importing growing amounts of soybeans, edible oils and, more recently, maize. In both countries, environmental degradation, growing water scarcity, the use of agricultural land for other purposes and declining productivity raise questions over future self-sufficiency. If both need to buy more food on the world market, there are clear implications for global food security.

Indeed, while much of Asia today is able to meet its demand for staple food grains through domestic production, there are concerns as to whether the region will remain able to do so as the overall demand for food continues to escalate and the consumption of animal products increases.

The United Nations forecasts that the global population will grow to more than nine billion by 2050.[9] The UN's Food and Agriculture Organization (FAO) estimates that food production worldwide will have to grow by around 70% to meet demand from this much larger, wealthier and more urban population.[10] Although population growth in Asia has been slowing since 2000,[11] the region is still expected to account for around 55% of the world's people by 2050[12] and Asian diets have already been moving towards more meat, eggs, fish, dairy, fruits and vegetables; for example, the average supply of meat per person in Asia increased from 8kg in 1972 to 27kg in 2002.[13]

Food systems in the region have been responding to this growing and changing demand. At the same time, however, critical resources such as arable land, fresh water, forestlands and fisheries are deteriorating under competing pressures from agriculture, urbanisation and industrialisation.

From the 1960s, when the technologically driven 'Green Revolution' began (see Chapter One), to the 1990s, agriculture in Asia boomed and agricultural growth exceeded population growth.[14] Since the 1990s, however, agricultural yields of staples have been stagnating or falling because of environmental degradation, declining soil fertility, inadequate irrigation infrastructure and damaging farming practices. Rice yield-growth rates in Southeast Asia, for example, dropped to 1.5% in 1990–2004, from 2.5% in 1970–90,[15] while wheat yield-growth rates have been stagnating or declining in major growing regions of South Asia.[16]

Rapid urbanisation and industrialisation have put tremendous pressure on agricultural land and freshwater resources; unsustainable land use and management have hurt land, soil and water systems. Parts of Indo-China, Myanmar, Malaysia, Indonesia and South China are hard hit by soil degradation. In South and Southeast Asia, only around a quarter of agricultural land remains unaffected by erosion or some form of pollution.[17]

Major food-producing regions, such as the Mekong and Irrawaddy deltas in Southeast Asia and the Ganges–Brahmaputra–Meghna Delta in South Asia, are vulnerable to the negative impacts of climate change. Rising temperatures, flooded coastlines and saltwater intrusion, changes in precipitation patterns and surface run-off volumes, and more frequent and intense natural disasters, such as droughts, floods and cyclones, directly threaten agriculture,[18] and with it the livelihoods and food security of hundreds of millions.

There are other phenomena, extending well beyond the region, that are affecting food security within Asia. The recent surge in global demand for biofuels has so far largely been met with crops from the United States and Brazil, but that has driven up global food prices and reduced access to food in poor food-importing countries (including in Asia). Many Asian countries have now also announced their own biofuel mandates and subsidies. As the demand for energy in Association of Southeast Asian Nations (ASEAN) member states China and India continues to burgeon, the search for clean, alternative sources of energy may lead to a greater regional reliance on biofuels (see Chapter Five).[19]

The spread of industrial agriculture is another defining feature of today's global food economy. This emphasises input-intensive, large-scale monocropping at the cost of biodiversity and environmental sustainability.[20]

Small farmers, typically working less than two hectares (ha) of land with limited capital resources and relying on household members for the bulk of the labour, produce up to 80% of Asia's food.[21] However, they face increasing challenges in raising productivity and, in turn, their income from farming. Farm-gate prices remain quite low compared to market prices, while the rising cost of fuel has pushed up the prices of some agricultural 'inputs', such as fertilisers, pesticides and transportation. Between 2000 and 2008, for example, the increase in the price of inputs exceeded the cost recouped by agricultural 'outputs', such as food and raw materials.[22]

Over the past few decades, agricultural trade has been fast-paced, although highly uneven between developed and developing countries. The latter have increasingly opened up their agricultural sectors to international trade and investment, but often on terms that favour rich farmers in developed countries seeking overseas markets for their agricultural exports, at the expense of local farmers who generally struggle to compete against lower-priced food imports. The growing presence of international conglomerates in the global food economy has resulted in the 'commodification' of food, as a handful of powerful corporations sets prices and wields considerable influence in policymaking on food and agriculture.[23] Financial speculation in agricultural commodities futures markets (betting on the price movements of agricultural crops) has also surged, especially for major crops such as wheat, maize, coffee and cocoa.[24] Some analysts believe that this played an important role in pushing up international food prices during the 2007–08 global food-price crisis and continues to play a role in increasing food-price volatility since.[25]

As the demand for food in Asia expands and diversifies, governments face the challenge of boosting agricultural productivity. Given the extent to which populations in developing Asian countries rely on agriculture for their livelihoods, it will be critical that this is done in an environmentally sustainable manner. Declining or stagnating yield-growth rates of staple crops in Asia are, to a large extent, a result of widespread environmental degradation and, under the adverse impacts of climate change, this will require even more attention. While most governments in Asia have been formulating national policies on climate-change adaptation and mitigation, there needs to be more local engagement with those on the frontline, such as coastal communities and small farming households in rural areas. Finally, both goals – increasing agricultural productivity and ensuring environmental sustainability – require secure and stable access to productive resources for farmers.

At the national level, governments will need to strike the right balance between protecting domestic agricultural producers, particularly small farmers, from unfair competition from low-cost or heavily subsidised imports, and providing them with adequate support and opportunities to earn by exporting their agricultural surplus abroad. They also need to determine the appropriate level of subsidies on farm inputs, public investment in agricultural infrastructure and government-backed research and development (R&D).

Governments will also need to determine how much agricultural produce to buy at minimum support prices from farmers, to be distributed to the public at subsidised costs. In developing countries in Asia with relatively high levels of poverty and hunger, food-distribution programmes are an important means of ensuring food security for the most vulnerable, especially during food-price spikes. Often, however, such programmes have been blighted by corruption and mismanagement. For example, in some cases, supplies have been siphoned off for private sale or grains have rotted in inadequate storage facilities. Such problems need to be addressed effectively for food-distribution programmes to reach intended beneficiaries.

Food security has several dimensions, and many of the issues surrounding it are interlinked. Rapid urbanisation, for example, increases demand for more and different types of food, but the resources to meet this growing and diversifying demand become scarcer as urban development encroaches on agricultural land and appropriates freshwater supplies. Rural areas, where most food is grown, are left with dwindling natural resources, deteriorating social and agricultural infrastructure, inadequate public services, insufficient investment and few alternative employment opportunities. The increased unviability of farming is an important reason behind the movement of people from rural areas to the cities, and could accelerate it as the competition for agricultural land and fresh water for food production, urbanisation and industrialisation intensifies. The growing number of urban poor itself has consequences for food security, as they must survive on meagre incomes and are therefore highly vulnerable to price shocks that can cause or worsen poverty and hunger.[26]

Given the complexity of food-security related challenges, it is not surprising that there is much debate over how best to tackle them. The World Bank, for example, focuses largely on industrial agriculture (including large-scale monocropping and input-intensive farming methods) as a way of boosting productivity and reducing poverty in developing countries. It advocates high-value crops for export to boost farmer incomes, and greater and more open trade to increasingly integrate local farmers into global supply chains – that is, further lowering barriers to agricultural trade and removing government agricultural subsidies. Biotechnology and other scientific disciplines are considered vital in increasing crop yields efficiently.[27] In this approach, agriculture is viewed primarily as an economic activity, and the role of large agribusinesses, international corporations and private financial institutions is encouraged, often over public-sector involvement.

Other experts argue that the emerging global food economy is shaped overwhelmingly by the interests of richer, developed countries, international financial institutions and corporations, and point to the inequalities within it.[28] In this view, greater access to markets in developing countries benefits heavily subsidised, richer farmers in developed countries, and the advocacy of biotechnology and other industrial agricultural methods raises serious environmental, health, socio-economic and ethical concerns.[29]

This book considers food security in Asia primarily through a focus on the smallholder farmers who produce the vast majority of the region's food, and who are being squeezed by rapid urbanisation, industrialisation, rising input costs, lopsided liberalisation and the commodification and financialisation of food and agriculture, among other things. The book underlines the importance of agriculture in developing countries in the region, where it remains a source of livelihood for up to 70% of national populations, the bulk of whom continue to live in rural areas. Developing Asian countries continue to battle relatively high levels of poverty and inequality. Most small farmers continue to face numerous challenges in attempting to boost productivity, including lack of access to productive resources, training and education, extension services, healthcare and adequate infrastructure. This book draws on the food-sovereignty approach to underscore the importance of 'agro-ecological' approaches to farming[30] – combining local farming knowledge with appropriate modern technologies – to provide a way forward for 'sustainable intensification' of agriculture to boost productivity.[31]

Clearly, this is not a wholesale rejection of the role of large-scale farming, modern technologies and international trade in meeting food-security needs. Instead, the book evaluates these issues as they emerge in broader food-security dynamics at the local, national and regional levels. Biotechnology per se is not the problem; rather its use in ways that exacerbate existing inequalities and environmental challenges is.[32] Allowing local communities to collectively own expertise, giving them equitable and stable access to productive resources, and helping them to sustainably increase productivity, remain key to resolving the problem of food insecurity in Asia.

Notes

1 Ambrose Evans-Pritchard, 'Egypt and Tunisia usher in the new era of global food revolutions', *Daily Telegraph*, 30 January 2011, http://www.telegraph.co.uk/finance/comment/ambroseevans_pritchard/8291470/Egypt-and-Tunisia-usher-in-the-new-era-of-global-food-revolutions.html.

2 Robert Darnton, 'What Was Revolutionary about the French Revolution?', *New York Review of Books*, vol. 35, no. 21–22, 19 January 1989, pp. 3–10.

3 Rex A. Wade, *The Russian Revolution, 1917* (Cambridge: Cambridge University Press, 2000), p. 4.

4 'Let them eat baklava: Today's policies are recipes for instability in the Middle East', *The Economist*, 17 March 2012, http://www.economist.com/node/21550328.

5 Rabah Arezki and Markus Brückner, 'Food prices and political instability', IMF Working Paper 11/62, March 2011, p. 4, http://www.imf.org/external/pubs/ft/wp/2011/wp1162.pdf.

6 'UPA's failure to control food prices risks voter wrath', LiveMint.com, 23 July 2013, http://www.livemint.com/Politics/n3gqSQgyzKeVqIDQHOavjP/UPAs-failure-to-control-food-prices-risks-voter-wrath.

7 Mindi Schneider, '"We are Hungry!" A Summary Report of Food Riots, Government Responses, and States of Democracy in 2008', December 2008, p. 30; 'Thousands protest against high food prices in Delhi', BBC News, 23 February 2011, http://www.bbc.co.uk/news/world-south-asia-12549050.

8 'Bangladesh hit by food price riots', Al Jazeera, 12 April 2008, http://www.aljazeera.com/

news/asia/2008/04/2008614228 21207204.html.

9 United Nations, *World Population to 2300* (New York: The Department of Economic and Social Affairs, Population Division, 2004), p. 4.

10 FAO, 'How to Feed the World in 2050', Executive Summary of the High-Level Experts Forum, held in Rome, 12–13 October 2009, p. 2, http://www.fao.org/fileadmin/templates/wsfs/docs/expert_paper/How_to_Feed_the_World_in_2050.pdf.

11 In South and Southeast Asia, the decline has been relatively quicker, while in East Asia population growth rates have remained relatively steady since 2003. See United Nations Economic and Social Commission for Asia and the Pacific (UNESCAP), *Statistical Year Book for Asia and the Pacific 2011* (United Nations, October 2011). Modernisation, social change and declining fertility rates (number of children born per woman) are some of the factors underpinning this gradual slowing of population growth in Asia. See also UN Public Administration Network, http://unpan1.un.org/intradoc/groups/public/documents/apcity/unpan010366.pdf.

12 United Nations, Department of Economic and Social Affairs, Population Division, *World Population Prospects: The 2012 Revision*, http://esa.un.org/unpd/wpp/index.htm.

13 Katinka Weinberger and Thomas A. Lumpkin, 'High value agricultural products in Asia and the Pacific for small-holder farmers: Trends, opportunities and research priorities', 'How Can the Poor Benefit from the Growing Markets for High Value Agricultural Products' Workshop, 3–5 October 2005, Chartered Institute of Agricultural Technologists, Cali, Colombia, p. 9, http://www.fao.org/docs/eims/upload/210973/regional_ap.pdf.

14 Angelina Briones, Jocelyn Cajiuat and Charmaine Ramos, 'Food Security Perspectives: Focus on Asia and the Philippines', paper presented at 'The United Nations and the Global Environment in the 21st Century: From Common Challenges to Shared Responsibilities' Conference, New York, 14–15 November 1997, p. 1, http://archive.unu.edu/ona/PDF/Papers/Briones,%20A%20PAPER.pdf.

15 ActionAid, 'Asia at the Crossroads: Prioritising Conventional Farming or Sustainable Agriculture?', February 2012, p. 14, http://www.actionaid.org/sites/files/actionaid/asia_at_the_crossroads_full_report_2012.pdf.

16 R. Chatrath et al., 'Challenges to wheat production in South Asia',

Euphytica, vol. 157, no. 3, October 2007, pp. 447–56.

17 UNESCAP, 'Sustainable Agriculture and Food Security in Asia and the Pacific', 2009, p. 60, http://bit.ly/11IX6M. See also Stanley Wood, Kate Sebastian and Sara J. Scherr, *Pilot Analysis of Global Ecosystems: Agroecosystems* (Washington DC: World Resources Institute, 2000), p. 50, http://www.ifpri.org/sites/default/files/publications/agroeco.pdf.

18 For example, see 'Food security and climate change', a report by the High Level Panel of Experts on Food Security and Nutrition, Committee on World Food Security, Rome, June 2012, http://www.fao.org/fileadmin/user_upload/hlpe/hlpe_documents/HLPE_Reports/HLPE-Report-3-Food_security_and_climate_change-June_2012.pdf; and Hugh Turrel, Jacob Burke and Jean-Marc Faurès, *Climate change, water and food security* (Rome: FAO, 2011), http://www.fao.org/docrep/014/i2096e/i2096e.pdf.

19 Jinyue Yan and Tun Lin, 'Biofuels in Asia', *Applied Energy*, vol. 86, supplement 1, November 2009, S1–S10, http://www.sciencedirect.com/science/article/pii/S0306261909002815.

20 Jennifer Clapp, *Food* (Cambridge: Polity Press, 2012), p. 12.

21 G. Thapa, 'Smallholder Farming in Transforming Economies of Asia and the Pacific: Challenges and Opportunities', discussion paper prepared for a side event of the 33rd session of the International Fund for Agricultural Development's Governing Council, 18 February 2009, p. 1, http://www.ifad.org/events/gc/33/roundtables/pl/pi_bg_e.pdf.

22 United Nations Conference on Trade and Development, 'Food Security and Agricultural Development in Times of High Commodity Prices', Discussion Paper No. 196, November 2009, p. 10, http://unctad.org/en/Docs/osgdp20094_en.pdf.

23 Clapp, *Food*, pp. 14–15.

24 *Ibid.*, p. 16.

25 Ann Berg, 'The rise of commodity speculation: from villainous to venerable', in Adam Prakash (ed.), *Safeguarding Food Security in Volatile Global Markets* (Rome: FAO, 2011).

26 'Food Security in Asia: A Report for Policymakers', Centre for International Security Studies, University of Sydney, February 2013, p. 11, http://sydney.edu.au/arts/ciss/downloads/CISS_Food_Security_Policy_Report.pdf.

27 Carey L. Biron, 'Regional Trade Key to African Food Security, World Bank Says', IPS News Agency, 25 October 2012, http://www.ipsnews.net/2012/10/regional-trade-key-to-african-food-security-world-bank-says/.

[28] For more, see Clapp, *Food.*

[29] Robert Bailey, *Growing a Better Future: Food justice in a resource-constrained world* (Oxford: Oxfam International, June 2011), pp. 52–3.

[30] Miguel A. Altieri, Peter Rosset, and Lori Ann Thrupp, 'The potential of agroecology to combat hunger in the developing world', IFPRI, 2020 Policy Brief No. 55, October 1998, p. 1, http://www.ifpri.org/publication/potential-agroecology-combat-hunger-developing-world. Agro-ecology refers to a scientific approach that 'provides ecological principles for the design and management of sustainable and resource-conserving agricultural systems'. The authors argue that by using local farming knowledge and appropriate modern technologies, it offers 'the only practical way to restore agricultural lands that have been degraded by conventional agronomic practices'. Agro-ecology offers a way forward for small farmers to boost production in environmentally fragile areas, they continue, and to potentially roll back 'the anti-peasant bias of strategies that emphasise purchased inputs as opposed to the assets that small farmers already possess'.

[31] Bailey, *Growing a Better Future,* p. 53.

[32] Here, the book agrees with the International Assessment of Agricultural Knowledge, Science and Technology for Development (IAASTD) report that advises governments to take a 'problem-oriented approach' to biotechnology R&D and to examine how such technologies affect the abilities of local communities to collectively own expertise and genetic resources such as seeds, as well as their capacity to undertake further research independently. For more, see 'IAASTD Executive Summary of the Synthesis Report', April 2008.

CHAPTER ONE

Understanding food security

Future global food security will require food production to keep pace with demand in an era of climate change, as populations continue to grow and diets diversify. However, there is more to the challenge than simply ensuring adequate supplies of food. Although enough is currently produced to feed everyone on the planet, nearly one billion people remain chronically undernourished.[1] Therefore, ensuring more equitable access to food is another vital part of the equation.

The Asian experience clearly proves that economic success alone does not alleviate vulnerability to food insecurity. Even after average annual economic growth of 7.6% across the region between 1990 and 2010 – much higher than the global average of 3.4% – 733 million Asians still live in absolute poverty, on less than US$1.25 a day, while 540m remain undernourished.[2]

Food security is a multidimensional issue, presenting different challenges when viewed from a regional, national or household perspective. National food security does not guarantee enough to eat in every home at the local level, nor does it ensure food security across a region. Multilateral organisations such as ASEAN and the South Asian Association for Regional Cooperation (SAARC), therefore, have a role to play in ensuring the continent's wider food security.

What is food security?

The notion of food security has evolved considerably over the past four decades. The first official definition put forward at the United Nations World Food Conference in 1974[3] described it as 'the availability at all times of adequate world food supplies of basic foodstuffs to sustain a steady expansion of food consumption and to offset fluctuations in production and prices'.[4] By the late 1970s and early 1980s, however, a more complex concept had emerged. The groundbreaking work of Indian economist Amartya Sen contributed significantly towards this by challenging the notion that famines were caused by a shortage of food – the Malthusian logic of 'too many people, too little food' – and shifting the focus to 'the inability of groups of people to acquire food'.[5] This underlined the importance of food distribution and citizens' access to food. In the late 1980s, other approaches further emphasised the roles of conflict and health, and the question of maintaining and sustaining livelihoods during famines.[6]

The UN's Food and Agriculture Organization (FAO) arrived at the prevailing definition of food security in 2001, stating that it exists 'when all people, at all times, have physical, social and economic access to sufficient, safe and nutritious food that meets their dietary needs and food preferences for an active and healthy life'.[7] Unlike earlier definitions, this underlines the significance of physical, social and economic access to food for those who are the most poor and malnourished. It says that food security is not just about food quantity (having enough to eat) but also about food quality (having access to safe, nutritious food as per one's dietary requirements and cultural tastes), integrating the problems of malnourishment[8] and food safety into the equation. The FAO also identified four elements of food security: availability, access, utilisation and stability (of the first three factors), insisting that 'a population, household or individual must have access to food at all times and should not risk losing access as a consequence of sudden shocks or cyclical events.'[9]

This official understanding of food security has been widely embraced, but it fails to grasp the larger issues underpinning food insecurity in the developing world. Although it emphasises the links between poverty and malnourishment, it underplays the wider social, economic and political factors that may give rise to food insecurity in the first place. For instance, in many developing countries where agriculture remains the single most important source of livelihood, small farmers usually have little or no influence over agricultural and food-related policies, even though they dominate the sector. They also tend to lack adequate access to agricultural resources such as land, fresh water, fisheries and forest lands. In such situations, it becomes particularly important to extend the current definition of food security to consider the control of food systems.

Towards food sovereignty

It is here that the concept of 'food sovereignty' has much to offer policymakers, as it highlights the gaps in the official food-security approach while emphasising agriculture's many functions.[10] Outlined by La Via Campesina (or the International Peasant Movement) that emerged in the 1990s,[11] food sovereignty refers to 'the right of peoples to healthy and culturally appropriate food produced through socially just and ecologically sensitive methods ... to participate in decision making and define their own food, agriculture, livestock and fisheries systems'.[12] It promotes sustainable agricultural practices based on small-scale, family-based production – which is predominant in developing countries in Asia – for the benefit of local communities and their environment. In doing so, it prioritises local and sustainable food production (using sound ecological practices) and consumption, and calls for those who produce, distribute and need wholesome, local food to be placed 'at the heart of food, agricultural, livestock and fisheries systems and policies, rather than the demands of markets and corporations that reduce food to internationally tradable commodities and components'.[13]

Although the concept of food sovereignty has some weaknesses,[14] it importantly moves the debate forward on how to effectively address food insecurity outside the narrow confines of the economic realm of supply and demand, into the wider socio-economic and political realms, to allow for a more nuanced understanding of the global food system. It also provides a more comprehensive view of the challenges involved in feeding those who are most hungry and poor (most of the world's small food producers), while ensuring environmental sustainability, particularly in the face of climate change. This book draws upon the concept of food sovereignty to inform its analysis of food security in Asia.

The Green Revolution

For many years before the idea of food sovereignty was articulated, technology and trade appeared to be answering Asia's dietary needs. Faced, in the early 1960s, with a looming regional crisis caused by rapid population growth, low agricultural investment and declining productivity,[15] the industrialised world responded with a large technology-transfer programme that led to the so-called 'Green Revolution'. Private US institutions, mainly the Rockefeller and Ford foundations, the US government and the World Bank[16] were behind 'a package of modern inputs', including irrigation and improved, high-yielding seed varieties, fertilisers and pesticides that 'together dramatically increased crop production' in parts of Asia.[17] This was helped by significant levels of public investment in agricultural research to develop new, higher-yielding varieties of wheat and rice, expand irrigation infrastructure and subsidise vital inputs such as fertilisers, electricity and water. Governments also intervened in markets to ensure that farmers were offered minimum support prices for their produce.[18]

The implementation of industrial farming technologies, backed by public investment and supportive policies, saw serious improvements in crops yields and helped to lift millions out of poverty. Between 1967 and 1982, total cereal production in the region grew at an annual rate of 3.6% and average growth rates for staple crops also increased, including wheat (5.4% per year), rice (3.2%) and maize (4.6%).[19] As a result of these year-on-year increases, cereal production in Asia doubled between 1970 and 1995, keeping ahead of population growth. Increases in agricultural yields were also recorded in many individual countries, and the use of high-yielding varieties of seeds was the main factor behind this surge. In Indonesia, for example, FAO figures show that rice-paddy yields grew from 1.76 tonnes per hectare (t/ha) in 1961 to 4.34t/ha in 1995 while wheat yields in India grew from 1.1t/ha in 1968 to 2.55t/ha in 1995. By the 1990s, almost three-quarters of rice areas and more than half of wheat areas in Asia were planted with high-yielding varieties.[20]

Agricultural trade liberalisation

As more developing countries began World Bank and IMF structural-adjustment programmes in the 1980s, they liberalised their agricultural sectors by adopting policies such as eliminating or reducing farmer subsidies and removing barriers to imports and exports. Although the impact of trade liberalisation on economic growth and food security remains an area of intense debate in academic and policy-making circles, a 2008 study claims that between 1950 and 1998 sample countries that opted for trade liberalisation emerged with average annual growth rates that beat pre-trade liberalisation growth rates by around 1.5 percentage points.[21] In countries such as Bangladesh, access to agricultural markets in other countries such as India, especially in times of domestic shortfalls in staples (such as rice), has provided an important means of ensuring food security at the national level in times of crisis.[22] At the same time, access to markets overseas has allowed many farmers to bolster their livelihoods and raise incomes. As Oxfam has pointed out, in many developing countries (for example, Vietnam in Southeast Asia and Uganda in East Africa), trade liberalisation has played a prominent role in poverty reduction, and global trade is potentially far more beneficial to the poor than financial aid, as the production of exports 'can concentrate income directly in the hands of the poor, creating new opportunities for employment and investment in the process'.[23]

In the current approach to food security, greater and more open international trade in food is considered vital in eradicating food insecurity in developing countries.[24] In this view, trade liberalisation helps boost small-farmer incomes in poorer countries by allowing greater access to overseas markets and fairer competition for their produce. At the same time, the availability of food imports at competitive prices helps address food insecurity amongst vulnerable populations. In 2002, for example, Director General of the WTO Supachai Panitchpakdi insisted that 'Agricultur[al] trade is of critical importance to the economic development of poor countries, both importers and exporters … trade liberalisation in agriculture is probably the single most important contribution the multilateral trading system can make to help developing countries … to trade their way out of poverty.'[25]

Here, the general belief is that developing countries have a strong competitive edge when it comes to agricultural production, and so liberalising trade in agricultural products is a certain path towards economic growth and higher incomes. Theoretically, by specialising in the production of those agricultural commodities that they are 'best' at producing, developing countries can earn foreign exchange that can then be ploughed back into boosting agricultural productivity.[26] Foreign investors can also play a role by providing vital funds to enhance agricultural productivity, in turn leading to higher incomes and boosting momentum for overall economic growth.

The 2007–08 food-price crisis

The Green Revolution and accelerated agricultural trade liberalisation were followed by decades of relatively low food prices, but a global food-price crisis in 2007–08 reawakened Malthusian fears about the world's long-term ability to feed its growing population. In developing Asia and elsewhere, this crisis laid bare some of the deep-rooted problems within agricultural and food systems, and exposed the extent to which poor households were vulnerable to volatile food prices.

Between January 2007 and June 2008, the FAO's Food Price Index rose by 54%. The real price of wheat and maize (corn) more than doubled, and that of rice tripled.[27] During those 18 months, there were violent protests in as many as 30 countries[28] – from Mexico, where tens of thousands protested in January 2007 against a 400% rise in tortilla prices,[29] to Indonesia, where the high cost of soybeans prompted demonstrations in Jakarta in January 2008.[30] Some of the demonstrations turned deadly, including in Egypt, Haiti[31] and India, where at least two people were killed and hundreds were injured in West Bengal during rationing protests.[32]

Both short-term and long-term factors have been deemed responsible for the sharp hike in prices. The World Bank subsequently singled out 'the large increase in biofuels production in the US and EU' in response to biofuel mandates and subsidies as the leading cause.[33] Demand for maize for biofuel production in the United States between 2006 and 2007, for example, surged by more than double the

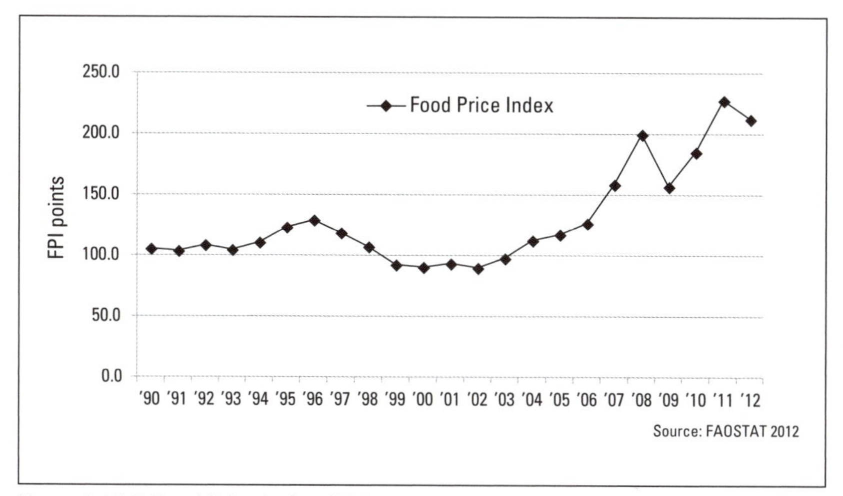

Figure 1. **FAO Food Price Index (FPI), 1990–2012**

yearly increase in global demand for the same.[34] This also propelled farmers to switch from wheat, soybean and other staple crops to lucrative maize. As the land available for cultivating these crops shrank, the World Bank said, their prices escalated. Because maize and soy are 'main ingredients for processed food and livestock feed', the increase in corn prices dramatically increased food prices worldwide.[35]

A surge in oil prices in 2008 to US$147 a barrel – the highest ever over the past century – also had an effect.[36] As oil prices surged, the cost of inputs such as fertilisers and of running farm machinery and transport, also increased.[37] Analysts consider excessive financial speculation in agricultural commodity futures markets another contributory factor. Many have also emphasised, to varying degrees, the role of historically low global food stocks.[38] Subsequent knee-jerk government policies, such as export bans in the face of perceived national shortages, exacerbated the situation, causing further global shortages and putting additional upwards pressure on world prices.

These short-term changes were seen as adding to long-term structural trends, such as population growth, rising incomes and changing diets in developing countries. Declining agricultural yield-growth rates; falling levels of public investment in agricultural infrastructure and in research and development; growing scarcity of arable land and water; and extreme weather have all been identified as background factors.[39]

For scholars such as Philip McMichael and Mindi Schneider, the 2007–08 crisis stemmed, in many ways, from the evolution of the global food economy in the decades preceding it.[40] They contend that while the falling global food prices of the 1990s may have ensured cheaper food 'to compensate for declining wages in the North', they worked against many small food producers in developing countries:

> The artificial cheapening of traded food put smallholders across the world under intense price competition in their home markets, producing an 'income deflation' which has rendered their farming increasing[ly] unviable, and generated land consolidation by agribusiness ... Such 'accumulation by encroachment' contributed to the stagnation in food supply over the past quarter century, undermining small farmer capacity to respond to agflation by increasing food production.[41]

However successful the Green Revolution was in raising crop yields between the 1950s and 1990s, by 2007–08 it had also produced many unintended negative consequences.

The industrial practices that it promoted – such as a shift away from traditional, mixed-crop farming and rotational cropping patterns to the singular production (namely monocropping) of high-yield varieties of wheat, rice and other crops – ultimately led to severe environmental degradation. High-yielding seed varieties require greater levels of capital and of technological expertise.[42] Such seeds rely heavily on irrigation and fertilisers, which many poorer farmers often could not afford during the Green Revolution, not even with government-subsidised credit. Intensive use of fertilisers and pesticides necessitated yet more use of fertilisers and pesticides, as natural soil fertility was depleted and pests developed chemical resistance.[43] The frequent overexploitation of land and mismanagement of natural resources caused air, water and soil pollution, and alarming losses in biodiversity.

Trade liberalisation also proved uneven. Agriculture remains a relatively protected sector in most developed and many developing countries,[44] but barriers to agricultural trade have fallen, and farmers' subsidies have been disappearing at a far greater pace in developing countries than in the developed world. Trade liberalisation has not automatically guaranteed positive outcomes; as Alan Winters, Neil McCulloch and Andrew McKay point out, its impact depends on 'its starting point, the precise trade reform measures undertaken, who the poor are, and how they sustain themselves'.[45] Alternative views on food security emphasise that global agricultural trade liberalisation has been highly skewed, benefitting richer countries while undermining the welfare and livelihoods of those who are amongst the poorest.[46] Jennifer Clapp, for example, suggests that the expansion of the global food economy is driven by four main factors, namely:

> state-led global expansion of both the industrial agricultural model and the transnational trade in food; agricultural trade liberalisation; the rise of transnational corporate actors in all aspects of the food and agricultural sector; and the intensification of the financialisation of food, such that food commodities have become increasingly like any other financial product bought and sold by investors.[47]

In her analysis, the growth of international trade since the 1970s has opened up 'new arenas of governance in the world food economy' shaped by 'rich developed countries, international development agencies and private foundations'.[48] Increasingly, 'the rules for imports and exports in food and agriculture were set by international development agencies.'[49]

The emergence of the WTO's 1994 Agreement on Agriculture (AoA) helped to perpetuate the advantage that richer industrialised countries had over poorer developing countries in international agricultural trade. The agreement's provisions on market access, for example, had very little impact in making Organisation for Economic Co-operation and Development (OECD) country markets more liberalised, and the ways in which OECD countries implemented those provisions further restricted developing countries' access to their markets. At the same time, there was a surge in food imports in developing countries, including meat and dairy items, after the AoA was concluded.[50]

Furthermore, the agreement required both developed and developing countries to reduce export subsidies. Historically, these have been a major feature of agricultural support in developed countries, while developing countries have usually taxed the agricultural sector. Carmen Gonzalez claims that in allowing 'past users of export subsidies to maintain these subsidies, subject to certain reduction obligations, while prohibiting the introduction of new subsidies, the Agreement institutionalized the unfair competitive advantage held by developed country producers'.[51]

Bill Pritchard argues that agricultural trade liberalisation has worsened the plight of small farmers in developing countries, by aggravating 'already-existing uneven opportunities in the world food system'.[52] As domestic markets were flooded with cheaper and heavily subsidised food from developed countries, many small farmers in the developing world were pushed out of farming as it became an increasingly unviable livelihood. Meanwhile, land consolidation and the expansion of large agribusiness continued rapidly, further skewing access to productive resources in favour of wealthier farmers and international corporations.[53]

In the past few decades, Cargill, Archer Daniels Midland (ADM), General Mills and other large corporations dealing in food and agricultural items (especially grain) have been quick to take advantage of the opportunities offered by the emerging global food economy. They have expanded rapidly, both horizontally and vertically, into newly opened markets, 'acquiring firms specialising in different food [and agricultural] commodities, and expanding up and down along the food supply chain into shipping and food processing'.[54] In doing so, Clapp argues, transnational corporations have been able to 'actively shape the global food system to fit their own needs'.[55] For example, they wield enormous influence in international markets, with the ability to determine prices for farmers (as suppliers) as well as consumers. They pump significant resources into lobbying.[56] This 'commodification' of food has now arguably reached 'a new and intangible level' through the 'financialisation of food and agriculture', whereby the global food economy has become increasingly linked to events in the realm of international finance.[57]

Major structural shifts in global commodity markets have sharply increased speculation in agricultural commodities futures markets, including the deregulation of the financial-services sector in the US, particularly at the start of the twenty-first century.[58] This happened alongside the growing liberalisation of international markets, the decline of farmer subsidies (such as direct price support), declining margins in securities trading, and the general 'restructuring of primary exchanges from member organisations to for-profit corporations', among other developments.[59] Consequently, the numbers of speculators and contract limits in agricultural commodities futures markets have boomed, particularly for crops such as wheat, maize, coffee and cocoa.[60] Large banks such as Goldman Sachs, Barclays and Morgan Stanley have been setting up and managing agricultural commodity funds that invest money from pension funds, insurance companies and wealthy individuals.[61]

Between 2006 and early 2011, total investment in agricultural commodities futures markets nearly doubled, from US$65bn to US$126bn.[62] This surge in speculative activity has become an important factor in pushing up prices and making them more volatile. As the International Food Policy Research Institute (IFPRI) points out:

> The excess price surges caused by speculation and possible hoarding could have severe effects on confidence in global grain markets, thereby hampering the market's performance in responding to fundamental changes in supply, demand and costs of production. More important, they could result in unreasonable or unwanted price fluctuations that can harm the poor and result in long-term, irreversible nutritional damage, especially among children.[63]

It is now widely believed that excessive speculation in agricultural commodity futures markets contributed to the global food price spike in 2007–08, although how much exactly remains a point of contention.[64]

Analysts argue that the growing volatility of global food prices has increased the risks involved in making farming decisions, since 'the world trade market in food has started to behave like any other financial market: it's full of asymmetry.'[65] For example, large international corporations have much more access to information, marketing expertise and technology, and much more political power than local small food producers in developing countries.[66] As these conglomerates have expanded globally, integrating and consolidating their marketing and production activities, they have gained a formidable stronghold in food supply chains, allowing them to 'dictate significantly the patterns of international trade through intra-firm trade under their globally integrated production and marketing strategy'. On the other hand, small farmers in developing countries are disadvantaged as they are increasingly isolated and often become victims of false or distorted information or lack of expertise. This leads to poor decisions about farm production and marketing.[67]

The forces shaping the emerging global food economy have also been deeply influenced by the official approach to food security adopted by rich industrialised donor countries, leading development organisations, philanthropic bodies, international financial institutions and large corporations. This approach tends to espouse greater and freer trade as a main route out of food insecurity in developing countries (but without, thus far, much impact on subsidies and other protectionist measures within developed markets).

Household, national and regional food security

Much of the debate about food security is focused at the national level. However, two other levels must be recognised – one below and one above. Food security and poverty are closely interlinked, and a nation can be 'food secure' without guaranteeing food security for all households within it. The vast majority of the world's food-insecure people remain concentrated in developing countries and significantly comprise rural farming households.[68] Such households may spend up to 70% of their monthly income on food, and are usually ill-equipped to increase food production when food prices rise, because the value chains they belong to are usually informal and characterised by 'spot market transactions, small percentages of production sold off the farm, weak road and communications infrastructure, weak information systems and limited coordination between input delivery, credit and sales'.[69]

Across Asia, experiences of food insecurity vary, as do national governments' views on which factors are most relevant and how to address them effectively. This can lead to policies that cancel each other out in a regional or even global crisis. The 2007–08 global food-price spike, in particular, demonstrated the difficulties in orchestrating regional approaches to tackling food insecurity in Asia, as measures taken by some countries – including export bans – worsened food insecurity in others.

During this period, major food exporters in Asia such as Cambodia, Thailand, Vietnam and India took measures to control domestic food prices, and some of them also tried to take advantage of the global increase in export prices of food grains. In Cambodia, for example, the prices of all varieties of rice doubled in March–July 2007 and in March–July 2008. Meat prices increased by 50–70%, while prices of fish and vegetables rose by 20–30%.[70] The Cambodian government imposed a brief ban on rice exports in March 2008, but lifted it two months later to capitalise on the soaring price of rice in the global market. India banned the export of all non-basmati rice as early as October 2007 in a bid to control spiralling rice prices at home.[71] In April 2008, Vietnam, another major global supplier of rice, banned all new rice-export contracts. The aim, as declared by Deputy Industry and Trade Minister Nguyen Thanh Bien, was twofold: to secure food for domestic consumption and to put further upward pressure on global rice prices to raise national export earnings over time.[72]

This, in turn, meant sharp increases in food bills for overall food-importing countries such as the Philippines,

Indonesia, Malaysia, Singapore, Bangladesh and Pakistan. Restrictions by food exporters threatened the ability of food-importing countries to procure enough on the global market to meet domestic demand. Inevitably, some rise in global food prices was transmitted down to the domestic level. In the Philippines, for example, food prices rose by around half between February and June 2008. The government had to enlist the army to deliver rice to poor neighbourhoods for safety reasons.[73]

Food-importing countries generally responded by reducing import duties, relaxing other import restrictions and, in some cases, building up extra reserves of rice. The volume of internationally traded rice is relatively low; less than 5% of the world's rice is traded across borders, compared to a quarter of its soybeans and around 18% of its wheat production. Therefore, the stockpiling of rice by exporting countries such as the Philippines and Malaysia caused anxiety in the global rice market. Both countries reduced import duties and relaxed restrictions on imports. Along with Indonesia, they also introduced measures to control domestic food prices for consumers, including restrictions on private grain trade.[74] As David Dawe and Tom Slayton point out, 'these policy decisions collectively created a speculative bubble that encouraged farmers, traders and consumers to hoard rice, further increasing prices.'[75]

Conclusion

The longer-term implications of the 2007–08 food-price crisis are yet to be fully realised. Yet, in the aftermath, the broad range of issues challenging food and agricultural systems, in Asia and the wider world, have again come to the fore.

Concerns around food security in the region are not entirely new; China's ability to feed itself, for example, and the impact of its food-security policies on the rest of the world have been subjects of debate since the 1990s.[76] However, the enormous socio-economic, environmental and political pressures on food systems in Asia are now being considered with a sense of renewed urgency. This is especially true when the effects of climate change are added to the mix.

Food security in the region is already a challenge, even before addressing how agricultural production may measure up against overall demand in future. Yet, as Asia's overall population grows and dietary tastes change, farmers in the region will need to produce more and different kinds of food on less land and in changing climatic conditions.

As a recent report on food security in the region points out, 'continuing population growth, even if it slows somewhat, declining rural agricultural populations, limited agricultural land, rapidly growing cities and ageing populations will – together with soaring food prices … impact on food resources and in some cases may increase the risk of famine and conflict.'[77]

Notes

1 FAO, *Unlocking the water potential of agriculture* (Rome: FAO, 2003), p. 1, http://www.fao.org/docrep/006/Y4525E/Y4525E00.HTM.

2 Asian Development Bank (ADB) and the Liu Institute for Global Issues at the University of British Columbia, *Food Security in Asia and the Pacific* (Mandaluyong City, Philippines: ADB, 2013), p. XV, http://www.adb.org/publications/food-security-asia-and-pacific.

3 FAO, *Trade Reforms and Food Security: Conceptualizing the linkages* (Rome: FAO, 2003), p. 26, http://www.fao.org/docrep/005/y4671e/y4671e00.htm. This chapter's brief

overview of the evolution of the official concept of food security is informed substantially by this FAO text.

[4] UN, 'Report of the World Food Conference', New York, 5–16 November 1974, in FAO, *Trade Reforms and Food Security*.

[5] Stephen Devereux, 'Sen's Entitlement Approach: Critiques and Counter-critiques', *Oxford Development Studies*, vol. 29, no. 3, 2001, pp. 246–63. For more, see Amartya Sen, 'Famines as failures of exchange entitlements', *Economic and Political Weekly*, vol. XI, no. 31–33, 1976, pp. 1,273–80. See also Amartya Sen, *Poverty and Famines: An Essay on Entitlement and Deprivation* (Oxford: Clarendon Press, 1981); Amartya Sen, *Resources, Values and Development* (Oxford: Basil Blackwell, 1984); and Amartya Sen, 'Food, economics and entitlements', *Lloyds Bank Review*, vol. 160, 1986, pp. 1–20.

[6] Simon Maxwell, 'Food Security: A post-modern perspective', *Food Policy*, vol. 19, no. 2, April 1994, p. 158.

[7] FAO, *The State of Food Insecurity in the World 2011* (Rome: FAO, 2011). This definition was very similar to the one offered by the FAO in its 1996 Rome Declaration on World Food Security, except it included a reference to 'social access' to food in addition to physical and economic access. For more, see FAO, 'Rome Declaration on World Food Security', Rome, 13–17 November 1996, http://www.fao.org/docrep/003/w3613e/w3613e00.htm.

[8] According to the FAO, malnourishment encompasses both undernourishment (namely energy deficiency) and micronutrient deficiencies (resulting from an unbalanced diet), as well as overnourishment (excessive energy intake).

[9] Saswati Bora et al., 'Food Security and Conflict', World Development Report 2011, Background Paper, 22 October 2010, p. 2, http://www.indiaenvironmentportal.org.in/files/food%20security%20and%20conflict.pdf.

[10] For more on food sovereignty, see Michael Windfuhr and Jennie Jonsén, *Food Sovereignty: Towards Democracy in Localized Food Systems* (Rugby: ITDG Publishing, 2005); Philip McMichael, 'Peasants Make Their Own History, But Not Just As They Please…', *Journal of Agrarian Change*, vol. 8, nos. 2 and 3, April and July 2008, pp. 205–28; and Peter Rosset, 'Moving forward: agrarian reform as part of food sovereignty', in Peter Rosset, Raj Patel and Michael Courville (eds), *Promised Land: Competing Visions of Agrarian Reform* (Oakland, CA: Food First Books, 2006), pp. 301–21.

[11] La Via Campesina is a grassroots movement of peasants, small farming households, fisherfolk, pastoralists, indigenous communities, rural women and other marginalised communities from more than 60 countries. It was founded in 1993, shortly before the conclusion of the Uruguay Round of the General Agreement on Tariffs and Trade (GATT), as major WTO agreements, including the 1994 Agreement on Agriculture, were about to come into existence. The movement opposes these developments and what its members perceive as the growing power of corporations and neoliberal international institutions in agriculture. According to its website, its main goal is 'to realize food sovereignty and stop the destructive neoliberal process. It is based on the conviction that small farmers, including peasant fisher-folk, pastoralists and indigenous people, who make up almost half the world's people, are capable of producing food for their communities and feeding the world in a sustainable and healthy way.' For more, see La Via Campesina, 'The international peasant's voice', http://viacampesina.org/en/index.php/organisation-mainmenu-44. See also Annette A. Desmarais, 'The Via Campesina: Peasant Women on the Frontiers of Food Sovereignty', *Canadian Woman Studies*, vol. 23, no. 1, 2003, pp. 140–45.

[12] Via Campesina, Nyéléni 2007 Synthesis Report, Sélingué, Mali, 23–27 February 2007, http://www.nyeleni.org/IMG/pdf/31Mar2007NyeleniSynthesisReport-en.pdf.

[13] *Ibid.*

[14] For example, as Raj Patel points out, one of the concept's inherent contradictions is the rejection of corporations and other market-driven actors on the one hand, while calling for a focus on *all* of those who 'produce, distribute and consume food' on the other. Another weakness Patel points out is a failure to distinguish between farm owners and farm workers, and recognise the tensions that may exist between the interests of each group. For more, see Raj Patel, 'Food Sovereignty', *The Journal of Peasant Studies*, vol. 36, no. 4, July 2009, pp. 663–706.

[15] Akinwumi A. Adesina, 'Solving the food crisis in Africa: achieving an African Green Revolution', in Baris Karapinar and Christian Häberli (eds), *Food Crises and the WTO* (Cambridge: Cambridge University Press, 2010), p. 84.

[16] Vandana Shiva, *The Violence of the Green Revolution: Third World Agriculture, Ecology and Politics* (London: Zed Books, 1991), p. 29.

[17] Peter B.R. Hazell, 'The Asian Green Revolution', IFPRI Discussion Paper, November 2009, p. 3, http://www.ifpri.org/sites/default/files/publications/ifpridp00911.pdf.

[18] *Ibid.* See also Adesina, 'Solving the food crisis in Africa', p. 84.

[19] *Ibid.*, p. 7.

[20] Peter Rosset, 'Lessons from the Green Revolution', The Institute for Food and Development Policy – Food First, 8 April 2000, http://www.foodfirst.org/media/opeds/2000/4-greenrev.html.

[21] Romain Wacziarg and Karen Horn Welch, 'Trade Liberalization and Growth: New Evidence', *The World Bank Economic Review*, vol. 22, no. 2, 2008, pp. 187–231.

[22] Paul A. Dorosh, 'Trade Liberalization and National Food Security: Rice Trade between Bangladesh and India', *World Development*, vol. 29, no. 4, 2001, pp. 673–89.

[23] Kevin Watkins and Penny Fowler, *Rigged Rules and Double Standards: Trade, globalisation and the fight against poverty* (Oxford: Oxfam, 2002), p. 8, http://policy-practice.oxfam.org.uk/publications/rigged-rules-and-double-standards-trade-globalisation-and-the-fight-against-pov-112391.

[24] Philip McMichael, 'A food regime analysis of the 'world food crisis', *Agriculture and Human Values*, vol. 26, no. 4, 2009, pp. 281–95; Philip McMichael and Mindi Schneider, 'Food security politics and the Millennium Development Goals', *Third World Quarterly*, vol. 32, no. 1, 2011, pp. 119–39.

[25] Supachai Panitchpakdi, 'Agriculture and the Doha Development Agenda', keynote address by the director general to the World Food and Farming Congress, London, 25 November 2002, http://www.wto.org/english/news_e/spsp_e/spsp06_e.htm.

[26] Unisféra International Centre, 'From Boom to Dust? Agricultural trade liberalization, poverty, and desertification in rural drylands: The role of UNCCD', April 2005, http://www.wto.org/english/forums_e/ngo_e/posp46_unisfera_e.pdf.

[27] ADB and Liu Institute, *Food Security in Asia and the Pacific*, p. 1.

[28] Raj Patel and Philip McMichael, 'A Political Economy of the Food Riot', *Review, A Journal of the Fernand Braudel Center*, vol. 32, no. 1, 2009, pp. 9–35, http://rajpatel.org/wp-content/uploads/2009/11/patel-mcmichael-2010Review321.pdf.

[29] Elisabeth Malkin, 'Thousands in Mexico City Protest Rising Food Prices', *New York Times*, 31 January 2007, http://www.nytimes.com/2007/02/01/world/americas/01mexico.html?_r=0.

[30] Fitri Wulandari, 'Indonesian tempeh makers struggle as soybean prices rise', Reuters,

4 February 2008, http://www.reuters.com/article/2008/02/05/us-soybean-indonesia-idUSJAK8152720080205.

[31] 'Global food riots turn deadly', *Washington Times*, 10 April 2008, http://www.washingtontimes.com/news/2008/apr/10/global-food-riots-turn-deadly/?page=all.

[32] Bappa Majumdar, 'Food riots expose how corruption hurts India's poor', Reuters, 12 October 2007, http://in.reuters.com/article/2007/10/12/idINIndia-29970920071012.

[33] World Bank, 'Double Jeopardy: Responding to High Food and Fuel Prices', working paper presented at G8 Hokkaido Toyako Summit, 2 July 2008, p. 2, footnote 2, http://siteresources.worldbank.org/NEWS/MiscContent/21828409/G8-HL-summit-paper.pdf.

[34] Eric Holt-Giménez and Isabella Kenfield, 'When Renewable Isn't Sustainable: Agrofuels and the Inconvenient Truths Behind the 2007 U.S. Energy Independence and Security Act', Policy Brief No. 13, Institute for Food and Development Policy, p. 3, http://www.foodfirst.org/files/pdf/PB13_Agrofuels-WhenRenewableIsntSustainable.pdf.

[35] *Ibid.*

[36] Alan Dupont and Mark Thirlwell, 'A New Era of Food Insecurity?', *Survival: Global Politics and Strategy*, vol. 51, no. 3, June–July 2009, p. 85.

[37] *Ibid.*

[38] Although, in a 2009 study, David Dawe makes a strong case against the importance of low global food stocks in the 2007–08 food-price crisis. For more, see David Dawe, 'The Unimportance of "Low" World Grain Stocks for Recent World Price Increases', FAO Agricultural Development Economics Division, ESA Working Paper No. 09–01, February 2009, http://www.agriskmanagementforum.org/sites/agriskmanagementforum.org/files/Documents/unimportance%20of%20low%20world%20grain%20stocks.pdf.

[39] Alex Evans, 'The Feeding of the Nine Billion: Global Food Security for the 21st Century', Chatham House Report, London, 2009; Philip C. Abbott, Christopher Hurt and Wallace E. Tyner, 'What's Driving Food Prices?', Farm Foundation Issue Report, July 2008, http://www.farmfoundation.org/news/articlefiles/404-FINAL%20WDFP%20REPORT%207-28-08.pdf; Ronald Trostle, 'Global Agricultural Supply and Demand: Factors Contributing to the Recent Increase in Food Commodity Prices', Economic Research Service, Outlook Report, US Department of Agriculture, Washington DC, May

2008, http://www1.eere.energy.gov/bioenergy/pdfs/global_agricultural_supply_and_demand.pdf; and Dupont and Thirlwell, 'A New Era of Food Insecurity?', pp. 71–98.

40 McMichael and Schneider, 'Food security politics and the Millennium Development Goals', p. 127.

41 *Ibid.*

42 Prabhu L. Pingali, 'Green Revolution: Impacts, limits, and the path ahead', *Proceedings of the National Academy of Sciences of the USA*, vol. 109, no. 31, 31 July 2012, pp. 12,302–08.

43 Rosset, 'Lessons from the Green Revolution'.

44 M. Ataman Aksoy and John C. Beghin, 'Introduction and Overview', in Aksoy and Beghin (eds), *Global Agricultural Trade and Developing Countries* (Washington DC: World Bank, 2005), p. 1.

45 L. Alan Winters, Neil McCulloch and Andrew McKay, 'Trade Liberalization and Poverty: The Evidence So Far', *Journal of Economic Literature*, vol. 42, March 2004, p. 107.

46 Jennifer Clapp, *Food* (Cambridge: Polity Press, 2012), p. 11.

47 *Ibid.*, p. 11.

48 *Ibid.*, p.12.

49 *Ibid.*

50 Carmen G. Gonzalez, 'Institutionalizing Inequality: The WTO Agreement on Agriculture, Food Security, and Developing Countries', *Columbia Journal of Environmental Law*, vol. 27, 2002, pp. 458–59, http://works.bepress.com/cgi/viewcontent.cgi?article=1018&context=carmen_gonzalez.

51 *Ibid.*, p. 462.

52 Bill Pritchard, 'The Long Hangover from the Second Food Regime: A World-Historical Interpretation of the Collapse of the WTO Doha Round', *Agriculture and Human Values*, vol. 26, no. 4, 2009, pp. 297–307; and Hannah Wittman, 'Food Sovereignty: A New Rights Framework for Food and Nature?', *Environment and Society: Advances in Research*, vol. 2, no. 1, 2011, p. 97.

53 McMichael and Schneider, 'Food security politics and the Millennium Development Goals'.

54 Clapp, *Food*, p. 14.

55 *Ibid.*

56 *Ibid.*, pp. 14–15.

57 *Ibid.*, p. 18.

58 Ann Berg, 'The rise of commodity speculation: from villainous to venerable', in Adam Prakash (ed.), *Safeguarding Food Security in Volatile Global Markets* (Rome: FAO, 2011), p. 258.

59 *Ibid.*

60 Clapp, *Food*, p. 16.

61 Tom Bawden, 'Goldman bankers get rich betting on food prices as millions starve', *Independent*, 20 January 2013, http://www.independent.co.uk/news/

business/news/goldman-bankers-get-rich-betting-on-food-prices-as-millions-starve-8459207.html.

[62] Murray Worthy, 'Broken markets: How financial market regulation can help prevent another global food crisis', World Development Movement, September 2011, p. 13, http://www.wdm.org.uk/sites/default/files/Broken-markets.pdf.

[63] Miguel Robles, Maximo Torero, and Joachim von Braun, 'When speculation matters', IFPRI Issue Brief 57, February 2009.

[64] Berg, 'The rise of commodity speculation', p. 258.

[65] Interview with Jayati Ghosh in http://www.therealnews.com, 2010, cited in *Ibid.*, p. 259.

[66] Adam Prakash and Christopher L. Gilbert, 'Rising vulnerability in the global food system: beyond market fundamentals', in Prakash (ed.), *Safeguarding Food Security in Volatile Global Markets*, p. 56.

[67] *Ibid.*, pp. 56, 272.

[68] *Ibid.*, pp. 18–19.

[69] FAO, *The State of Agricultural Commodity Markets 2009* (Rome: FAO, 2009), p. 34, http://www.fao.org/docrep/012/i0854e/i0854e00.htm.

[70] Cambodian Development Research Council (CDRI), 'Impact of high food prices in Cambodia', CDRI Survey Report, November 2008, p. 9, http://www.cdri.org.kh/webdata/download/conpap/hfp-survey.pdf.

[71] 'India introduces rice export ban', BBC News, 1 April 2008, http://news.bbc.co.uk/1/hi/7323713.stm. See also Christine Stebbins, 'Tight global supplies to keep rice on the boil', Reuters, 16 April 2008, http://www.reuters.com/article/2008/04/16/us-food-rice-idUSN1634613420080416.

[72] 'Vietnam reaffirms rice export curb through June', Reuters, 26 April 2008, http://www.reuters.com/article/2008/04/26/us-vietnam-rice-export-idUSHAN2698220080426.

[73] Lawrence Ong, 'Rice prices hit Philippines poor', BBC News, 6 April 2008, http://news.bbc.co.uk/1/hi/business/7330168.stm.

[74] Alexander C. Chandra and Lucky A. Lontoh, 'Regional Food Security and Trade Policy in Southeast Asia: The Role of ASEAN', Trade Knowledge Network Policy Brief No. 3, June 2010, p. 3, http://www.iisd.org/tkn/pdf/regional_food_trade_asean_brief.pdf.

[75] David Dawe and Tom Slayton, 'The World Rice Market Crisis of 2007–2008', in Dawe (ed.), *The Rice Crisis: Markets, Policies and Food Security* (London: Earthscan and FAO, 2010), p. 24.

[76] Lester Brown, *Who Will Feed China? Wake-Up Call for a Small Planet* (New York: W.W. Norton and Company, 1995).

[77] 'Food Security in Asia: A Report for Policymakers', Centre for

International Security Studies, University of Sydney, March 2013, p. 11, http://sydney.edu.au/arts/ciss/downloads/CISS_Food_Security_Policy_Report.pdf.

CHAPTER TWO

What is driving food insecurity in Asia?

Asia is at the heart of the many different changes in food consumption and production that are driving twenty-first century concerns about food security. Although the rate of population growth in Asia has slowed,[1] the number of people continues to rise, and by 2050 the region is still expected to account for around 55% of the world's 9.6 billion people.[2] More Asians are also moving to cities, with implications for food supply and demand. In 2013, around 40% of Asians lived in urban areas. By 2050, nearly two-thirds of Asia's population – or 3.3bn people – will be urban dwellers, with the largest numbers in India (497 million), China (341m) and Indonesia (92m).[3]

Rapid economic growth and rising incomes in Asia also mean a fast-expanding middle class.[4] According to the Asian Development Bank (ADB), if the current growth trajectory continues, developing Asia will account for more than half of the world's GDP by 2050.[5] In the intervening period, an extra 3bn people in the region will become affluent by current standards.[6] However, millions are already being left behind in poverty and this inequality gap is likely to widen. The division is sometimes referred to as the 'two faces of Asia'.[7]

The growth in population will mean an overall increase in the demand for food, putting pressure on limited land resources that are also increasingly in demand for industrial use and urban development. Rising incomes and urbanisation will accelerate ongoing shifts in lifestyles and diets, putting yet more strain on the system. Urban dwellers are situated further from traditional sites of food production in rural areas, requiring more storage and transportation of foodstuffs. Also, urban diets are different, generally requiring a wider range of ingredients and including more processed foods.

All of these pressures are increasing just as gains in crop yields brought by the Green Revolution are starting to fade, more crops are being taken to produce biofuels, land is increasingly sought after for competing uses and the unpredictable effects of climate change are casting great uncertainty over future food security.

According to one estimate, continuing population growth and changing food consumption will require cereal production in Asia to increase by half by 2030.[8] As China and India, in particular, turn increasingly to the international market to satisfy their rising demand – for cereal grains like maize, vegetable oils and non-cereal grains such as soybean – this will have a significant effect on both global stocks and food prices.

China's imports of edible oils have already surged, and imports of other key crops, such as maize and soybean, have also been escalating, thanks largely to a booming livestock sector and the associated need for animal feed. The country has become the world's largest importer of soybean, buying in more than 58m tonnes in 2012.[9] Wheat imports are projected to increase from 1.2m tonnes in 2011 to around 2.8m tonnes per year by 2022.[10]

Changing dietary patterns

The 'nutrition transition' brought about by rising incomes and urbanisation means people have a smaller amount of grains in their diets, and instead eat more meat, eggs and dairy products. The consumption of other higher-value agricultural products, such as fish, vegetables, fruits and vegetable oils, also rises. Urban lifestyles demand shorter times for meal preparation, leading to a higher consumption of processed foods and the growing importance of super-

Figure 1. **Supply of select food items in Asia, 1972 and 2002**

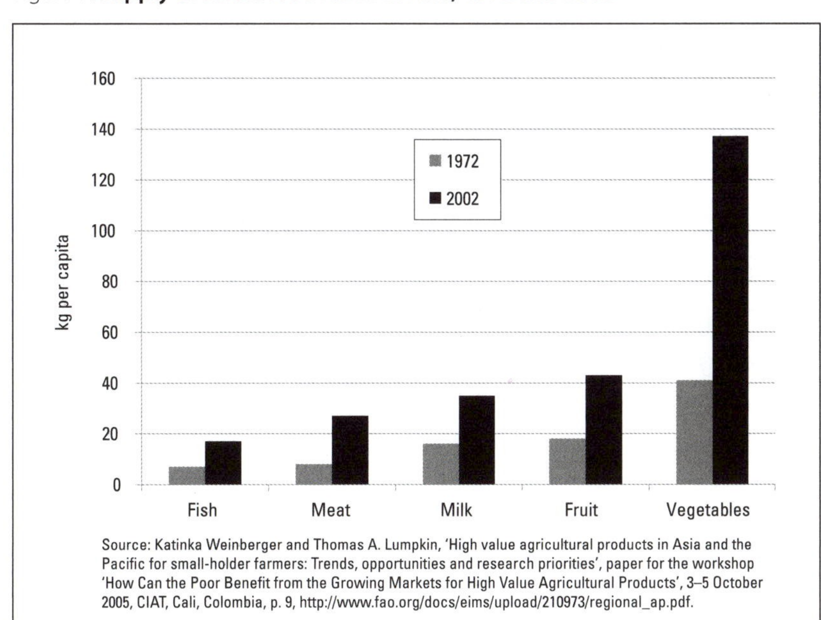

Source: Katinka Weinberger and Thomas A. Lumpkin, 'High value agricultural products in Asia and the Pacific for small-holder farmers: Trends, opportunities and research priorities', paper for the workshop 'How Can the Poor Benefit from the Growing Markets for High Value Agricultural Products', 3–5 October 2005, CIAT, Cali, Colombia, p. 9, http://www.fao.org/docs/eims/upload/210973/regional_ap.pdf.

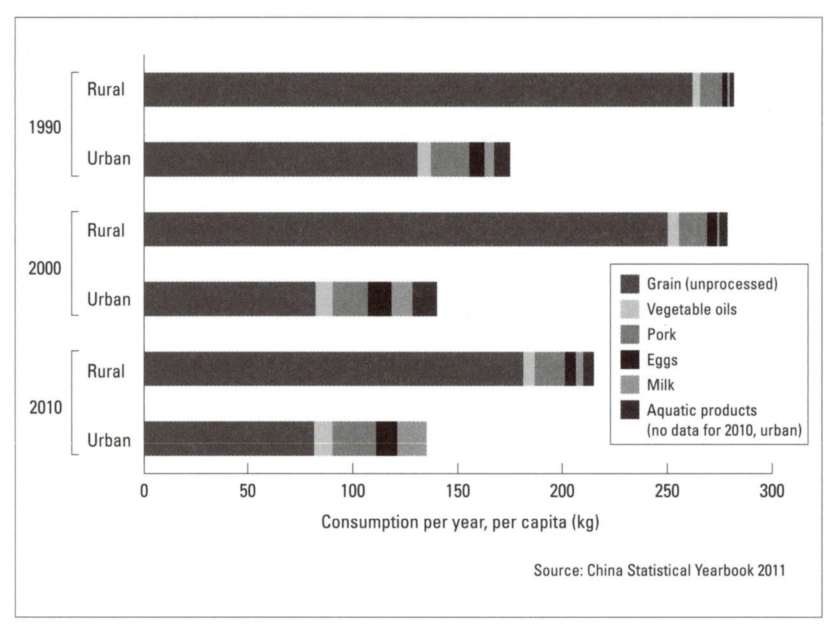

Figure 2. **Changing food-consumption patterns in China, 1990–2010**

market chains.[11] Retail giants such as Carrefour, Walmart and Tesco have all been expanding across the region.[12]

In Asia, average daily consumption of food has gradually risen, from 2,379 kilocalories (kcal) per person in 1990 to 2,665kcal in 2009.[13] Food-consumption patterns have also been changing over the past few decades, with distinct increases in fish, meat, dairy and vegetable consumption (see Figure 1). Between 1970 and 2007, the proportion of total daily calories consumed from rice by people in the average Asian household dropped from 38.2% to 29.3%.[14]

This shift is important because the production of meat is much more land intensive than cereal production, and diverts grains from human consumption into use in livestock feed. It takes around 7kg of grain to produce 1kg of beef and 2kg of grain for every 1kg of chicken.[15] UN agencies estimate that a single hectare planted with rice can feed around 19 people for a year, compared with just one or two people for beef or lamb raised on one hectare of land.[16]

In Asia, the decline in grain consumption has been most prominent in the industrialised countries of Japan, Singapore and South Korea, where imports of livestock products, edible oils and oil seeds have increased sharply.[17] Developing

Changing eating habits in China and India

In most booming Asian countries, with the exception of India,[20] the average person is consuming more calories a day than 20 years ago.[21] In 2009, the average Chinese, for example, consumed 3,036 kilocalories (kcal) per day, up from 2,562kcal in 1990. Throughout Asia, people are consuming more meat, fish, dairy and vegetables – making rice and other grains a smaller proportion of national diets.[22] Increased buying power allows consumers to buy refrigerators to store more meat and milk;[23] it also enables them to eat food prepared and purchased outside of the home.

In China, annual meat consumption rose from 8 million tons in 1978 to 71m tons in 2012.[24] The fast-food restaurant industry and confectionery market have also grown – the former was valued at US$94.2 billion in 2012, having grown at an average rate of 13% a year since 2008.[25] Better-off Chinese consumers were calculated to have spent approximately US$10.2bn on confectionery in 2011, a 20% increase in five years.[26]

Likewise, Indians in both rural and urban areas are now eating fewer grains, such as rice and wheat, in favour of more higher-value agricultural products, such as meat (mainly chicken), eggs, fish, fruits and edible oils.[27] In fact, because of its large vegetarian population, India has been consuming more dairy products than meat. The country is now the world's largest producer of milk (if one excludes the European Union) and although some projections indicate that it will be able to meet domestic demand until 2020,[28] other analysts note that this cannot be guaranteed.[29]

Increasing disposable income and the subsequent embrace of Western-style diets in China, India and other Asian nations have contributed to a twin-pronged problem: even as hundreds of millions continue to live in poverty and hunger, the number of overweight and obese people has risen rapidly. Diet-related, non-communicable illnesses, including type-2 diabetes, cardiovascular disease and certain types of cancer, are becoming more prevalent, posing a significant public-health burden.[30]

Asian countries, such as China, India, Indonesia and the Philippines, are experiencing similar dietary changes, albeit to varying degrees.[18]

In India, for example, between 2004/05 and 2009/10, imports of edible vegetable oils increased by 67% and those of pulses by almost 85%[19] (see text box). In 2010, China produced more than 50m tonnes of pork (around half of global pork production) for domestic consumption.

Agricultural decline and shifts

Since the successes of the Green Revolution approach of the 1940–70s – in which flagging food production after the Second World War was lifted, particularly with the use of hybrid seeds and chemical fertilisers – the two most populous Asian countries, China and India, have remained largely self-sufficient in cereal grains. However, there are signs that this is changing. Food imports are increasing or liable to increase.

In India in the 1980s, compound-growth rates of production and yields for two staple grains – rice and wheat – hovered above 3%. Between 2000/01 and 2011/12, by comparison, rice production grew at a much lower rate of 1.72% and yields only grew by 1.68%. The compound-growth rate of wheat production declined to 2.37% during this period and to 1.14% for wheat yields.[31] Overall, agricultural growth slowed from around 3.5% between the early 1980s and mid-1990s, to an estimated 2.5% in 2011/12 (short of a targeted 4%).

In China, too, yields are still growing but at a reduced rate. The annual yield-growth rate for cereals fell from 4% in the 1970s to 1.9% in the 1990s.[32] Since 2000, yield-growth

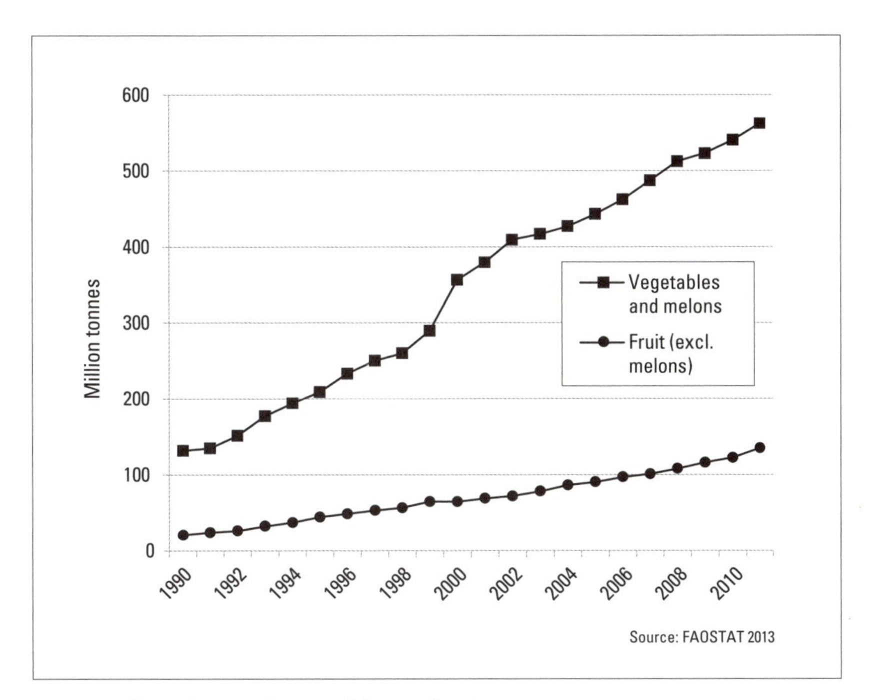

Figure 3. **China fruit and vegetable production, 1990–2011**

rates of both rice and maize stagnated or decelerated in most parts of China (although improvements have been noted in wheat yields).[33]

While yield-growth rates for major cereals have begun to slow, there have also been distinct structural shifts in Asian agriculture to accommodate changing demand.[34] This is particularly true in China, where the production of fruits and vegetables has increased significantly in recent decades (see Figure 3) as has that of meat and eggs. For example, between 1990 and 2011, the production of hen eggs increased by around 275%, chicken meat by 425%, pig meat by around 124% and cattle meat by more than 470%.[35]

Moreover, the very nature of farming is beginning to change. Pork, for example, accounts for roughly three-quarters of all meat eaten in China. Until the mid-1980s, up to

95% of China's pork was produced by small farming households, from pigs fed on kitchen scraps and locally sourced feedstuff. These pigs were raised mainly for consumption by the household, not only providing an important source of protein to those living in rural areas but also fulfilling an important ecological function by converting weeds, kitchen waste and residues from crops into manure for farm use.[36] Since 2007, however, these 'backyard farms' have been decreasing, while industrial-scale commercial pork farms and specialised household farms (with up to 500 pigs) have been expanding.[37]

Commercial farms rely on feedstuff manufactured from oil seeds and grains (mainly soybean and maize).[38] The pork industry's heavy reliance on soybean from North and South America to feed its animals helps explain why China has become the world's largest importer of the crop.

Poultry production in China has also become increasingly industrialised. One academic reports that the total amount of land occupied by large industrial farms is still only 17%, but this is a much more significant proportion than the 2% of land that such farms occupied in the 1980s.[39] The shift has not only had implications for smaller farmers, but has caused concerns about greenhouse-gas emissions, pollution from animal waste, over-grazing, and chemical and antibiotic use. China's livestock industry has been at the centre of numerous disease outbreaks and other food scares in recent years.[40]

Competing land uses in Asia

With relatively high levels of population growth and economic development, there has been increasing competition for land across Asia from agriculture on the one hand and industry and urban development on the other. Urban expansion usually happens on arable land, and in China and India such expansion has been occurring at an astonishing pace. According to one study, urban areas in India expanded by around 1.5m ha between 1955 and 1985, primarily by encroaching on arable land.[41] In China, arable land area shrank by more than 6% between 1997 and 2009, from just under 130m ha to 121.7m ha.[42]

In South Asia, there is now little or no spare land available for agricultural expansion within countries. Around 45% of the land with the potential to grow food but not used for this purpose instead houses human settlements, leaving 'little doubt that population growth and further urbanisation will be a significant factor in reducing land availability for agricultural use in this region'.[43] Assuming that population growth begins to stabilise in the next two decades, continuing changes in food consumption are expected to put considerable extra pressure on limited natural resources.[44]

Environmental degradation and water shortages

Across Asia, the unsustainable use of land, fresh water, fisheries and forests has resulted in high levels of environmental degradation. The benefits of the Green Revolution in Asian countries are widely known. Between 1970 and 1995, cereal production (mainly rice and wheat) in the region doubled, lifting millions out of poverty and hunger and contributing substantially to overall economic growth.[45] However, at its worst, the Green Revolution 'increased inequality, worsened absolute poverty, and resulted in environmental degradation'.[46] In doing so, it contributed to the conditions behind the current food insecurity in the region, including the mismanagement of the environment and an overemphasis on industrial agriculture. As the International Food Policy Research Institute (IFPRI) points out:

> Excessive and inappropriate use of fertilizers and pesticides ... has polluted waterways, poisoned agricultural workers, and killed beneficial insects and other wildlife. Irrigation practices have led to salt build-up and eventual abandonment of some of the best agriculture lands. Heavy dependence on a few major cereal varieties has led to the loss of biodiversity on farm.[47]

Soil fertility is essential for growing any kind of crop. The physical, chemical or biological degradation of soil threatens its ability to produce crops and affects productivity. According to one study, 24% of the world's land area is affected by degradation, 11% of which is in Indo-China, Myanmar, Malaysia, Indonesia and South China.[48] In South Asia, the arid and semi-arid regions of India, Pakistan and Afghanistan are particularly prone to desertification, while water erosion is a serious problem in humid climates, including in Bangladesh, Nepal, Sri Lanka and much of India.[49] In Bangladesh, riverbank erosion is the most serious form of soil degradation. Rain-fed parts of South Asia are also affected by declining soil fertility and deforestation. In China, more than 35% of land is now affected by degradation, and it is estimated that unless this trend is checked, crop production in northeast China could drop by as much as 40% over the next 50 years.[50] In South and Southeast

Asia, almost three-quarters of total agricultural land is now affected 'by erosion, by wind or water or chemical pollution'.[51]

Much of Asia's environmental degradation problem is rooted in the excessive use of agro-chemicals such as fertilisers and pesticides. Between 1992 and 2002, the use of chemical fertilisers grew by as much as 90% in countries such as India, Laos, Myanmar, the Philippines, Sri Lanka, Thailand and Vietnam, with much damage to soil structure and nutrient balance.[52] In China, chemical-fertiliser use per hectare doubled between 1980 and 2000.[53]

Irrigation has expanded rapidly since the 1960s. Today, Asia accounts for around 70% of the world's 277m ha of irrigated cropland.[54] Due to over-extraction and other poor irrigation practices, there has been widespread waterlogging and salinisation of irrigated land in the region. Almost 40% of cropland under irrigation in Asia's drylands is affected by salinisation.[55] The problem is of particular concern where monocropping of rice and wheat is widespread and relies on intensive irrigation practices, such as in the 13.5m-hectare Indo-Gangetic Plains across Bangladesh, India, Nepal and Pakistan. It is estimated that in India and Pakistan around 4.6m ha and 4.2m ha respectively of irrigated land are affected by salinisation.[56] In the Mekong River Delta, some of the most productive agricultural lands have been damaged because of saltwater intrusion and the natural leaching of rock salt into soils.[57]

Although the use of fertilisers and pesticides has brought great benefits to agriculture in Asia, it has also caused widespread contamination of aquifers, rivers and lakes in the region through run-off water containing nitrogen, phos-

Environmental degradation of fisheries

Fish is vital in Asian diets, accounting for up to 50% of all dietary protein consumed in countries such as Sri Lanka and Indonesia and around one-third in countries such as Bangladesh, Malaysia, Vietnam, Thailand and the Philippines.[68] Fisheries are also large contributors to GDP and a major source of livelihood for small-scale producers. The Asia-Pacific has been the world's largest producer of fish for decades; in 2008, 51% of all fish caught (marine and inland) were captured in the region, while 89% of farmed fish originated there.[69]

However, environmental degradation is challenging the health of Asia's fisheries. The FAO reports that in the last three decades or so there have been significant changes in fish stocks in the South China Sea and the Gulf of Thailand. While the abundance of larger, more valuable species (for example, groupers, snappers, sharks and rays) has dropped sharply, that of smaller and less valuable species (such as cardinal and trigger fish) has grown.[70] In general, many coastal fisheries in South and Southeast Asia have experienced severe and continuing declines as a result of overfishing.[71] Environmental degradation has exacerbated these declines and threatened biodiversity. Water quality and fish habitats in coastal areas have been reduced especially, as urban development and other land-based activities have polluted and silted up coastal waters.[72] Equally, 'irresponsible fishing practices, habitat loss and degradation, water abstraction, drainage of wetlands, dam construction and pollution' have threatened inland fisheries.[73] Even when these developments do not affect overall fish production, they harm the composition and value of fish produced.[74]

The Mekong River Basin, for example, is home to the world's largest inland fisheries. In 2008, these fisheries had a total production of 3.9 million tonnes: 1.9m tonnes from caught fish and 2m tonnes from aquaculture or fish farms.[75] The basin's fisheries generate up to US$7 billion per year and sustain millions of people, each of whom consumes between 41kg and 51kg of fish and other aquatic produce annually. Those who live near the Tonle Sap lake and river system in Cambodia consume considerably higher quantities – among the highest in the world.[76] According to the Mekong River Commission, declining catches are being reported throughout the basin, as well as there being fewer and smaller fish from the most popular predatory species. In the Tonle Sap, as commercial fishing increases the pressure on local fisherfolk, there are declining catches of larger carnivorous fish, while a greater proportion of smaller species are being caught.[77] Plans to further dam the mainstream Mekong River in the lower-basin countries of Cambodia, Vietnam and Laos have raised fears that the movements of migratory fish – which make up a large proportion of the basin's catch – will be blocked. The potential decline in fish production would have serious basin-wide economic and social impacts.[78]

phorous and highly toxic heavy metals such as copper and zinc.[58] The boom in Southeast Asia's livestock sector has not only led to a surging demand for cereals as animal feed, but has also resulted in rising contamination of freshwater resources from animal waste. This is now a serious problem in countries such as China and Vietnam.[59] Urbanisation and industrialisation have also contributed to water degradation through the discharge of industrial and household effluents into freshwater systems.

Water shortages in Asia are growing, and many areas are now water stressed[60] or water scarce.[61] Groundwater overuse rates are particularly high in China (more than 25%) and in parts of India (around 56%).[62] At the same time, demand for water is escalating steadily for agricultural, domestic and industrial use. Although agriculture remains the single largest use for fresh water in Asia, accounting for around 70% of all water consumed,[63] domestic and industrial demand has been growing, placing enormous pressure on regional river systems. Indeed, some major rivers, such as the Ganges in India, the Yellow River in China and the Chao Phraya in Thailand, are suffering from reduced flows. In China and South Asia, water tables have been declining alarmingly as annual groundwater withdrawals have increased more than twelvefold since the 1950s.[64] In some countries, government subsidies in the agricultural sector have worsened the situation. In parts of India, for example, fuel and electricity use for agricultural purposes is heavily subsidised by regional governments, leading to unsustainable rates of freshwater extraction from rivers and groundwater, as well as to huge wastage.[65]

Land and water degradation both have an adverse impact on agricultural productivity, and may contribute significantly to lower agricultural yields with a direct negative effect on agricultural incomes. Across Asia, there have been signs of declining productivity for staple crops such as rice in the last two decades. In Southeast and East Asia, for example, rice yields increased by an average of 2.5% annually from 1970–90 but slowed to 1.5% in Southeast Asia and 0.5% in East Asia from 1990–2004.[66] This slowdown is largely due to soil and water degradation caused by the expansion of intensive rice and wheat monocropping.[67]

Climate change

In the longer term, climate change is expected to further threaten agricultural production and productivity (discussed in further detail in Chapter Four). Climate change is 'now evident from observations of increases in global average air and ocean temperatures, widespread melting of snow and ice, and rising global mean sea level'.[79] Current trends indicate that average global temperatures are set to increase by 2–3°C in the latter half of this century.[80] Across Asia, increasing trends in surface-air temperatures have already led to observable changes in climate trends and variability, and extreme weather events.[81] Not only will these changes affect the availability of natural resources required to increase food production and to raise crop productivity, but they also threaten to undermine agricultural livelihoods, further push up food prices and cause the displacement of millions of people across the region.

Agriculture in South and Southeast Asia continues to rely heavily on rainfall, but monsoon patterns in the region are being disrupted, and most climate projections suggest that rising temperatures will see future monsoons with more rain falling in fewer days, increasing flooding risks, particularly in such densely populated areas as the Ganges–Brahmaputra–Meghna River Delta in South Asia and in the Mekong and Irrawaddy deltas in Southeast Asia.[82]

The dry season is also likely to last longer and become more intense, causing more droughts. Droughts have already caused substantial yield losses in India and China. In India, for example, the drought years of 1987 and 2002–03 affected over half the total cropped area and almost 300m people in the country.[83] Low precipitation is a threat to the region's winter wheat, and water availability for both people and livestock has also been declining.[84] A variety of extreme weather events – storms, typhoons and droughts – have caused widespread crop damage in the past few decades, in the Philippines in particular.[85]

Climate change, together with population growth and rising standards of living, is expected to continue to reduce freshwater availability across the region, and could affect more than 1bn people by 2050.[86] Saltwater intrusion into freshwater resources is already escalating because of rising sea levels and retreating river flows. This is a significant problem not just in the coastal parts of the Mekong Delta, but also in the Bay of Bengal region and the coastal plains of China in the dry season.[87]

Growing energy demand and biofuels

The production of biofuels has affected food prices in Asia (as in the rest of the world) and the availability of cereals on the international market. Because the United States, EU and Brazil together produce about 90% of the world's biodiesel and ethanol,[88] such production has so far only had a minor impact on land use within Asia. However, this could change as high economic growth escalates energy demands. The International Energy Agency estimates that energy demand in ASEAN states will expand by 90% between 2009 and 2035.[89] China and India will together account for more than half the increase in global energy demand to 2035.[90] The pursuit of energy self-sufficiency in the face of rising demand, as well as the imperative to lower carbon emissions through the use of 'green' fuel, may see developing Asian countries turn increasingly to biofuel production.[91]

Already, the production of first-generation liquid biofuels such as bioethanol (from food crops such as cereals, sugar cane and root crops) and biodiesel (from oil crops such as oil palm, rapeseed and soybeans) has increased substantially in Asia, from 2bn litres in 2004 to 12bn litres in 2008.[92] Major biofuel producers in the region include China, India, Indonesia, Malaysia, the Philippines, Thailand and Vietnam. Bioethanol is the main focus of production in China (from maize, wheat and cassava) and India and Thailand (mainly from molasses and sugar cane), while Indonesia, Malaysia and the Philippines are the main producers of biodiesel, using predominantly crude palm oil (CPO) as feedstock.[93] Other countries in the region are also producing biofuels, either on a more limited scale (in Vietnam and Myanmar) or at an experimental level (in Cambodia and Laos).[94]

As well as diverting land away from food production, biofuel production is seen as contributing to the concentration of land ownership and forced evictions. Since it requires large tracts of land and is reliant on monocropping by large agribusinesses, the FAO states that biofuel production leads to 'a much higher degree of external investors in land ownership and production than under more traditional forms of production'.[95]

Poverty and urbanisation

Great steps have been made in reducing poverty in Asia.[96] Since 1990, the number of people living on less than US$1.25 a day has dropped from 1.57bn to 733m people.[97] However, many in the region remain poor and malnourished, and in many areas life is becoming more difficult for farmers. In Asia, households living in poverty spend an average 60–70% of their household budgets on food.[98] This makes them extremely vulnerable to the kind of food-price inflation that has been seen globally since the mid-2000s; sudden increases in food prices are enough to push them over the edge. According to a study by the ADB, in the late 2000s an extra 112m Asians remained in poverty every year because of the food-price increases of this period.[99]

Poverty remains a predominantly rural phenomenon in Asia, and agriculture is a major source of livelihood for the rural poor. In East Asia, the proportion of poor people living in rural areas has declined to just over 50%. In South and Southeast Asia, however, the rural poor still account for around three-quarters of those living in extreme poverty.[100]

To cope with high food prices, poor households often resort to measures such as selling assets, mortgaging land, taking excessively high interest loans, pulling children out of school or spending less on food.[101] All of these have implications for their long-term ability to escape poverty.

Despite being food producers, small farmers are rarely net sellers of food and usually have little capacity to respond to higher food prices – by trying to increase production – in time to be able to benefit from them. Food-price volatility also deters farmers from making 'productive agricultural investments', because it makes it seem riskier to invest precious resources in better technology or other inputs with higher returns.[102] Consequently, small farmers in developing countries in Asia have largely been unable to respond to price spikes in the recent past, when 'not only did higher prices fail to reach the farm gate in many cases, but even where they did, smallholders were … unable to seize the opportunity because of long-standing production and marketing constraints, coupled with higher costs for fuel and fertilizers.'[103]

Landlessness is another growing problem, and farm sizes continue to shrink across the region. In India, for example, average farm sizes in 1960 were 2.6ha. At present, however, more than 80% of agricultural land holdings are smaller than two hectares, and more than 60% of farmers cultivate less than one hectare of land.[104] Over the past 25 years, farm sizes have shrunk and landlessness has also increased in Bangladesh, Cambodia, the Philippines, Thailand and Indonesia.[105] As rural populations in parts of Southeast Asia and in South Asia are still expanding, these trends are set to continue over the coming decades.

Poor and marginalised communities are often pushed off their traditional lands into areas where land is more difficult to cultivate and ecologically very sensitive to input-intensive farming. This results in both dwindling incomes for these communities and damage to the environment. While nobody is really clear on how much farmland has been 'grabbed' worldwide, at least 29m ha of agricultural land in Asia has been documented as being sold to wealthy outside investors.[106] Many of these sales have not only forced small farmers off their lands without sufficient compensation to restore local livelihoods,[107] but have also targeted uncultivated, 'marginal' land collectively owned by rural communities under indigenous land-tenure systems. In Indonesia and parts of Malaysia, for example, millions of hectares of customary forestlands are reportedly being acquired for the production of palm oil, which is exported to China, India and the EU in large quantities.[108] In the Philippines, 'idle, under-utilised lands' traditionally belonging to local communities have been allocated for plantation-style agriculture for biofuels and rubber.[109] Such land acquisitions have also been reported in Special Economic Zones (SEZs) in India, Nepal, Bangladesh, Cambodia and Laos.

In a region where most of the poor live in rural areas and rely on small-scale farming, these acquisitions are limiting access to land and worsening tenure insecurity. Despite decades of land reforms, land tenure remains a complex challenge in most developing Asian countries. The unequal distribution of land leads to poor production output, paltry income for the less privileged, indebtedness and ultimately poverty in the countryside.

The difficulties of making a living on the land have contributed to the urban migration that continues unabated across Asia. This move to the cities is predominantly by men and younger people, resulting in a surge in the number of rural households headed by women. Along with other 'marginalised farmers and tenants, indigenous peoples, pastoralists and herders, fisherfolk and internally displaced persons', rural women suffer disproportionately from socio-economic inequalities in Asia.[110] Throughout the region, they lack sufficient access to productive resources and relevant support services, deeply undermining their ability to earn a decent living that enables them to provide adequate and nutritious food to themselves and those dependent on them.[111]

Conclusion

Asia is central to the world's ability to feed itself in the future. Its rapidly growing middle classes and their shifting diets have triggered fundamental structural changes in agricultural sectors in the region. Yet, as governments strive to meet their citizens' growing and diversifying demand for food, they also face huge environmental and socio-economic challenges. Asia's limited arable land and water resources have been degraded by decades of misuse and industrial pollution. Land is increasingly being deployed for purposes other than growing food, from the building of homes and factories to the production of biofuels. Both of the region's giants, China and India, are already importing more food to feed their livestock and people; if this trend continues, it will inevitably affect global food prices and the food security of hundreds of millions worldwide.

Even as efforts to achieve greater food security at home become more urgent, many in Asia are still being left behind in hunger and poverty. Life is proving increasingly difficult for small farmers, accelerating migration to the cities and widening the gap between the growing demand for food and the capacity of those left behind in the countryside to grow more food on dwindling resources. The unpredictable effects of climate change will undeniably compound these difficulties.

So far, Asia has managed to grow enough food to feed its people. China and India have maintained a reasonable degree of self-sufficiency, while countries such as Vietnam and Thailand have turned themselves into food exporters. However, food systems in the region are fast approaching the limits of their ability to sufficiently feed the continent. The situation urgently demands sustainable and more resilient forms of agriculture. Action needs to be taken to ensure local communities are protected from threats to their livelihoods and food security, including forced land evictions, harmful climate-change impacts, inequitable food and agricultural policies, inadequate infrastructure and high levels of food wastage on and off farms. These are just some of the challenges that Asian governments must come to terms with quickly if they are to have any success in safeguarding the future food security of their people.

Notes

1 In South and Southeast Asia, the decline has been quicker, while in East Asia population growth rates have remained relatively steady since 2003. See United Nations Economic and Social Commission for Asia and the Pacific (UNESCAP), *Statistical Year Book for Asia and the Pacific 2011*, October 2011, http://www.unescap.org/stat/data/syb2011/I-People/Population.asp. Modernisation, social change and declining fertility rates (number of children born per woman) are some of the factors underpinning this gradual slowing of population growth in Asia.

2 Population Division of the Department of Economic and Social Affairs of the United Nations Secretariat, *World Population Prospects: The 2012 Revision*, http://esa.un.org/unpd/wpp/index.htm.

3 'Africa and Asia to lead urban population growth in next 40 years – UN report', UN News Centre, 5 April 2012, http://www.un.org/apps/news/story.asp?NewsID=41722.

4 ADB, *Food security and poverty in Asia and the Pacific: Key challenges*

and policy issues (Mandaluyong City: ADB, 2012), p. 3, http://www.adb.org/sites/default/files/pub/2012/food-security-poverty.pdf.

5 The IMF's definition of 'developing Asia' includes all of the region except Japan and the 'newly industrialised countries' of South Korea, Singapore, Hong Kong and Taiwan; see 'Asia Rising: Patterns of Economic Development and Growth', IMF World Economic Outlook, Chapter 3, p.1. The ADB definition is broader, referring to 45 developing member countries of the ADB, in East, Southeast, South and Central Asia, as well as Pacific island countries. The definition excludes Japan but includes: Afghanistan, Armenia, Azerbaijan, Bangladesh, Bhutan, Brunei Darussalam, Cambodia, Cook Islands, People's Republic of China, Georgia, India, Indonesia, Fiji, Hong Kong, China, Kazakhstan, Kiribati, the Republic of Korea, Kyrgyz Republic, Lao People's Democratic Republic, Malaysia, Maldives, Marshall Islands, Federated States of Micronesia, Mongolia, Myanmar, Nauru, Nepal, Pakistan, Palau, Papua New Guinea, Philippines, Samoa, Singapore, Solomon Islands, Sri Lanka, Taipei, China, Tajikistan, Thailand, Timor Leste, Tonga, Turkmenistan, Tuvalu, Uzbekistan, Vanuatu, Vietnam. See http://www.adb.org/countries/main.

6 ADB, *Food security and poverty in Asia and the Pacific*, p. 3.

7 See, for example, Harinder Kohli, Ashok Sharma and Anil Sood (eds), *Asia 2050: Realizing the Asian Century* (Mandaluyong City, Philippines: ADB, 2011).

8 Sanderine Nonhebel, 'Global food supply and the impacts of increased use of biofuels', *Energy*, vol. 37, no. 1, January 2012, pp. 115–21, http://www.sciencedirect.com/science/article/pii/S0360544211006165.

9 Zhong Nan, 'Demand drives soybean imports', *China Daily*, 28 October 2013, http://www.chinadaily.com.cn/business/2013-10/28/content_17064657.htm. See also Mindi Schneider, 'Feeding China's Pigs: Implications for the Environment, China's Smallholder Farmers and Food Security', Institute for Agriculture and Trade Policy, May 2011, p. 4, http://pigpenning.files.wordpress.com/2011/05/schneider_feeding-chinas-pigs-2011.pdf.

10 'OECD–FAO Agricultural Outlook 2013–2022: Highlights', OECD–FAO, 2013, p. 72, http://www.oecd.org/site/oecd-fao agriculturaloutlook/highlights-2013-EN.pdf.

11 ADB, *Food security and poverty in Asia and the Pacific*, p. 3.

[12] For more, see KPMG, 'Grocery Retailing in Asia Pacific', 25 October 2006, http://www.kpmg.com/cn/en/issuesandinsights/articlespublications/pages/retailing-asia-pacific-200610.aspx.

[13] ADB, *Food Security in Asia and the Pacific*, report from Symposium on Food Security in Asia and the Pacific: Key Policy Issues and Options, 17–18 September 2012 at the Liu Institute for Global Issues, UBC, p. xv, http://www.adb.org/sites/default/files/pub/2013/food-security-asia-pacific.pdf.

[14] C. Peter Timmer, 'The Changing Role of Rice in Asia's Food Security', ADB Working Paper Series No. 15, September 2010, p. 8, http://www.agriskmanagementforum.org/sites/agriskmanagementforum.org/files/Documents/adb-wp15-rice-food-security.pdf.

[15] FAO, 'Livestock's Long Shadow: Environmental issues and options', 2006, p. 45, http://www.fao.org/docrep/010/a0701e/a0701e00.htm.

[16] See, for example, WHO and FAO, 'Diet, Nutrition and the Prevention of Chronic Diseases', 2003, p. 21, http://www.fao.org/docrep/005/AC911E/ac911e05.htm#bm05.4. See also, C.R.W. Spedding, 'The effect of dietary changes on agriculture', in Barry Lewis and Gerd Assmann (eds), *The social and economic contexts of coronary prevention* (London: Current Medical Literature, 1990).

[17] ADB, *Food security and poverty in Asia and the Pacific*, p. 4.

[18] *Ibid.*

[19] Indian Ministry of Agriculture, 'Agriculture at a Glance 2010', http://eands.dacnet.nic.in/Advance_Estimate-2010.htm.

[20] Curiously, the average number of calories consumed by Indians since the early 1980s has reportedly declined, especially in rural areas where consumption has dropped from around 2,150kcal in 1993/94 to 2,028kcal in 2009/10. See Deepankar Basu and Amit Basole, 'The Calorie Consumption Puzzle in India: An Empirical Investigation', Working Paper No. 285, Political Economy Research Institute, University of Massachusetts Amherst, 12 July 2012, http://www.peri.umass.edu/fileadmin/pdf/working_papers/working_papers_251-300/WP285.pdf. Some analysts argue that household food budgets have stagnated or shrunk as non-food items have become costlier, and that families have been spending more on eating fewer calories (for example, more from fruits and vegetables and less from grains). Others insist that national agencies are failing to measure all of the processed or pre-prepared food being eaten in and outside of the home. In any case,

Nikos Alexandratos and Jelle Bruinsma estimate that even with modest economic growth in the medium term, average individual daily intake of food is likely to grow considerably, to around 2,825kcal by 2050. See Nikos Alexandratos and Jelle Bruinsma, 'World Agriculture towards 2030/2050: The 2012 Revision', ESA Working Paper No. 12-03, Global Perspective Studies Team, FAO Agricultural Development Economics Division, June 2012 (a remake of Chapters 1–3 of FAO, *Interim Report World Agriculture: towards 2030/2050* (Rome: FAO, 2006), http://www.fao.org/fileadmin/templates/esa/Global_persepctives/world_ag_2030_50_2012_rev.pdf).

21 Economic growth in countries such as China and Vietnam has resulted in considerable increases in per-capita calorie consumption. See Nikos Alexandratos and Jelle Bruinsma, 'World Agriculture towards 2030/2050: The 2012 Revision'.

22 Fengying Zhai et al., 'Prospective study on nutrition transition in China', *Nutrition Reviews*, vol. 67, Special Issue on 'World Congress of Public Health Nutrition', issue supplement S1, May 2009, pp. S56–S61.

23 Penn State Extension, 'India: Milk's New Horizon', College of Agricultural Sciences, 13 September 2013, http://extension.psu.edu/animals/dairy/news/2013/india-milk2019s-new-horizon.

24 Janet Larsen, 'Meat Consumption in China Now Double That in the United States', Plan B Update, Earth Policy Institute, 24 April 2012, http://www.earth-policy.org/plan_b_updates/2012/update102.

25 IBIS World Fast-Food Restaurants Market Research Report, August 2013.

26 Oliver Nieberg, 'Chocolate driving growth in Chinese confectionery market – Euromonitor' Confectionery News, 9 November 2011, http://www.confectionerynews.com/Markets/Chocolate-driving-growth-in-Chinese-confectionery-market-Euromonitor.

27 Government of India (GoI), *Economic Survey 2011–12* (New Delhi: Ministry of Finance, 2012). See also Srikanta Chatterjee, Allan Rae and Ranjan Ray, 'Food Consumption and Calorie Intake in Contemporary India', April 2007, https://editorialexpress.com/cgi-bin/conference/download.cgi?db_name=NZAE2007&paper_id=72; and Raghav Gaiha et al., 'Has Dietary Transition Slowed Down in India: An analysis based on 50th, 61st and 66th rounds of NSS', Research Institute for Economics and Business Administration, Kobe University, Japan, 8 June 2012, http://www.rieb.

kobe-u.ac.jp/academic/ra/dp/English/DP2012-15.pdf.

[28] OECD–FAO, Country statistical profiles 2011, http://stats.oecd.org/index.aspx, as quoted in Penn State Extension, 'India: Milk's New Horizon'.

[29] Wenge Fu et al., 'Rising consumption of animal products in China and India: National and global implications', *China & World Economy*, vol. 20, no. 3, pp.88–106.

[30] Zhai et al., 'Prospective study on nutrition transition in China'.

[31] GoI, *Economic Survey 2011–12*, pp. 181–2, http://indiabudget.nic.in/es2011-12/echap-08.pdf. See also Angus Deaton and Jean Drèze, 'Food and Nutrition in India: Facts and interpretation', *Economic and Political Weekly*, vol. XLIV, no. 7, 14 February 2009.

[32] Mingsheng Fan et al., 'Improving crop productivity and resource use efficiency to ensure food security and environmental quality in China', *Journal of Experimental Botany Advance Access*, published online 30 September 2011, p. 3.

[33] *Ibid.*

[34] Jikun Huang, Jun Yang and Scott Rozelle, 'China's agriculture: drivers of change and implications for China and the rest of world', *Agricultural Economics*, vol. 41, no. 1, 2010, p. 48.

[35] Based on figures from FAOSTAT 2013.

[36] Schneider, 'Feeding China's Pigs', p. 6.

[37] Fred Gale, Daniel Marti, and Dinghuan Hu, 'China's Volatile Pork Industry', USDA Economic Research Service (ERS), February 2012, p. 8, http://usda01.library.cornell.edu/usda/ers/LDP-M/2010s/2012/LDP-M-02-07-2012_Special_Report.pdf.

[38] *Ibid.*, and Schneider, 'Feeding China's Pigs', p. 10.

[39] See Wen Tiejun, dean of Renmin University's agriculture school, quoted in Malcolm Moore, 'China now eats twice as much meat as the United States', *Daily Telegraph*, 12 October 2012, http://www.telegraph.co.uk/news/worldnews/asia/china/9605048/China-now-eats-twice-as-much-meat-as-the-United-States.html.

[40] For example, see Gale, Marti and Hu, 'China's Volatile Pork Industry', p. 21.

[41] Shuqing Zhao et al., 'Land use change in Asia and the ecological consequences', *Ecological Research*, vol. 21, no. 6, November 2006, pp. 890–6, http://link.springer.com/article/10.1007%2Fs11284-006-0048-2.

[42] PRC, China Statistical Yearbook 2012. See also 'Shrinking arable land threatens grain security', *Xinhua*, 18 October 2010, http://www.chinadaily.com.cn/china/2010-10/18/content_11423618.htm; and

Shuhao Tan, 'Impacts of Cultivated Land Conversion on Environmental Sustainability and Grain Self-sufficiency in China', *China & World Economy*, vol. 16, no. 3, 2008, p. 79 for a discussion of declining agricultural land availability in China between 1988 and 2005.

[43] Jelle Bruinsma, 'The Resource Outlook to 2050: By how much do land, water and crop yields need to increase by 2050?', paper presented at the 'Expert Meeting on How to Feed the World in 2050', FAO Economic and Social Development Department, 24–26 June 2009, ftp://ftp.fao.org/docrep/fao/012/ak971e/ak971e00.pdf.

[44] Thomas Kastner et al., 'Global changes in diets and the consequences for land requirements for food', *Proceedings of the National Academy of Sciences of the United States of America (PNAS)*, vol. 109, no. 18, 1 May 2012, pp. 6,868–72.

[45] Peter B.R. Hazell, 'The Asian Green Revolution', IFPRI Discussion Paper 00911, November 2009, p. 1, http://www.ifpri.org/sites/default/files/publications/ifpridp00911.pdf.

[46] Sununtar Setboonsarng, 'Organic Agriculture, Poverty Reduction, and the Millennium Development Goals', ADB Institute Discussion Paper No. 54, August 2006, p. 5, http://www.undpegov.org/w/images/b/b2/ADBI_study_shows_potential_of_organic_agriculture_to_contribute_to_the_MDGs.pdf.

[47] *Ibid.*, p. 6.

[48] Z.G. Bai et al., 'Proxy global assessment of land degradation', *Soil Use and Management*, vol. 24, no. 3, September 2008, pp. 223–34, http://www.geo.uzh.ch/microsite/rsl-documents/research/publications/peer-reviewed-articles/2008_ProxyGlobal_SoilUseMgmt_ZB-0471031552/2008_ProxyGlobal_SoilUseMgmt_ZB.pdf.

[49] Tapan J. Purakayastha et al., 'Soil Resources Affecting Food Security and Safety in South Asia', in Lal R. and B.A. Stewart (eds), *World Soil Resources and Food Security* (Boca Raton, FL: CRC Press/Taylor and Francis, 2012), p. 281.

[50] United Nations Economic and Social Commission for Asia and the Pacific (UNESCAP), *Sustainable Agriculture and Food Security in Asia and the Pacific* (Bangkok: United Nations, 2009), p. 60, http://www.unescap.org/65/documents/Theme-Study/st-escap-2535.pdf.

[51] *Ibid.* See also Stanley Woods, Kate Sebastian and Sarah Scherr, *Pilot Analysis of Global Ecosystem: Agroecosystems* (Washington DC: World Resources Institute, 2000), p. 50, http://www.ifpri.org/sites/default/files/publications/agroeco.pdf.

52 UNESCAP, *Sustainable Agriculture and Food Security in Asia and the Pacific*.

53 Mark Curtis and Sameer Dostani, 'Asia at the Crossroads', ActionAid, 28 February 2012, p. 20, http://www.actionaid.org/publications/asia-crossroads.

54 Aditi Mukherji et al., *Revitalizing Asia's Irrigation: To sustainably meet tomorrow's food needs* (Rome: International Water Management Institute and FAO, 2009), http://www.fao.org/nr/water/docs/Revitalizing_Asias_Irrigation.pdf.

55 Hazell, 'The Asian Green Revolution', p. 16.

56 Rajat Gupta and Ashok Seth, 'A Review of Resource Conserving Technologies for Sustainable Management of the Rice–Wheat Cropping Systems of the Indo-Gangetic Plains (IGP)', *Crop Protection*, vol. 26, no. 3, March 2007, p. 436.

57 United Nations Environment Programme (UNEP), *Global Environmental Outlook 2000*.

58 Mukherji et al., *Revitalizing Asia's Irrigation*, pp. 250–1.

59 UNESCAP, *Sustainable Agriculture and Food Security in Asia and the Pacific*, p. 63

60 United Nations Development Programme (UNDP), 'Beyond scarcity: Power, poverty and the global water crisis', *Human Development Report 2006*, p. 176, http://hdr.undp.org/en/media/HDR06-complete.pdf. A country is water stressed when its per-capita availability of water falls to 1,700 cubic metres or less.

61 *Ibid*. Water scarcity is achieved when per-capita availability drops to less than 1,000 cubic metres, and absolute water scarcity is reached when this availability falls below 500 cubic metres.

62 *Ibid.*

63 UNESCAP, *Sustainable Agriculture and Food Security in Asia and the Pacific*, p. 63.

64 *Ibid.*

65 *Ibid.*, p. 62.

66 Curtis and Dostani, 'Asia at the Crossroads', p. 14.

67 *Ibid.*

68 Ilona C. Stobutzki, Geronimo T. Silvestre and Len R. Garces, 'Key issues in coastal fisheries in South and Southeast Asia, outcomes of a regional initiative', *Fisheries Research*, vol. 78, no. 2–3, May 2006, p. 109, http://www.sciencedirect.com/science/article/pii/S0165783606000567.

69 FAO, 'Status and potential of fisheries and aquaculture in Asia and the Pacific 2010', Asia-Pacific Fishery Commission, RAP Publication 2010/17, pp. 5, 45, http://www.fao.org/docrep/013/i1924e/i1924e00.pdf.

70 *Ibid.*, p. 14.

71 *Ibid.*

72 I.C. Stobutzki et al., 'Decline of demersal coastal fisheries res-

ources in three developing Asian countries', *Fisheries Research*, vol. 78, no. 2–3, May 2006, p. 138, http://www.sciencedirect.com/science/article/pii/S0165783606000580.

[73] FAO, *The State of World Fisheries and Aquaculture 2010* (Rome: FAO Fisheries and Aquaculture Department, 2010), p. 8, http://www.fao.org/docrep/013/i1820e/i1820e01.pdf.

[74] *Ibid.*

[75] Mekong River Commission, 'State of the Basin Report 2010 – Summary', 2010, p. 12, http://www.mrcmekong.org/assets/Publications/basin-reports/MRC-SOB-Summary-reportEnglish.pdf.

[76] *Ibid.*

[77] *Ibid.*

[78] *Ibid.*, p. 13. See also Christopher Baker, 'Dams, Power and Security in the Mekong: Non-Traditional Security Assessment of Hydro-Development in the Mekong River Basin', NTS-Asia Research Paper No. 8, Centre for Non-Traditional Security Studies, S. Rajaratnam School of International Studies Singapore, 2012, http://www.rsis.edu.sg/nts/HTML-Newsletter/Report/pdf/NTS-Asia_Christopher%20G.%20Baker.pdf.

[79] IPCC, *Climate Change 2007: Synthesis Report. Contribution of Working Groups I, II and III to the Fourth Assessment Report of the Intergovernmental Panel on Climate Change* (Geneva: IPCC, 2008), p. 72.

[80] Nicholas Stern, *The Economics of Climate Change: The Stern Review* (Cambridge: Cambridge University Press, 2006), p. 63. See also Ian Allison et al., *The Copenhagen Diagnosis, 2009: Updating the World on the Latest Climate Science* (Sydney: The University of New South Wales, 2009); and IPCC, *Climate Change 2007: Synthesis Report*.

[81] IPCC, *Climate Change 2007: Working Group II: Impacts, Adaptation and Vulnerability* (Cambridge, UK, and New York: Cambridge University Press, 2007), pp. 472–506.

[82] IPCC, *Climate Change 2007: Working Group II*. See also IPCC, *Climate Change 2001: Working Group II: Impacts, Adaptation and Vulnerability* (Cambridge: Cambridge University Press, 2001), p. 578.

[83] Reiner Wassmann et al., 'Regional Vulnerability of Climate Change Impacts on Asian Rice Production and Scope for Adaptation', *Advances in Agronomy*, vol. 102, no. 9, 2009, p. 103, http://www.sciencedirect.com/science/article/pii/S0065211309010037.

[84] See, for example, 'UN: Drought endangers Chinese winter wheat harvest', Associated Press, 11 February 2011, http://www.businessweek.com/ap/financialnews/D9L8JFGG1.htm.

[85] Caesar B. Cororaton and Erwin L. Corong, 'Philippine Agricultural and Food Policies: Implications on Poverty and Income Distribution', IFPRI Draft Research Report, Annual Meeting of International Agricultural Trade Research Consortium, 7–9 December 2008, Scottsdale, Arizona, p. 23.

[86] IPCC, *Climate Change 2007: Working Group II.*

[87] *Ibid.*

[88] USAID, 'Biofuels in Asia: An analysis of sustainability options', March 2009, p. 17, http://pdf.usaid.gov/pdf_docs/PNADS887.pdf.

[89] International Energy Agency (IEA), 'Southeast Asia likely to play increasingly significant role in the world's energy markets', 31 May 2012, http://www.iea.org/newsroomandevents/news/2012/may/name,27338,en.html.

[90] IEA, *World Energy Outlook 2012*, 12 November 2012, http://www.worldenergyoutlook.org/publications/weo-2012/.

[91] Jinyue Yan and Tun Lin, 'Biofuels in Asia', *Applied Energy*, vol. 86, supplement 1, November 2009, S1–S10, http://www.sciencedirect.com/science/article/pii/S0306261909002815.

[92] USAID, 'Biofuels in Asia', p. 16.

[93] Yan and Lin, 'Biofuels in Asia', S8.

[94] *Ibid.*

[95] Asbjørn Eide, *The Right to Food and the Impact of Liquid Biofuels (Agrofuels)* (Rome: FAO Right to Food Unit, 2009), p. 12, http://www.fao.org/docrep/016/ap550e/ap550e.pdf.

[96] This reduction, however, has been uneven across and within sub-regions. For more, see ADB, *Food security and poverty*.

[97] ADB, *Food Security in Asia and the Pacific*, p. xv.

[98] ADB, *Food security and poverty*, p. 9.

[99] *Ibid.*

[100] While the rural population in Southeast Asia is already declining, South Asia's rural population continues to grow, albeit at a gradually decreasing rate. It is expected to start to decline only in 2025. See International Fund for Agricultural Development (IFAD), 'Rural Poverty Report 2011 - New realities, new challenges: new opportunities for tomorrow's generation' (Rome: IFAD, November 2010), p. 16, http://www.ifad.org/rpr2011/report/e/rpr2011.pdf.

[101] Swati Narayan, 'Nourish South Asia', Oxfam Report, September 2011, p. 14, http://www.oxfam.org/sites/www.oxfam.org/files/cr-nourish-south-asia-grow-101111-en.pdf.

[102] ADB, *Food security and poverty*, p. 12.

[103] IFAD, 'Rural Poverty Report 2011', p. 33.

[104] GoI, 'Report of the Steering Committee on Agriculture and Allied

Sectors for the Formulation of the Eleventh Five Year Plan (2007–2012)', Planning Commission of India, 15 April 2007, p. 20, http://planningcommission.nic.in/aboutus/committee/strgrp11/str11_agriall.pdf.

[105] IFAD, 'Improving access to land and tenure security', IFAD policy paper, December 2008, p. 7, http://www.ifad.org/pub/policy/land/e.pdf.

[106] Ward Anseeuw et al., and Michael Taylor, 'Land Rights and the Rush for Land', in the Findings of the Global Commercial Pressures on Land Research Project, International Land Coalition (ILC), January 2012, p. 4.

[107] *Ibid.*

[108] Marcus Colchester, 'Palm oil and indigenous peoples in South East Asia', ILC, 2011, http://www.landcoalition.org/publications/palm-oil-and-indigenous-peoples-south-east-asia.

[109] *Ibid.*

[110] Asian NGO Coalition for Agrarian Reform and Rural Development (ANGOC), 'Securing the Right to Land: A CSO Overview on Access to Land in Asia', 2009, http://www.angoc.org/portal/wp-content/uploads/2010/04/12/securing-the-right-to-land-a-cso-overview-on-access-to-land-in-asia/Securing-the-Right-to-Land-FULL.pdf.

[111] *Ibid.*

CHAPTER THREE

How Asia has fed its citizens

Despite dire predictions in the mid-1990s that some leading Asian nations would become a burden on the global food system, many have so far managed to remain largely self-sufficient in major grains. In recent decades, great steps have also been made in reducing poverty in Asia.[1] Between 1990 and 2009, for example, those living on less than US$1.25 a day fell from 1.57 billion to 733 million people.[2] Granted, the region's food and agricultural systems are now under tremendous stress, creating concerns for the future; and despite years of economic boom, many Asians remain undernourished. However, before analysing these problems, it is worth examining the policies that have kept most of Asia fed over the past five decades.

In many ways, China has been at the forefront of this success. Since then-leader Deng Xiaoping ushered in an era of economic reforms in the late 1970s,[3] the country has defied fears around its ability to feed itself as its population grows, incomes rise, diets change and natural resources dwindle.[4] Deng's economic reforms saw significant structural changes in the agricultural sector, including the decentralisation of land from collectives to individual households and the re-establishment of rural markets. Rapid agricultural growth and gains in productivity followed.[5]

According to Jikun Huang and Scott Rozelle, increased productivity 'enabled China to release its large pool of abundant rural labour, providing cheap labour for industrialisation', thereby assisting the country's transition from an agrarian, centrally planned economy to a market-oriented one dominated by industry and services.[6] Industrialisation was also fuelled by aggressive policies designed to lower trade barriers and attract foreign direct investment.[7]

The Chinese economy has grown at an average rate of around 10% per year since 1990, and this has helped the country to reduce poverty and undernourishment. Between 1990 and 2009, the proportion of people living on less than US$2 a day plunged from 84.6% (or more than 968m) to less than 27.2% (around 360m).[8] The proportion of children under five suffering from stunting and those underweight both dropped by nearly two-thirds.[9]

Industrialisation in China has meant agriculture now contributes less to GDP – just 10.1% in 2010, down from 27.1% in 1990. Nevertheless, sectoral output has continued to grow fairly quickly, staying ahead of population growth.[10] Technological advances since the 1960s – with integrated planting technologies involving the use of greater planting density, chemical fertilisers, pesticides and herbicides, and soil-quality improvements – have been critical to this achievement, following substantial increases in investment in agricultural research and development (R&D), as have improvements in transport, market infrastructure and inte-

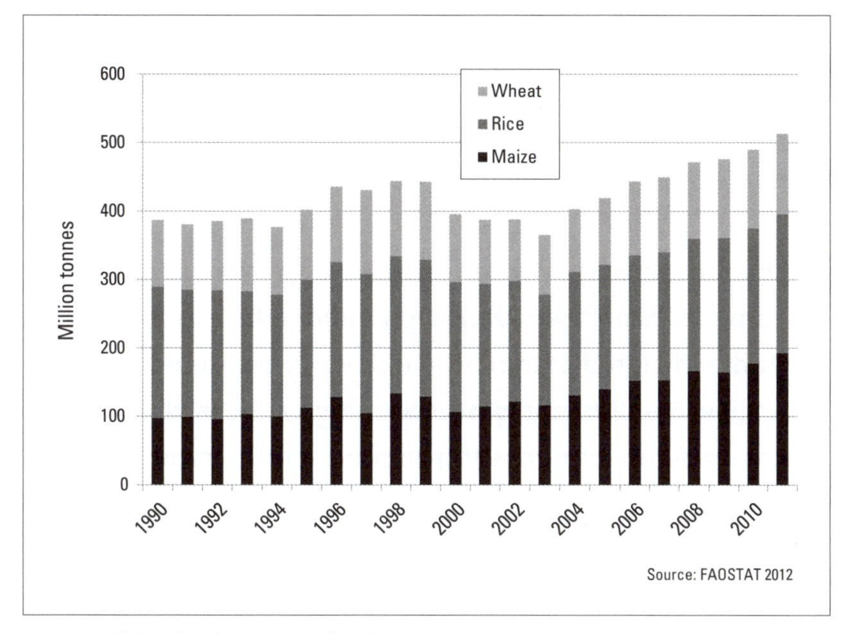

Figure 1. **China food grain production, 1990–2011**

gration, and an expansion in irrigation.[11] Between 1990 and 2011, production of rice, wheat and maize jumped from around 387m tonnes to almost 513m tonnes (see Figure 1), mainly due to increases in yields, as total area under cultivation shrank during this period. The production of meat (especially pork) and eggs has also increased significantly, as has that of fruits and vegetables.[12]

These trends indicate a distinct structural shift in China's agricultural sector.[13] There has also been a growing focus on value-added agriculture. At the household level, the share of land sown for grains has dropped, from 75.8% in 1985 to 68.4% in 2010,[14] although there is considerable regional variation in these figures, and for China's poorest farmers cereal production still remains the most reliable source of food.

China's continued heavy emphasis on maintaining near self-sufficiency in cereals such as rice, wheat and maize relies on, among other things: the maintenance of a significant buffer stock (at least 150–200m tonnes); boosting domestic grain production to 540m tonnes by 2020; and preserving 121.2m ha of the 121.7m ha of farmland cultivated today.[15]

Over the past decade, the need to strongly support all farmers has been recognised and addressed through several policies. In 2004, for example, nationwide direct subsidies to farmers were introduced as part of larger efforts to support agricultural production, promote rural development and raise the incomes of small farmers. These subsidies included direct payments to farmers for cultivating grain crops and assistance in buying high-quality seeds and agricultural machinery. By 2006, all agricultural taxes and fees had been phased out, price-support programmes for government procurement were amended, and a subsidy for fuel and fertilisers was introduced.[16] Between 2005 and 2010, the amount allocated for government-support programmes for agriculture grew from RMB17.4bn to RMB133.49bn.[17] The government's substantial investment in agricultural R&D, which began in the mid-1990s, continues to grow.[18]

China's 12th Five-Year Plan stresses the development of modern agriculture that is technologically advanced and ecologically safe. This is based on increasing farm incomes and providing farmers with new income channels and greater subsidies, improving rural infrastructure and services such as health and social security, and more.[19] In 2012, China's annual 'No. 1' policy document outlining government priorities looked at rural issues, emphasising the importance of technological innovation in ensuring sustained agricultural growth.[20] Such policies reflect the government's growing sense of urgency around the need to address the expanding income gap in China, and the imperative of keeping a sufficient number of small farmers engaged in food production – vital at a time when more than half of the population is already residing in urban areas.

In addition to rural development, the government has also strengthened its focus on environmental sustainability. For some time now, it has been enforcing water conservation and efficiency measures for urban, industrial and agricultural purposes, including wastewater recycling in cities such as Beijing and improvement in irrigation practices.[21] The 12th Five-Year Plan has been called the 'greenest' of all such plans, with ambitious targets for reducing pollution, improving energy efficiency and increasing the use of clean energy and the rate of forest coverage.[22] In 2011, the 'No. 1' policy document, for the first time, focused on water conservation and the development of adequate relevant rural infrastructure.[23] A budget of RMB4 trillion (around US$620bn) was announced to fund these efforts to tackle China's growing water shortage over the next decade.

Additionally, Beijing has tried to safeguard fish stocks. China is the world's largest fish producer, accounting for around 35% of global production.[24] Domestic demand has been growing rapidly, but several factors have contributed to a decline in the country's inshore fishing industry. These include overfishing and government-imposed limits on fishing in response to industrial pollution, as well as bilateral fishing agreements and the establishment of Exclusive Economic Zones (EEZs) by neighbouring countries.[25] To counter this decline and provide livelihoods to unemployed fisherfolk, the Chinese government has been increasingly focusing on the development of aquaculture and distant-water fishing. Today, China's distant-water fishing fleet lands more seafood than any other country's, and China has signed many bilateral agreements that permit its vessels to fish in foreign EEZs.[26] In Asia, more than 730 Chinese vessels are running off the coast of eight Asian countries, 'with 456 off the east coast of North Korea (predominantly squid jiggers), 133 vessels in Indonesia, 72 vessels in Myanmar, and additional vessels in Malaysia, India, Thailand, the Philippines, and Bangladesh'.[27]

'Outsourcing' food production

Apart from looking for domestic solutions, China is increasingly looking abroad for assistance with its rising food-security challenges. This firstly involves importing certain food items to free up scarce land and water resources for its more strategic crops. Beijing recognised long ago, for example, that boosting domestic cereal production would not be enough to meet the growing demand for animal feed to sustain its mushrooming livestock industries (see Chapter Two). As Mindi Schneider puts it, 'to increase meat consumption for 1.3 billion people on only 120 million hectares of arable land, something's got to give. For China's central authorities, a major "something" has been soybeans.'[28]

The surge in soybean imports is, therefore, not just an indication of the growth in meat production and consumption in China over recent decades. It is also a reflection of the government's awareness of its limitations with respect to food-growing resources, and its deliberate move to 'outsource' its soybean production. In 2002, China slashed import tariffs on

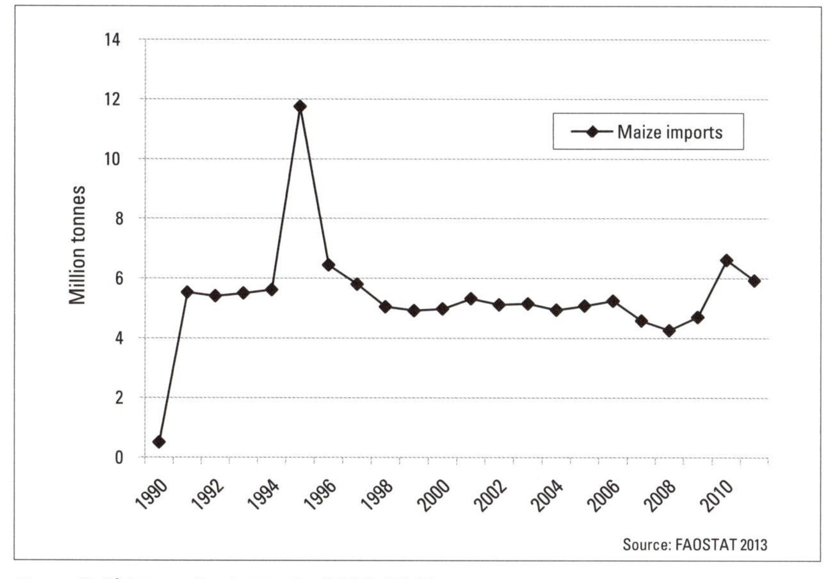

Figure 2. **China maize imports, 1990–2011**

soybeans drastically and today around 60% of the world's soybean exports – mainly from the United States, Argentina and Brazil – find their way to China.[29] China is also now the world's largest importer of palm oil (as cooking oil), most of which is supplied by Indonesia and Malaysia.

In a sign of looming challenges for the global food market, the deputy director of the China National Grain and Oils Information Center admitted in 2011 that China's maize imports were likely to increase.[30] According to FAO data, China imported 6.6m tonnes of maize in 2010, its largest intake since the mid-1990s when crop failure led to a huge spike in maize imports (see Figure 2).[31] Analysts project that maize imports may grow to as much as 7m tonnes in 2013–14.[32] Perhaps anticipating its growing need for overseas-produced maize to meet demand at home, China signed an agreement in early 2012 to import maize from Argentina, which is already a major supplier of soybean to China. In the same year, China imported wheat and, for the first time, maize from Ukraine.[33]

China's reliance on imports for maize, wheat and edible oils looks likely to increase over the long term, as there is still plenty of scope for incomes to rise in China, especially in rural areas. China also appears to have been buying agricultural land in other developing countries. In 2008, media reports suggested that the Chinese Ministry of Agriculture had drafted a policy to buy and lease agricultural land overseas for the purpose of growing food for domestic markets.[34] This was denied by the Chinese government, which has since insisted that China's food-security strategy does not include such a policy. In the same year, however, a report by an international NGO, GRAIN, alleged that China had secured around 30 'agricultural cooperation' deals that guaranteed it 'access to "friendly country" farmland in exchange for Chinese technologies, training and infrastructure development funds' in Asia and Africa.[35]

Certainly, China's largest farming company, the Heilongjiang Beidahuang Nongken Group,[36] the large state-owned Chongqing Grain Group Co Ltd (CGG), Zhejiang Fudi Agriculture Group and the agricultural bureau of Heilongjiang province[37] all have agricultural interests in South America. CGG, for example, has been growing soybeans on a 200,000ha farm in the northeastern Brazilian state of Bahia since 2008 and reportedly shipped 400,000 tonnes of soybeans back to China in 2011, where they were converted into 80,000 tonnes of cooking oil. It is said to be investing $US500m in building a soybean industrial base in Bahia to produce 1.5m tonnes of cooking oil a year for both the Chinese and Brazilian markets.[38]

Meanwhile, China National Cereals, Oils and Foodstuffs Corporation, the country's largest cotton and soybean trader by revenue, is reportedly involved in palm-oil production in Indonesia,[39] while other Chinese companies have supposedly invested in agricultural production of crops such as soybean, maize, rubber, rice and tropical fruit in other Southeast Asian countries such as the Philippines, Cambodia, Malaysia, Laos and Myanmar.[40]

Some argue that such investments in foreign agricultural land by China and other countries are not 'land grabs' but vital development opportunities for host countries. However, while some industrial-scale farmers in those countries are benefitting economically both from Beijing's inward investment and from access to China's vast markets, many smaller farmers are not. Moreover, the practice is detrimental to local food security where land acquisition for such projects results in loss of livelihoods or where the bulk of the food produced is exported.

Raising yields in Southeast Asia

Vietnam is also an Asian success story in terms of national food security. Between 1989 and 2012, it went from a rice-importing nation to one of the world's largest exporters of rice, alongside Thailand and India.[41] Rice production more than doubled from 19.2m tonnes to 42.3m tonnes (see Figure 3), while exports grew from 1.6m tonnes in 1990 to 7.72m tonnes in 2012. The transformation occurred on the back of the 'Doi Moi' policy introduced in 1986, when the government responded to economic stagnation and food deficits by identifying households as the main unit of agricultural production and privatising agricultural markets – thus helping to move

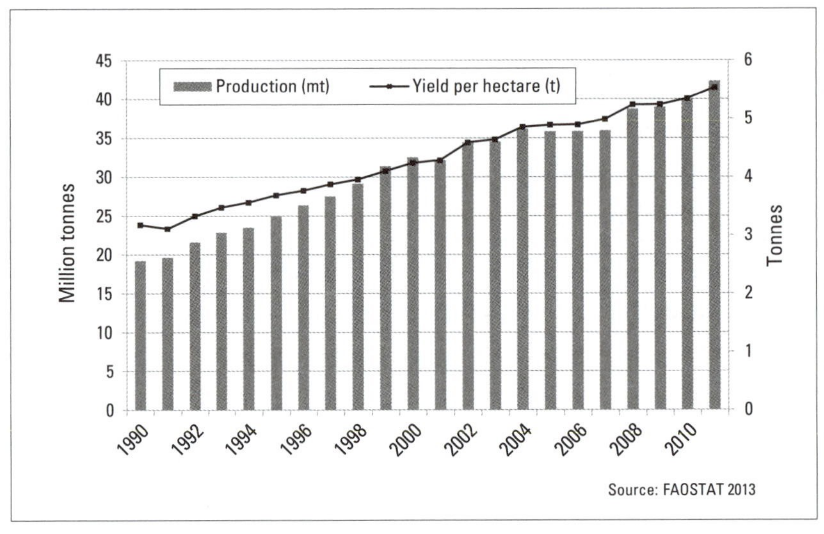

Figure 3. **Vietnam rice (paddy) production and yields, 1990–2011**

Vietnam's centrally planned economy to a decentralised one, founded on market-based competition.[42] With further developments in high-yielding rice varieties[43] plus substantial investment in agricultural infrastructure, extension and credit services, rice productivity in Vietnam grew rapidly.[44] Hanoi now exports around one-third of its rice output, mainly through government-to-government contracts.

However, this national success has not guaranteed household food security; despite more than two decades of relative abundance in rice and ever-increasing rice exports, around 11% of the Vietnamese population remains malnourished.[45] Rice exports bring in more than US$3bn annually, so they are a significant foreign-exchange earner for the Vietnamese economy, but the government's continued emphasis on producing rice for export leaves insufficient focus on local food security (see Chapter Five).

In Cambodia, rice production has increased at a brisk pace, allowing the country to become self-sufficient in the grain in 1995,[46] and to start exporting it the following year.[47] More than 90% of the country's total cultivated area is planted with rice. The Cambodian government realises the importance of raising rice productivity in improving farm incomes and contributing towards wider socio-economic development in the country through export earnings. In recent years, it has been working to rehabilitate and expand irrigation infrastructure, and plans to turn Cambodia into a major rice exporter by 2015.[48] Attracting private investment in the agricultural sector is viewed as a major plank of this strategy. In 2010, for example, the government announced it would invest US$310m to boost irrigation infrastructure; this included US$240m in loans from China, one of the largest foreign investors in Cambodia.[49]

In the Philippines, the use of modern rice varieties, together with the expansion of irrigation facilities and the use of fertilisers, contributed to substantial improvements in the yields of crops such as rice and maize during its Green Revolution.[50] Between 1980 and 1990, rice yields grew at an average of 3.39% and maize yields grew at an average of 2.45%.

In Indonesia, the world's third-largest producer of rice after China and India, policies have been more ad hoc. Since the mid-1990s, rice production has grown only because of increases in cropping intensity (the number of crops grown per year).[51] However, as Pantjar Simatupang and Peter Timmer point out, the scope for raising crop intensity is limited, and this approach may be exhausted very quickly. 'If the recent trends in both productivity and land area devoted to paddy persist, it is reasonable to predict that rice production will continue to stagnate, and will

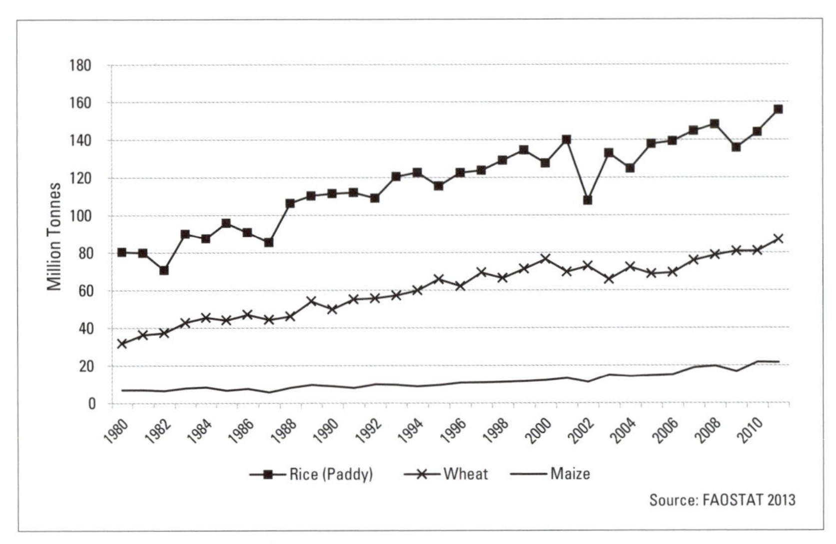

Figure 4. **India cereal production, 1980–2011**

even decline,' they report.[52] As population growth increases future demand for rice, there will need to be a significant increase in rice production in Indonesia, or dependence on rice imports may escalate.[53] In 2005, the government began allocating substantial resources to make Indonesia's agricultural sector more competitive, by increasing productivity, added value and self-reliance in production.[54] This included higher subsidies for inputs, such as fertilisers and seed, and better credit facilities, among other measures.[55]

Multi-pronged approaches in India

Despite continuing high levels of hunger and malnourishment, India also witnessed tremendous gains in the productivity of cereal crops, mainly rice and wheat, in the latter half of the twentieth century. Between 1950/51 and 2006/07, cereal production increased at an annual rate of 2.5%, higher than the average rate of population growth (2.1%).[56] Rice production more than doubled, while wheat production grew more than seven times. Since the 1970s, India has remained largely self-sufficient in cereals and exports many crops, including rice and maize, in substantial quantities, notwithstanding growing imports of vegetable oils (mainly palm oil but also soybean and sunflower oils), sugar (raw and refined), cashew nuts, pulses, dry beans and peas.[57] India is already the world's largest importer of vegetable oils; by 2021, it is expected to import up to 60% of the vegetable oil it needs.[58] Indian companies, supported by the Indian government, have also emerged as important agricultural investors in other countries in Asia, Africa and South America.[59]

Efforts to boost declining productivity have increased in recent years, with some improvements in public investment and growth in the agricultural sector. Farmer-friendly schemes have been launched to provide technological support to farmers to help increase production. In 2007, for example, New Delhi launched the Rashtriya Krishi Vikas Yojana (RKVY, or the National Agriculture Development Scheme), which provides financial incentives to state governments to boost agricultural investment and formulate more environmentally sound and technologically advanced plans for their agricultural sectors;[60] it seeks to raise yields and boost farm incomes through targeted interventions tailored to local conditions and needs. The government has also been promoting technologies such as the 'system of rice intensification',[61] an agro-ecological method for increasing the productivity of irrigated rice while reducing the use of chemical fertilisers and conserving water.[62] In 2005–06, the National Horticulture Mission[63] set out to promote the holistic growth of the horticulture sector through regionally differentiated strategies, using research, technology promotion, extensions, post-harvest management, processing and marketing appropriate for each state or region.[64]

India has long viewed national food security in terms of being self-sufficient in major cereal crops such as rice and wheat. Core policies have included: offering farmers a minimum support price for harvests; maintaining a sufficient buffer stock (on average 20m tonnes in the year) of rice and wheat; and distributing subsidised food grains to the poorest Indians through its targeted Public Distribution System (PDS) and other mechanisms.[65]

The minimum support price for food grains (focused on rice and wheat) is one way in which the Indian government has attempted to improve farmers' incomes. By offering them an attractive price for their crops, it also acts as an incentive for farmers to adopt new technologies and maximise production.[66] In recent years, the government has substantially increased minimum prices for both rice and wheat, and procurement has surged.[67] In July 2012, the central government was sitting on record stocks of more than 80m tonnes of rice and wheat, compared to the usual combined amount of just under 32m tonnes.[68]

India's food-security policies also aim to make sufficient staple food grains available to domestic consumers at affordable prices.[69] Since 1997, India's targeted PDS has been the main vehicle for providing subsidised food to the country's poor.[70] Under this system, the Food Corporation of India, a central government agency, buys food grains directly from farmers at established minimum prices and transports them to its storage depots across India. This grain is then distributed by state governments through 'fair-price shops' to

Rice is life

Rice enjoys a special place in Asian diets. Even as meat consumption increases in the region, rice remains the most vital foodstuff – a staple for half of the world's population. Across Asia, the proportion of total daily calories consumed from rice still averages nearly 30%[73] and in some countries accounts for as much as 48% (Indonesia)[74] and 55% (Vietnam).[75] Some 90% of the world's rice is grown and eaten in Asia; less than 5% of the global harvest is traded internationally, compared to 20% for wheat.[76] Rice farming is also a way of life for most rural Asian households and a principal source of income. This central role means that countries such as Vietnam, Indonesia, Cambodia and the Philippines have concentrated on boosting rice production and raising rice productivity. China, Cambodia and Vietnam have long pursued policies of rice self-sufficiency, while the Philippines and Indonesia have more recently renewed their focus on it. The Philippines, where rice paddies spread out across almost one-third of the land but imports are still needed, has aimed to be self-sufficient by 2013/14. Indonesia has the official goal of achieving rice self-sufficiency by 2014, after decades of yo-yoing imports hurt domestic prices for farmers. In 2004, Jakarta effectively banned private rice imports.[77]

Nevertheless, rice is a good case study in how an emphasis on national self-sufficiency can often come at the expense of both household (see Chapter Five) and regional food security. During the global food-price crisis of 2007–08, major rice-producing nations China, India and Vietnam banned exports – in India's case, of non-basmati rice – to ensure their own populations would have enough to eat. Meanwhile, importers, such as the Philippines and many Middle Eastern countries, hoarded supplies. In effect, rice export bans in Asia helped push the international price for rice up from US$200–400 per tonne to more than US$1,000 per tonne.[78]

The politicisation of rice in Asia meant that even though there was no actual rice shortage in the region, the market reacted as if there was. Rising prices of other key staples, such as wheat, soybean and maize, prompted governments to take pre-emptive measures to protect domestic prices of rice from escalating and to safeguard supplies, which had direct implications for international prices.

The fact that rice comes in many varieties – long-grain, short-grain, aromatic, basmati, jasmine and so on – and that consumers tend to have local preferences further complicates the situation. While organisations such as the FAO and IFPRI may promote 'sustainable intensification' to further increase rice yields, and others may offer up 'flood-tolerant' rice varieties to guard against climate change,[79] it is clear that political agreements are also vital to ensuring regional food security.

households with ration cards, at heavily subsidised prices. However, there are several major problems with the PDS. Historically, it has failed to reach all of those it should, as well as suffering significant losses of grain through corruption. A 2005 government study found that only 57% of intended recipients were reached by the system. Fair-price shops selling subsidised food grains were largely financially unviable, and survived mainly through diverting stock to sell on the open and black markets.[71] Despite these difficulties, India chose to use the PDS to implement its 2013 food bill, which makes access to food a legal right (see Chapter Five for more on the PDS and the bill).

Other Indian safety-net programmes for tackling poverty and hunger have included the Integrated Child Development Services (ICDS 1975), focused on improving health and nutrition amongst young children and pregnant and nursing mothers; the Mid Day Meal Scheme (MDMS) that provides primary students with cooked midday meals in government and local authority public schools; and the National Rural Employment Guarantee Act (NREGA 2005) that guarantees 100 days of wage employment in a financial year to all rural households who volunteer to do unskilled manual work. Indonesia also has a subsidised rice procurement and distribution programme for the poor, called Raskin.[72]

Conclusion

Asian governments have largely succeeded in feeding their growing, increasingly demanding populations in the last half century by raising crop production, through agricultural expansion and higher yields, as well as running subsidised food programmes for their poorest citizens. Where policies have sometimes been fitful, governments have often redoubled their efforts after long periods of declining productivity or dependence on imported food, with schemes to provide farmers technological assistance, credit facilities, extension services and subsidies for costly agricultural inputs such as fertiliser.

However, as discussed in more detail in the following chapter, developing countries in Asia now face multiple challenges to food security. The region has little unused arable land left, non-replenishable water resources are declining and intensive farming has caused environmental degradation and pollution. Climate change is casting a shadow over future crop yields and the availability of natural resources, and enduring inequalities prevent universal access to sufficient food. Moves by governments and government-backed private companies to purchase agricultural land abroad have not only proved controversial but are also riddled with risks for investors and may undermine local food security, peace and stability.[80]

Given the scale and complexity of the challenges, what has worked in the past is unlikely to work in the future. Strains are already beginning to show, not only in the region's agricultural systems but also in the social fabric of some Asian countries – where smaller farmers have begun to protest about agricultural policies that result in the loss of their land and livelihoods.

Ensuring food security – and ultimately political stability – requires sustainable policies to assure the livelihoods of the small farmers who produce so much of Asia's food, as well as access to food for poorer citizens. A much more holistic approach is needed rather than ad-hoc plans, focused narrowly on raising production, which have largely driven food-security and agricultural policies in Asia in recent decades.

Notes

1 This reduction, however, has been uneven across and within sub-regions, and in many countries, economic growth has come with growing income inequality. East Asia has made the most progress – largely thanks to China's achievements in poverty reduction – followed by Southeast Asia, where countries such as Indonesia, Vietnam and Thailand have registered good progress, although others such as Cambodia, Laos, Myanmar, and the Philippines continue to lag behind. For South Asia, the inclusion of India in the calculation skews the proportion of poor people in the sub-region considerably, whereby it accounts for around 65% of Asia's extremely poor. At the national level, extreme poverty rates in the region vary as much as from nil in Malaysia to 55% in Nepal. For more, see ADB, 'Food Security and Poverty in Asia and the Pacific: Key Challenges and Policy Issues', April 2012, Manila, p. 3, http://www.adb.org/sites/default/files/pub/2012/food-security-poverty.pdf.

2 ADB, 'Food Security in Asia and the Pacific', report from Symposium on Food Security in Asia and the Pacific: Key Policy Issues and Options, 17–18 September 2012 at the Liu Institute for Global Issues, UBC, p. xv, http://www.adb.org/sites/default/files/pub/2013/food-security-asia-pacific.pdf.

3 For example, see Yingyi Qian, 'The Process of China's Market Transition (1978–1998): The Evolutionary, Historical, and Comparative Perspectives', *Journal of Institutional and Theoretical Economics (JITE)/Zeitschrift für die gesamte Staatswissenschaft*, vol. 156, no. 1, 17th International Seminar on the New Institutional Economics: Big-Bang Transformations of Economic Systems as a Challenge to New Institutional Economics, March 2000, pp. 151–71, http://www.jstor.org/discover/10.2307/40752194?uid=3738032&uid=2&uid=4&sid=21103320475551.

4 For example, see Lester Brown, *Who Will Feed China? Wake-up Call for a Small Planet* (New York: Norton, 1995).

[5] Alejandro Nin-Pratt, Bingxin Yu and Shenggen Fan, 'Comparisons of agricultural productivity growth in China and India', *Journal of Productivity Analysis*, vol. 33, no. 3, June 2010, pp. 209–23.

[6] Jikun Huang and Scott Rozelle, 'Agriculture, Food Security, and Poverty in China: Past Performance, Future Prospects, and Implications for Agricultural R&D Policy', IFPRI and Centre for Chinese Agricultural Policy, June 2009.

[7] Nin-Pratt, Yu and Fan, 'Comparisons of agricultural productivity growth in China and India', p. 212.

[8] World Bank, Worldwide Development Indicators (WDIs), November 2013.

[9] World Bank WDIs, July 2012.

[10] Jikun Huang, Xiaobing Wang and Huanguang Qiu, *Small-scale farmers in China in the face of modernisation and globalisation* (London and The Hague: International Institute for Environment and Development, in conjunction with HIVOS, 2012), p. 7.

[11] Mingsheng Fan et al., 'Improving crop productivity and resource use efficiency to ensure food security and environmental quality in China', *Journal of Experimental Botany Advance Access*, 2011, pp. 1–2, http://jxb.oxfordjournals.org/content/early/2011/09/30/jxb.err248.full.

[12] According to FAOSTAT (2013), between 1990 and 2011 China's production of hen eggs (in shell) increased from 6.56m tonnes to 24.2m tonnes; pork meat from 23.5m tonnes to 51.5m tonnes; fruits (excluding melons) from 20.9m tonnes to 134.4m tonnes; and vegetables and melons from 131.8m tonnes to 565.3m tonnes.

[13] Jikun Huang, Jun Yang and Scott Rozelle, 'China's agriculture: drivers of change and implications for China and the rest of world', *Agricultural Economics*, vol. 41, no. 1, 2010, p. 48.

[14] *Ibid.*

[15] 'Key targets of China's 12th five-year plan', *People's Daily Online*, 5 March 2011, http://english.peopledaily.com.cn/90001/90776/7309132.html. See also Liming Ye and Eric Van Ranst, 'Production scenarios and the effect of soil degradation on long-term food security in China', *Global Environmental Change*, vol. 9, no. 4, October 2009.

[16] 'China Grain and Feed Annual 2011', United States Department of Agriculture (USDA) GAIN Report, 3 August 2011, http://gain.fas.usda.gov/Recent%20GAIN%20Publications/Grain%20and%20Feed%20Annual_Beijing_China%20-%20Peoples%20Republic%20of_3-8-2011.pdf.

[17] *Ibid.*

[18] Jikun Huang et al., 'Agricultural Trade Reform and Rural Prosperity: Lessons from China', in Robert C. Feenstra and Shang-Jin Wei (eds), *China's Growing Role in World Trade* (Chicago, IL: University of Chicago Press, 2008), pp. 397–423.

[19] 'China's 12th Five-Year Plan (Agricultural Section)', USDA GAIN Report, 3 May 2011, http://gain.fas.usda.gov/Recent%20GAIN%20Publications/China's%2012th%20Five-Year%20Plan%20(Agricultural%20Section)_Beijing_China%20-%20Peoples%20Republic%20of_5-3-2011.pdf.

[20] 'No.1 central document targets rural issues for 9th year', China.org.cn, 1 February 2012, http://www.china.org.cn/china/2012-02/01/content_24526692.htm.

[21] Keith Schneider et al., 'Choke Point China: Confronting water scarcity and energy demand in the world's largest country', *Vermont Journal of Environmental Law*, vol. 12, no. 3, Spring 2011, pp. 713–34, http://vjel.vermontlaw.edu/files/2013/06/Volume-12-Issue-31.pdf.

[22] 'Key goals of China's five-year-plan', *Daily Telegraph*, 21 August 2011,http://www.telegraph.co.uk/finance/economics/ 8714299/Key-goals-of-Chinas-five-year-plan.html.

[23] 'China Grain and Feed Annual 2011'.

[24] FAO, *The State of World Fisheries and Aquaculture 2012* (Rome: FAO, 2012), pp. 4–5.

[25] Tabitha Grace Mallory, 'China's distant water fishing industry: Evolving policies and implications', *Marine Policy*, vol. 38 (March 2013), pp. 100–01.

[26] *Ibid.*

[27] *Ibid.*, p. 102.

[28] Mindi Schneider, 'Feeding China's Pigs: Implications for the Environment, China's Smallholder Farmers and Food Security', Institute for Agriculture and Trade Policy, May 2011, p. 11, http://pigpenning.files.wordpress.com/2011/05/schneider_feeding-chinas-pigs-2011.pdf.

[29] Janet Larsen, 'Meat Consumption in China Now Double That in the United States', *Earth Policy Institute*, 24 April 2012, http://www.earth-policy.org/plan_b_updates/2012/update102.

[30] 'China acknowledges need for sizeable corn imports', Agrimoney.com, 25 October 2011, http://bit.ly/ujUfjf; and Aya Takada and Yasumasa Song, 'China May Become Top Corn Importer by 2014, Displacing Japan', Bloomberg, 17 April 2012, http://www.bloomberg.com/news/2012-04-17/china-may-become-top-corn-importer-by-2014-displacing-japan.html.

[31] Javier Blas, 'Chinese corn imports forecast to soar', *Finan-*

cial Times, 4 February 2011, http://www.ft.com/cms/s/be204aa2-304f-11e0-8d80-00144feabdco,Authorised=false.html?_i_location=http%3A%2F%2Fwww.ft.com%2Fcms%2Fs%2F0%2Fbe204aa2-304f-11e0-8d80-00144feabdco.html%3Fsiteedition%3Duk&siteedition=uk&_i_referer=#axzz2ltAUTNND.

32 'China corn imports could reach 20–30 million tonnes – govt researcher', Reuters, 5 September 2013, http://www.cnbc.com/id/101010513.

33 Zhou Siyu, 'China imports Ukrainian corn for 1st time', *China Daily*, 7 April 2012, http://www.chinadaily.com.cn/bizchina/2012-04/07/content_14996559.htm.

34 Duncan Freeman, Jonathan Holslag and Steffi Weil, 'China's foreign farming policy: can land provide security?', Brussels Institute of Contemporary China Studies (BICCS) Asia Paper, vol. 3, no. 9, 11 March 2008, pp. 11–12.

35 'Seized! The 2008 land grab for food and financial security', Genetic Resources Action International (GRAIN), 24 October 2008, http://www.grain.org/article/entries/93-seized-the-2008-land-grab-for-food-and-financial-security#sdfootnote6sym.

36 Shane Romig, 'Hungry China Shops in Argentina', *Wall Street Journal*, 20 June 2011, http://online.wsj.com/news/articles/SB10001424052702303823104576391621352528138?mg=reno64-wsj&url=http%3A%2F%2Fonline.wsj.com%2Farticle%2FSB10001424052702303823104576391621352528138.html.

37 Zhong Nan, 'Growing in greener pastures', *China Daily*, 8 June 2012, http://europe.chinadaily.com.cn/epaper/2012-06/08/content_15486250.htm.

38 *Ibid.*

39 Muklis Ali and Hari Suhartono, 'China's CNOOC in $5.5 bln Indonesian biofuel deal', Reuters, 9 January 2007, http://uk.reuters.com/article/2007/01/09/indonesia-bioenergy-venture-idUKJAK17155320070109.

40 For example, see Shepard Daniel with Anuradha Mittal, 'The Great Land Grab: Rush for World's Farmland Threatens Food Security for the Poor', The Oakland Institute, 2009, p. 4, http://www.oaklandinstitute.org/sites/oaklandinstitute.org/files/LandGrab_final_web.pdf; and Antonio B. Quizon, 'The rush for Asia's farmland: Its impact on land rights and security of the rural poor', *Lokniti*, vol. 18, no. 1, March 2012, pp. 3–4, http://www.angoc.org/portal/wp-content/uploads/2012/10/01/the_rush_abquizon.pdf.

41 'Thailand loses top rice exporter title', *The Nation*, 4 January 2013,

http://www.nationmultimedia.com/national/Thailands-loses-top-rice-exporter-title-30197275.html.

42 Kazunari Tsukada, 'Vietnam: Food Security in a Rice Exporting Country', in Shinichi Shigetomi, Kensuke Kubo and Kazunari Tsukada, *The World Food Crisis and the Strategies of Asian Rice Exporters* (Chiba: Institute of Developing Economics and Japan External Trade Organisation, 2011), p. 55.

43 For popular rice varieties used in 1998 in the Mekong and Red River deltas, including from IR50404-57 to Xuan 11, see Bui Ba Bong, 'Bridging the Rice Yield Gap in Vietnam', from the collected papers of the FAO's expert consultation 'Bridging the Rice Yield Gap in the Asia-Pacific Region', held in Bangkok, Thailand, 5–7 October 1999, http://www.fao.org/docrep/003/x6905e/x6905e0e.htm.

44 Steven Jaffee et al., 'Moving the Goal Posts: Vietnam's Evolving Rice Balance and Other Food Security Considerations', paper given at the 7th Asian Society of Agricultural Economists (ASAE) International Conference on 'Meeting the Challenges Facing Asian Agriculture and Agricultural Economics Towards a Sustainable Future', held in Hanoi, 13–15 October 2011.

45 World Bank WDIs 2012 (using 2008 figures).

46 According to FAOSTAT (2013), rice paddy production reached 3.44m tonnes in Cambodia.

47 See FAOSTAT (2013), in which Cambodia's rice exports reached 174,045 tonnes 2011, from just over 51,178 tonnes in 2010.

48 Ek Madra, 'Irrigation advances fuel Cambodian rice dream', Reuters, 7 October 2008, http://uk.reuters.com/article/2008/10/08/us-cambodia-rice-idUKTRE49702L20081008.

49 'Cambodia to Invest US$310 Million in Irrigations to Boost Rice Exports – PM', Dap-news.com, 5 February 2010, http://khmerforkhmer.blogspot.com.au/2010/02/cambodia-to-invest-us-310-million-in.html.

50 Amelia Bello, 'Food Security, Agricultural Efficiency and Regional Integration', Philippine Institute for Development Studies, Discussion Paper Series No. 2004-38, p. 18, http://dirp4.pids.gov.ph/ris/dps/pidsdps0438.pdf.

51 Pantjar Simatupang and C. Peter Timmer, 'Indonesian Rice Production: Policies and Realities', *Bulletin of Indonesian Economic Studies*, vol. 44, no. 1, April 2008, p. 68.

52 *Ibid.*, p. 69.

53 *Ibid.*, p. 77.

54 FAO, 'Summary of selected and relevant Indonesia's National Development Policies and Agricultural (incl. Forestry and Fish-

eries) Strategies and Goals', ftp://ftp.fao.org/TC/CPF/Country%20NMTPF/Indonesia/Process/Policies.pdf.

[55] Simatupang and Timmer, 'Indonesian Rice Production: Policies and Realities', p. 68.

[56] Government of India (GoI), *Union Budget and Economic Survey 2007–08* (New Delhi: Ministry of Finance, 2008), p. 156, http://indiabudget.nic.in/es2007-08/esmain.htm.

[57] FAOSTAT 2012.

[58] OECD and FAO, 'OECD–FAO Agricultural Outlook 2012–2021', p. 140, http://www.fao.org/fileadmin/templates/est/COMM_MARKETS_MONITORING/Oilcrops/Documents/OECD_Reports/Ch5StatAnnex.pdf.

[59] See Rick Rowden, 'India's Role in the New Global Farmland Grab', GRAIN and the Economic Research Foundation, August 2011, http://www.networkideas.org/featart/aug2011/Rick_Rowden.pdf.

[60] GoI, 'Rashtriya Krishi Vikas Yojna', http://rkvy.nic.in/#.

[61] The system of rice intensification (SRI) is an agro-ecological methodology for growing more rice with fewer inputs, by changing the management of plants, soil, water and nutrients. For a detailed explanation, see the International Fund for Agricultural Development: http://www.ifad.org/english/sri/index.htm.

[62] GoI, 'State of Indian Agriculture 2011–12', http://agricoop.nic.in/sia111213312.pdf. Around 90,000 demonstrations of SRI and 50,000 demonstrations of hybrid rice have been organised under the National Food Security Mission in the past five years.

[63] The scheme does not cover the eight northeastern states including Sikkim and the states of Jammu and Kashmir, Himachal Pradesh and Uttrakhand, which are covered under the Horticulture Mission for North East and Himalayan States.

[64] Indian Ministry of Agriculture, 'National Horticulture Mission: Operational Guidelines 2010', p. 1, http://www.nhm.nic.in/Horticulture/NHMGuidelines_English.pdf.

[65] Uttam Kumar Deb, Mahabub Hossain and Steve Jones, *Rethinking Food Security Strategy: Self-sufficiency or Self-reliance* (Dhaka: BRAC, 2009).

[66] S. Mahendra Dev and Alakh N. Sharma, 'Food Security in India: Performances, Challenges and Policies', Oxfam India Working Paper Series (OIWPS) VII, September 2010, http://www.oxfamindia.org/sites/www.oxfamindia.org/files/working_paper_7.pdf.

[67] *Ibid.*

[68] Department of Food and Public Distribution, February 2013

Bulletin, p. 6, http://dfpd.nic.in/fcamin/bulletion/FEB_2013.pdf.

69 World Bank, *Food Price Increases in South Asia: National responses and regional dimensions* (Washington DC: World Bank, 2010), p. 101.

70 The targeted PDS replaced India's universal PDS, which existed until the early 1990s, and was dismantled as the country embraced economic reforms under the structural-adjustment programmes of the IMF and World Bank. For more, see Madhura Swaminathan, 'Structural Adjustment, Food Security and System of Public Distribution of Food', *Economic and Political Weekly*, vol. 31, no. 26, 29 June 1996, pp. 1,665–72.

71 GoI, 'Performance Evaluation of Targeted Public Distribution System (TPDS)', Programme Eval uation Organisation, Planning Commission, March 2005, http://planningcommission.nic.in/reports/peoreport/peo/peo_tpds.pdf.

72 Simatupang and Timmer, 'Indonesian Rice Production', p. 68.

73 C. Peter Timmer, 'The Changing Role of Rice in Asia's Food Security', ADB Sustainable Development Working Paper No. 15, September 2010, p. 8, http://www.adb.org/sites/default/files/pub/2010/adb-wp15-rice-food-security.pdf.

74 *Ibid.*, p. 9.

75 See, for example, 'Rice Value Chain in Viet Nam', 18 February 2013, hosted on the ADB Institute website at http://www.adbi.org/files/2013.02.18.cpp.day1.ses3.2.kien.rice.value.chain.viet.nam.pdf.

76 'Asia's rice bowls', *The Economist*, 12 November 2011, http://www.economist.com/node/21538099.

77 George Fane and Peter Warr, 'Agricultural protection in Indonesia', *Bulletin of Indonesian Economic Studies*, vol. 44, no. 1, April 2008, p. 136. The private sector is only allowed to import speciality rice varieties, but the government reverted to an open import policy during the 2007–08 global food-price crisis. For more, see Agus Saifullah, 'Indonesia's Rice Policy and Price Stabilization Programme: Managing Domestic Prices during the 2008 Crisis', in Dave Dawe (ed.), *The Rice Crisis: Markets, Prices and Food Security* (London and Washington: Earthscan and FAO, 2010), pp. 109–22.

78 Javier Blas, 'Indian exports cap rice prices', *Financial Times*, 14 November 2011, http://www.ft.com/cms/s/03ea994a-070d-11e1-90de-00144feabdco,Authorised=false.html?_i_location=http%3A%2F%2Fwww.ft.com%2Fcms%2Fs%2F0%2F03ea994a-070d-11e1-90de-00144feabdco.html%3Fsiteedition%3Duk&siteedition=uk&_i_referer=#axzz2kia3PUZz.

79 Pia Ranada, 'IRRI to give "flood-tolerant" rice to Haiyan-stricken farmers', The Rappler, 14 November 2013, http://www.rappler.com/move-ph/issues/disasters/typhoon-yolanda/43682-irri-flood-tolerant-rice-haiyan.

80 See, for example, Benjamin Shepherd, 'GCC's Land Investments Abroad: The Case of Cambodia', Center for International and Regional Studies, Georgetown University School of Foreign Service in Qatar, Summary Report No. 5, http://www12.georgetown.edu/sfs/qatar/cirs/CambodiaSummaryReport.pdf.

CHAPTER FOUR

Challenges of sustainability, resilience and adaptation

The Green Revolution that swept through much of Asia from the 1960s onwards allowed many countries in the region to become self-sufficient in staples. However, some of these countries are now reaching a tipping point where their continued ability to feed themselves is no longer assured. The challenges are greater than during the Green Revolution because the world now needs to feed more people with rapidly diversifying diets, using less – and more degraded – natural resources such as farmland and fresh water.

The competition for land between industry, urban development and agriculture has left little spare arable land in Asia. This means, for example, that China – which feeds about 20% of the global population with less than 9% of the world's farmland – has little scope for expanding the area already under cultivation.[1] Across the continent, intensive farming practices have damaged soil fertility and depleted freshwater sources, while recent underinvestment in agricultural infrastructure has failed to counter the effects of this environmental degradation. Climate change is predicted to further impact agricultural productivity in Asia.

The consequences are particularly serious for the small farmers who provide the vast majority of the region's food. Already among the poorest communities, they find their livelihoods under threat from declining agricultural productivity, low farm-gate prices and a lack of land rights. Yet, as an examination of the issues shows, smallholder farmers are central to improving Asia's food security.

Declining investment in agriculture

Across Asia, a degree of complacency set in after the boosts in production and yields brought by the Green Revolution. Declining agricultural productivity in the Philippines, for example, has been linked to very low public or private investment in agriculture since the 1990s compared to other sectors, especially in irrigation, rural infrastructure development (such as transport infrastructure for access to agricultural markets) and agricultural research and development (R&D).[2] Lack of sufficient investment is a constraint on productivity in Cambodia. India also needs to substantially boost investment in agriculture to increase farm productivity and improve agricultural infrastructure.

Productivity growth made during the Green Revolution years in staples, such as rice and wheat, have been declining in India for some time now, raising questions about the country's future ability to remain self-sufficient. In the 1980s, compound-growth rates of production and yields for both rice and wheat hovered above 3%. Between 2000/01 and 2011/12, rice production grew at a much lower rate of 1.72% and yields only grew by 1.68%. The compound-growth rate of wheat production declined to 2.37% during this period, and to 1.14% for wheat yields.[3] Overall, agricultural growth remained at an average annual rate of 3.6% between 2007 and 2012 (short of a targeted 4% for this period).[4]

Since the 1980s, agricultural investment in India has fallen as a share of both total investment and GDP, although subsidies for agricultural inputs such as fertilisers, fuel, irrigation and electricity increased substantially.[5] Input subsidies remain important for small farmers, and have had a positive impact on poverty reduction, but as Shenggen Fan, Ashok Gulati and Sukhadeo Thorat point out, 'their effects are only half to one-third of those of investments in agricultural [R&D], roads, and education.'[6] Input subsidies also seem to have widely encouraged the inefficient use of resources, contributing to widespread soil degradation, polluted waterways and over-extraction of groundwater.[7]

Limited land and water

It is no longer easy to expand cultivated land in Asia to increase food production, as almost all of it is already accounted for. Shrinking arable land and declining soil quality are now major problems. In 2010, just 13% of China's land – 121.7 million ha, or just 0.09 ha per person – was under cultivation, giving the country the world's lowest cultivated-land-to-person ratio.[8] Years of urbanisation and industrialisation have taken their toll. Between 1995 and 2003, more than 1m ha of cultivated land in China was converted to other uses each year,[9] although the rate of decline has since slowed, thanks to government measures to protect farmland. Increases in grain production have been made mainly on the back of productivity growth and expansion in total sown area as a result of multi-cropping (more than two crops being grown per year on the same land) in some regions.[10]

Intensive use of this limited arable land has caused widespread soil degradation, including loss of fertility and structure, wind and water erosion, and salinisation. All of these have undermined productive capacity.[11] China still aims to be 95% self-sufficient in major cereals and intends to produce at least 540m tonnes of food grains annually under its 12th Five-Year Plan for 2011–15. However, the country's grain needs may grow to 648m tonnes by 2020 and 700m by 2050,[12] and output could struggle to keep up. According to one study, if soil degradation continues at the current pace, China's grain production will suffer a 9% fall by 2030, with an annual output of no more than 424m tonnes – significantly less than the 680m tonnes some forecast will then be necessary for self-sufficiency.[13]

India, likewise, has limited arable land available: at 0.13 ha per person, this is well below the world average of 0.23 ha, and it is expected to decline further soon because of population growth, and urban and industrial expansion.[14] This scarcity of arable land is being compounded by widespread degradation caused by poor land management, inefficient irrigation practices and input-intensive agricultural methods. Around 120m ha of arable land and open forest – roughly 36% of India's land mass – has been degraded by water and wind erosion or chemical pollution.[15] Declining soil fertility is a major problem. Indian soil suffers from nutrient imbalance and micronutrient deficiency, declining biodiversity, serious levels of water-logging, poor drainage and salinity.[16]

In both China and India, limited water is an even more pressing problem than limited land. Although China has the sixth-largest total annual renewable water resources globally, its annual per-capita freshwater resources are only one-quarter of the world average, at around 2,156 cubic metres.[17] According to Jianguo Liu and Wu Yang, two-thirds of China's 669 cities have water shortages, more than 40% of its rivers are severely polluted, 80% of its lakes suffer from 'eutrophication' (meaning they are covered in algae bloom), and about 300m rural residents lack access to safe drinking water.[18] Since 1949, the country has suffered 17 severe and widespread droughts.[19] These include the serious droughts that hit Chongqing and Sichuan provinces in 2006, seriously damaged winter wheat crops in 12 provinces across the north in 2008/09 and ravaged the central and northern parts of the Yangtze River Basin in 2011, affecting the drinking water of 3.5m people.[20] From 2009–13, drought plagued the southwestern provinces of Yunnan, Guizhou and Sichuan, harming crops and hurting millions of people.[21]

As with arable land, China's water resources are unevenly distributed.[22] Most arable land (around 64%) is in the dry north, while 81% of the country's water resources are located in southern China (36.5% of China's total area).[23] The north therefore relies heavily on groundwater for irrigation, accounting for almost half of national use.[24]

As Liming Ye and Eric Van Ranst highlight, poor irrigation practices and inadequate infrastructure have resulted in overuse of surface water resources and over-pumping of groundwater, causing 'water table decline, seawater intrusion, and land subsidence'. Moreover, 'pumping costs have risen … and, in many cases, agricultural wells have been abandoned and replaced by new deeper tubewells.'[25] Water pollution is another serious problem, both inland and along the coast. Around 20 billion cubic metres of untreated wastewater continues to be discharged into rivers, lakes and other stretches of water annually. Municipal wastewater discharge has overtaken industrial discharge.[26] However, agriculture remains the top polluter, especially with the excessive and inefficient use of fertilisers and pesticides, and billions of tonnes of manure being produced by China's burgeoning livestock industry.[27]

Beijing has realised the need to take action on environmental sustainability. In 2011, the 'No. 1' policy document[28] for the first time focused on water conservation and the development of adequate rural infrastructure for this. A budget of RMB4 trillion (more than US$600bn) was announced to fund these efforts to tackle China's growing water shortage over the next decade.

Growing attention to China's worsening water crisis is a positive development, but more is needed. The imposition of rigid limitations on national water consumption – no more than 670bn cubic metres in 2020 or 700bn cubic metres in 2030[29] – is, for example, widely considered a superficial response to a problem rooted in a lack of clarity around water rights, the need for strong new laws around the use of rivers and river basins, and incentives that promote water conservation for future use.[30] As in India, China's water resource-management approach is fragmented, spread across various bureaucracies and lacking much-needed coordination across organisational levels and sectors.[31]

Also, much of the budget allocated for water-related projects is actually earmarked for repairing and reinforcing more than half of China's 87,000 dams, which are, or soon will be, past their design lives, as well as building new dams, reservoirs and canals.[32] The government wants to speed up water-resource allocation measures, including that of the South–North Water Transfer (SNWT) project already under construction. Within China, the decision to move water to where demand is, rather than the other way around, has been criticised for risking 'much higher municipal, agricultural, and industrial water prices' and 'damage to aquatic environments'.[33] However, it has also created tensions with neighbouring India (see text box). Additional treatment facilities may be needed for Yangtze water that is currently too polluted to use, while water shortages in northern and possibly southern China may continue, even after the SNWT is completed.

In India, meanwhile, attempts to raise productivity have been hampered by a lack of adequate agricultural infrastructure, especially with respect to irrigation. About 60% of farming in India is rain-fed[34], and about 80% of annual rainfall occurs during the June–September monsoon season, when rainfall is often erratic and increasingly prone to variation.[35] This makes more surface irrigation vital for raising productivity, but the rate at which it is expanding has slowed considerably.[36] Also, the central government admits there are 'extreme inefficiencies in the use of available irrigation water', including surface and groundwater.[37]

Around one-third of India's population lives in areas with absolute water scarcity – where human water use has exceeded the limits of sustainability.[38] The over-extraction of groundwater through pump irrigation is a major factor in the depletion of water tables, and 'almost everywhere

Sino-Indian tensions over water

By 2050, China's huge South–North Water Transfer (SNWT) project is expected to divert 44.8 billion cubic metres of water annually from the Yangtze River in southern China to the parched Yellow River Basin in the north. This 'replumbing' of the country will be achieved via three channels: eastern, central and western.[41] Plans for the western route have caused alarm in India, where initial plans were seen as taking water not just from the Yangtze's upper reaches, but also from rivers on the Tibetan plateau, including the Yarlung Tsangpo that flows around the 'Great Bend' before entering India as the Brahmaputra.

Both India and Bangladesh rely heavily on the Brahmaputra. It accounts for almost 30% of India's water-resources potential and 41% of its hydropower reserves.[42] Any diversion in the river's upper reaches could have devastating effects on hundreds of millions of people living downstream.

Therefore, Beijing's 'choke hold' over the Brahmaputra and other major rivers originating on the Tibetan plateau is viewed in India as a potential threat to national water security.[43] Beijing's previous refusal to pass New Delhi hydrological data, despite a Memorandum of Understanding to share this information, has only served to reinforce suspicions.[44] According to Brahma Chellany, knowing that potential peer rival India 'is the main beneficiary of transboundary river flows from Tibet, China may only see an incentive to aggressively exploit or divert Tibetan river-water resources' in the future.[45]

Such views from India are set against a background of long-term Indo-Chinese rivalry, a border war in 1962 (that India lost) and unresolved border disputes. China claims the northeastern Indian state of Arunachal Pradesh, as 'Southern Tibet', and although both sides signed an agreement in 2005 outlining the 'Political Parameters and Guiding Principles for the Settlement of the Boundary Question', China's continued demands for major territorial concessions in populated (and water-rich) areas of Arunachal Pradesh, and related behaviour, have kept relations with India on edge in recent years.[46]

In 2011, China denied it was still considering diverting water from the Yarlung Tsangpo, citing environmental costs and technical difficulties, as well as 'state-to-state' relations.[47] Experts have also suggested it would be almost technically impossible to divert the Yarlung Tsangpo. However, not everyone in New Delhi has been convinced.[48] Separately from the SNWT, China has set out plans for dams on the river.[49] It is possible that India's recent revival of its National River Linking Project, including the diversion of water from the Ganges and Brahmaputra to its rivers in the south, is in part a response to China's unilateral approach to the management of the Yarlung Tsangpo.[50]

Military clashes between China and India in Arunachal Pradesh remain unlikely but not impossible.[51] The tussle over the state underlines the dangerous convergence between growing anxieties over water, food and energy security on the one hand and geopolitical concerns on the other. In such conditions, the absence of any institutional mechanism on the joint management of transboundary water resources is a glaring oversight.

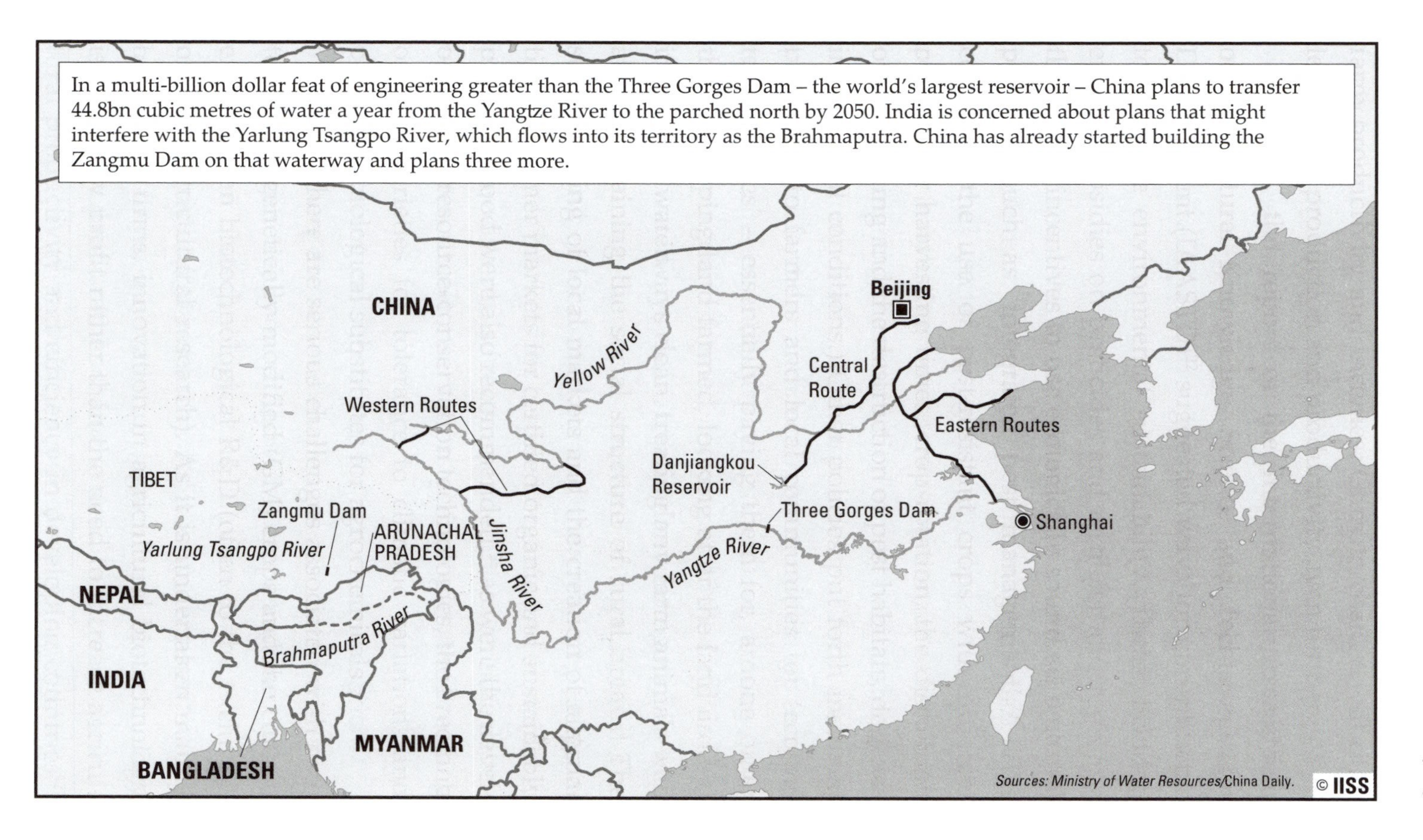

In a multi-billion dollar feat of engineering greater than the Three Gorges Dam – the world's largest reservoir – China plans to transfer 44.8bn cubic metres of water a year from the Yangtze River to the parched north by 2050. India is concerned about plans that might interfere with the Yarlung Tsangpo River, which flows into its territory as the Brahmaputra. China has already started building the Zangmu Dam on that waterway and plans three more.

*Sources: Ministry of Water Resources/*China Daily.

in India, freshwater aquifers are being pulled down by 1–3 metres per year' – faster than the rate of recharge.[39] If current practices continue, the dwindling availability of fresh water will almost certainly have devastating long-term impacts on agricultural production, livelihoods, health, and social and political stability.[40]

Extreme weather and climate change

With Asia already facing difficulties of degraded land and water resources, climate change (see also Chapter Two) is predicted to further threaten future agricultural production and productivity. While the evidence surrounding projected increases in CO_2 levels and their impact on agriculture remains the subject of debate, many studies agree that cereal production in parts of Asia in mid- to high-latitude regions is likely to benefit moderately from temperature increases of 1–3°C (together with rainfall changes). In seasonally dry and tropical regions, however, even moderate temperature increases of 1–2°C are expected to lead to declines in yields of major crops such as rice, wheat and maize.[52] As mentioned earlier, yields of these crops are already showing signs of decline or stagnation in parts of East, South and Southeast Asia.[53]

Changes in the climate are expected, for example, to compound both China and India's water problems. One study concludes that, through a complex mix of socio-economic, environmental and climatic factors, in China 'the gap between water scarcity in the north and abundance in the south will widen even further.'[54] By 2050, the annual run-off of the Brahmaputra and the Indus, both major rivers in South Asia, is projected to decrease by 14% and 27%

respectively.[55] These rivers underpin the food security of hundreds of millions, so the implications are serious.

Because agriculture in India continues to rely so heavily on rainfall, extreme weather events, prolonged dry spells and increased risk of severe flooding during the monsoons are expected to hurt crop yields in major food-growing regions. Changes in monsoon patterns, with rising temperatures predicted to cause more rain to fall in fewer days, threaten serious flooding in such densely populated areas as the Ganges–Brahmaputra–Meghna River Delta. The same can be expected in the Mekong and Irrawaddy deltas in Southeast Asia.[56]

More frequent droughts are expected if dry seasons become longer and more intense, as predicted. Droughts have already caused substantial yield losses in recent times. In India, for example, drought in 1987 and 2002–03 affected over half the total cropped area.[57] Although it appears that increasing temperatures have benefitted crop yields in northern China over the last six decades or so, the country has also seen an increasing number of droughts over the same period. Low precipitation is a threat to the region's winter wheat, and water availability for both people and livestock has also been declining (see 'Limited land and water' in this chapter). The total area of land affected annually by flooding in China has grown from 5m ha in the 1970s to up to 10m ha per year in the 2000s.[58] From 2000 to 2007, drought and flood together caused harvest failure of up to 5m ha.[59]

At the same time as changes in precipitation will affect water availability for both rain-fed and irrigated crops in Asia (particularly South and Southeast Asia), higher temperatures and increased evaporation will also raise the amount of water required for crop production.[60] Declines in soil quality (in terms of moisture and nutrient content), and increases in pests, plagues and crop diseases are also expected.[61]

Saltwater intrusion into freshwater resources is already escalating along the coasts, because of rising sea levels and retreating river flows. This is a significant problem in the Mekong Delta, the Bay of Bengal region and the coastal plains of China in the dry season.[62] The FAO states that rising sea levels are also worsening upstream salinity, affecting inland fisheries, where climate change is most likely to have 'a disproportionately negative impact on the economies and livelihoods of nations and communities in Asia'.[63]

The Philippines and Vietnam are also extremely vulnerable to the possible effects of climate change. After the 2007–08 global food-price crisis, Manila embarked on a quest for rice self-sufficiency (see Chapter Five). However, its plans have been hampered by the adverse effects on rice production that El Niño–Southern Oscillation[64] events such as storms, typhoons and droughts have had in the past few decades.[65] In 1998, for example, the El Niño phenomenon caused a severe drought, leading to a 10% drop in rice yields across the country.[66] In late 2009, storms hit crucial farming areas in Luzon, northern Philippines, costing the agricultural sector around US$90m in damaged paddy and submerged rice lands.[67] In 2010, a short drought cut paddy output and area harvested by 1.5% and 3.7% respectively (from 2009 levels). Rice imports that year reached 2.37m tonnes, almost as much as was imported in 2008 during the global food-price spike.[68] With climate change, El Niño events are expected to become more frequent and intense, further threatening food production and agricultural resources.

Vietnam's food-security policies will also need to be re-evaluated in the light of climate change. Vietnam is a highly disaster-prone country, suffering most from tropical storms, floods, droughts, storm surges and landslides.[69] It is also one of the most vulnerable to climate-change impacts worldwide, especially because of its heavy dependence on agriculture and low levels of development in rural areas.[70] Changing rainfall patterns mean natural disasters such as typhoons and floods are becoming more frequent and intense in Vietnam. Crops of the country's leading grain, rice, are 'particularly vulnerable to damage caused by long periods of inundation'.[71] Rising sea levels also pose a serious challenge to rice production in the country, as saltwater intrusion into freshwater resources in coastal areas will worsen in the coming years. According to the United Nations Development Programme (UNDP), as sea level continues to rise, parts of the low-lying Mekong Delta region could face complete inundation for parts of the year.[72] Changing temperatures will also affect '[crop] growing periods, crop calendars and crop distribution, increase pest and virus activity' and are expected to have a detrimental impact on spring and summer rice yields.[73] By 2050, Vietnam's total rice production could drop by 2.75m tonnes to 9.1m tonnes and, unless adaptation measures are taken, the output of other major crops like maize, cassava and sugar cane could also suffer.[74]

In this context, the route to ensuring food security (and raising farm incomes) is not so much dependent on increasing overall rice production, but largely intertwined with addressing local vulnerabilities to climate change.[75] This involves bolstering the resilience of individual communities through effective plans to mitigate and adapt to water-related disasters, while increasing institutional capacity, income diversification, poverty-reduction and other measures. At present, most adaptive measures are concerned with short-term response capacity and disaster-risk reduction activities – such as weather forecasting and erecting 'climate-proof physical infrastructure'. What is largely missing is more long-term action to tackle the root causes of vulnerability to climate change and food insecurity, such as poverty-reduction and adaptive measures to incorporate efforts to tackle climate change into wider rural and agricultural development programmes – including changes in housing styles to mitigate damage from floods and winds; adjustments in crop varieties and calendars; and a broadening of safety-net programmes to accommodate those forced to flee in the face of climate change.[76]

On a broader note, extreme weather and other climatic factors could lead to the widespread displacement of people within and across Asian countries. In 2010, the ADB reported that more than 30m people were at least temporarily displaced by environmental and weather-related disasters in the region.[77] As climate change results in more frequent and intense adverse weather events, tens of millions more are likely to be similarly displaced. Asia is home to seven of the ten countries in the world with populations most likely to be at risk from rising sea levels in 2050 – India, China, Bangladesh, Indonesia, Japan, the Philippines and Vietnam.[78] Policies adopted and implemented by governments and other regional authorities will determine the

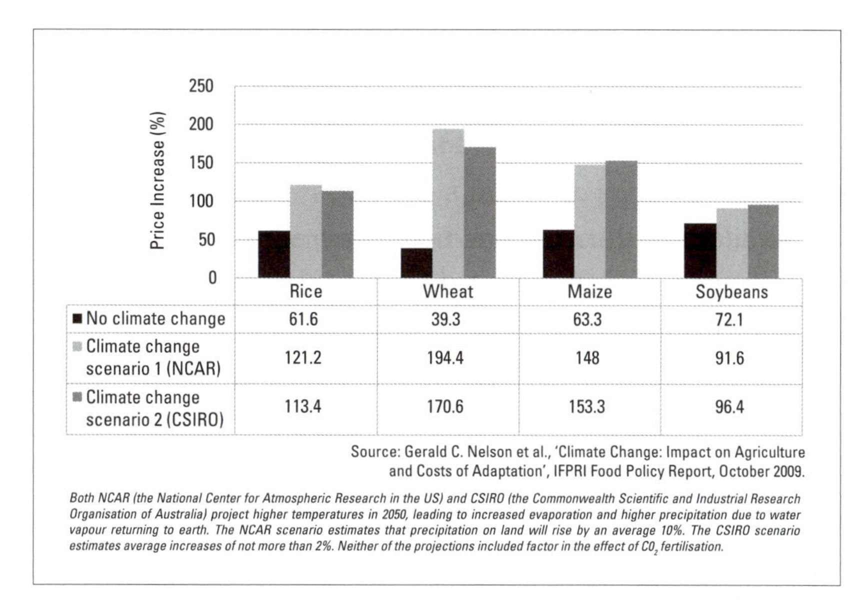

	Rice	Wheat	Maize	Soybeans
■ No climate change	61.6	39.3	63.3	72.1
■ Climate change scenario 1 (NCAR)	121.2	194.4	148	91.6
■ Climate change scenario 2 (CSIRO)	113.4	170.6	153.3	96.4

Source: Gerald C. Nelson et al., 'Climate Change: Impact on Agriculture and Costs of Adaptation', IFPRI Food Policy Report, October 2009.

Both NCAR (the National Center for Atmospheric Research in the US) and CSIRO (the Commonwealth Scientific and Industrial Research Organisation of Australia) project higher temperatures in 2050, leading to increased evaporation and higher precipitation due to water vapour returning to earth. The NCAR scenario estimates that precipitation on land will rise by an average 10%. The CSIRO scenario estimates average increases of not more than 2%. Neither of the projections included factor in the effect of CO_2 fertilisation.

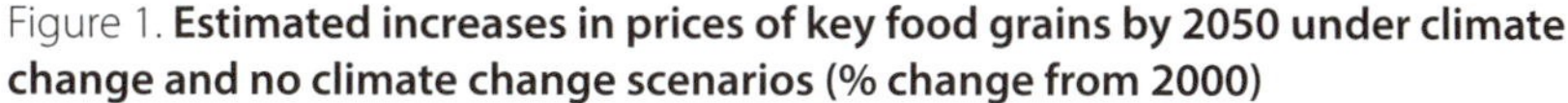
Figure 1. **Estimated increases in prices of key food grains by 2050 under climate change and no climate change scenarios (% change from 2000)**

extent to which vulnerable communities are left exposed to these threats.

Finally, as the effects of climate change make themselves felt globally, food prices are expected to further escalate. According to a 2009 IFPRI study examining the costs to agriculture of climate change between 2000 and 2050, prices were anticipated to rise by 62% for rice and 40% for wheat without climate change, but by 113–121% for rice and 170–195% for wheat under various climate-change projections (see Figure 1). Higher costs of feed would also have an impact on livestock prices and production costs. For example, price increases for beef and pork between 2000 and 2050 are expected to be 65–91% greater because of climate change.[79] Again, those most hurt by these increases will be smallholder farmers in the region who are net food consumers, rely on rain-fed agriculture and have little capacity

Fish as a strategic flashpoint

With the rapid expansion of China's distant-water fishing fleet, and Beijing's growing assertiveness over disputed seas and the resources they contain – meaning fish as well as oil and gas – maritime tensions have increased in East and Southeast Asia.[80] Incidents involving fishing vessels have exacerbated existing territorial disputes, including in the South China Sea between Beijing, on the one hand, and Manila,[81] Hanoi and others. As instances of illegal fishing by Chinese vessels (knowingly or unknowingly) in the Exclusive Economic Zones (EEZs) of neighbouring countries have increased, so too have clashes. According to official Chinese statistics, in the South China Sea during 1989–2010, there were 380 cases of Chinese fisherfolk being attacked, robbed, detailed or killed by neighbouring countries, involving more than 750 fishing vessels and 11,300 crew.[82] Filipino and Vietnamese fisherfolk have also been detained and their boats seized on numerous occasions.

A Philippine vessel was involved in a stand-off with Chinese vessels from April to June 2012, when the Philippines sent its largest naval vessel to inspect eight Chinese fishing boats in the South China Sea's disputed Scarborough Shoal and China responded by sending its own surveillance ships.[83] In May 2013, Taiwan imposed sanctions against the Philippines after the latter's coastguard killed a Taiwanese fisherman in disputed waters. Beijing, unusually, offered verbal support for Taipei in the dispute.[84]

China's fishing fleet is the world's largest. In 2010, more than 13 million people worked in China's fishing sector, among them nearly 7.5m traditional fisherfolk.[85] Their increasing involvement in distant-water fishing 'is also one of the drivers for the expansion of the PLA navy' to protect the country's fishing vessels.[86] More than that, Sarah Raine and Christian Le Mière report in *Regional Disorder: The South China Sea Disputes*, some have threatened the militarisation of the fishing fleet.[87] In June 2012, for example, He Jianbin, chief of the state-run Baosha Fishing Corporation, said: 'If we put 5,000 Chinese fishing boats in the South China Sea, there will be 10,000 fishermen. And if we make all of them militiamen, give them weapons, we will have a military force stronger than all the combined forces of the countries in the South China Sea.'[88]

There is certainly much at stake for both China and Southeast Asian nations with claims in the South China Sea; according to one set of statistics the sea provides 25% of the protein requirements for 500m people and up to 80% of the Philippine diet.[89] China has long imposed unilateral fishing bans, a tactic taken up by the Philippines since 2012. With national maritime patrols enforcing bans, as well as protecting their own country's fisherfolk, 'a greater incidence of confrontations becomes, to some extent, inevitable,' suggest Raine and Le Mière.[90]

to adapt quickly and adequately to the effects of climate change.

Rural farmers under threat

Small farmers produce 80% of Asia's food but are increasingly struggling to maintain their livelihoods. In recent years, riots have erupted in China, Indonesia, Cambodia and elsewhere over forced land acquisitions. Indigenous communities have frequently been forced off ancestral land that has provided them with livelihoods and food for generations. In India, more than 200,000 farmers have committed suicide since 1997.[91]

Despite decades of economic growth and poverty-reduction schemes, millions of Asians remain poor (see Table 1). The vast majority of them live in rural farming households, in areas where infrastructure has been neglected and alternative economic opportunities are slim to non-existent. In several countries in the region, including India, farm incomes have stagnated. Meanwhile input costs have universally soared and farm-gate prices have been kept low. The combination has forced many farmers into debt.[92] Lack of equal access to irrigation, and inadequate extension (that is, advisory) services, credit facilities and risk insurance have made their lives more difficult,[93] while insufficient post-harvest processing facilities and access to markets also

Table 1. **Poverty levels in Asia**

Country	Less than $2 a day (% of population)	Less than $1.25 a day (% of population)
China	27.2% (2009)	11.8% (2009)
India	68.8% (2010)	32.7% (2010)
Indonesia	43.3% (2011)	16.2% (2011)
Philippines	41.5% (2009)	18.4% (2009)
Vietnam	43% (2008)	17% (2008)
Cambodia	49.5% (2009)	18.6% (2009)

Source: World Bank

mean that waste levels remain high and less food makes it to the end of the supply chain.[94]

Furthermore, as 'distress migration' from rural to urban areas has increased, the number of rural households headed by women has grown in many developing Asian countries, as has the burden rural women face.[95] In 2004/05 in India, for example, women accounted for an unprecedented 34% of principal and 89% of subsidiary workers in agriculture.[96] Still, agricultural policies across the region treat women unequally, including the widespread denial of land rights, and inadequate access to natural and financial resources, skills and training.[97]

All of this has implications for the region's food security, because if there is no extra arable land to cultivate in Asia, and the land already under cultivation is degraded, then encouraging farm productivity – by assisting those who already produce most of the region's food – is one of the surest ways to raise overall productivity.

Poverty levels remain especially high in India. In 2011, more than 211m people – or nearly one-fifth of the population – remained undernourished.[98] Although Indians in both urban and rural areas are now eating more meat, dairy, fruits and vegetables, the average amount of calories consumed has seen a decline since the 1980s.[99] India also has the world's worst malnourishment figures for children under the age of five. Today, 42% of under-fives remain underweight and 59% are stunted.[100] Indian Prime Minister Manmohan Singh has called the scale of the problem 'unacceptably high' and 'a matter of national shame'.[101]

To a lesser extent, the patterns seen in India are mirrored across Asia. High economic growth has been accompanied by growing income inequality. Much of the region's boom has come on the back of expanding service sectors,[102] or in China's case manufacturing. However, agriculture remains a major source of livelihoods in China (38% of the workforce),[103] India (51%), the Philippines (33%), Vietnam (48%), Indonesia (36%) and Cambodia (56%).[104]

Moreover, small farmers and fisherfolk are often 'net food consumers', spending more on meals than they make by selling produce. This means they must supplement their income with other activities or face growing indebtedness. Poor Asian households also spend a disproportionate amount of their income on food. The problem is least marked in China, where people in rural areas were spending around 40% on food in 2009.[105] However, in countries like Cambodia, India, Indonesia, the Philippines and Vietnam, the poor continue to spend well above half of their incomes on food.[106]

This makes them particularly vulnerable to high and volatile food prices. Price shocks may force them to cut back on the quantity and quality of foodstuffs they eat, worsening short-term hunger and longer-term malnutrition, which in turn has implications for health, education and economic productivity. In theory, because they are food producers, poor rural farmers should also benefit from higher prices. In reality, however, small farmers have largely been unable to seize the opportunity presented by recent price spikes, because higher prices frequently failed to reach the farm gate, and even where they did, smallholders lacked access to quick, reliable information, faced real hurdles in both harvesting crops and getting them to market more rapidly, and were unable to afford the accompanying higher costs of oil and fertilisers.[107]

To improve poorer citizens' access to food, many Asian countries run social safety-net programmes, from food-price subsidies and cash transfers to food-for-work and food-distribution schemes. India, for example, operates a targeted Public Distribution System (PDS) for food grains, Indonesia dispenses subsidised rice via its 'Raskin' scheme and the Philippines' National Food Authority issues subsidised rice. However, to varying degrees, these programmes suffer from serious inefficiencies, and even corruption in some instances (see Chapter Five).

Land tenure

For extremely poor rural households, access to land and land tenure are among the main factors 'representing a stable basis of food security and income' in limited, seasonal and poorly paid rural labour markets.[108] Secure property rights are considered essential for equal economic growth, as they usually lead to greater investment by farmers into food-production processes. They encourage farmers to sustainably use natural resources, new technologies and innovations, leading to greater farm productivity (as well as overall poverty reduction).[109]

Unequal distribution of land, on the other hand, contributes to poor production output, meagre income for the less privileged, indebtedness and ultimately poverty in the countryside. The decline in agricultural investment in recent decades has exacerbated these problems.[110] Experts argue that schemes to boost productivity are unlikely to have the intended benefits without addressing deteriorating access to land and rising tenure insecurity for small farmers in rural areas.[111]

Yet despite decades of land reforms, land tenure remains a complex challenge in many Asian countries. In China, for example, around 4m rural families a year have their land confiscated by local government officials to be sold to developers.[112] This is despite laws preventing farmland conversion and promising land-use rights to farming households, suggesting that the rights of small farmers under China's current land-tenure system need to be strengthened and better enforced.[113] In 2011, a survey of 1,791 farmers in 17 of China's provinces found that land acquisitions had steadily increased since 2005. While more than 75% of affected farmers were promised compensation, fewer than 10% received any. Those who did received only a fraction of the true value of their land.[114] Land documentation remains incomplete, and women's names continue to be largely excluded from land certificates, despite their having the same land rights as men. This is particularly problematic when there are more women working in the fields than men.[115]

Add other challenges – such as a glaring lack of agricultural extension and support services, and inadequate and dilapidated rural infrastructure[116] – and it is hardly surprising that the discontents of China's small farmers have been rising. In 2009, there were around 90,000 reported 'mass incidents' such as riots, protests, demonstrations and other forms of social unrest in the country.[117] Protests in rural areas against forced land acquisitions have also increased. In April 2011, for example, when trying to force 2,000 villagers in Suijiang county in Yunnan from their land to make way for a large hydroelectricity project,[118] the government had to deploy 400 paramilitary troops, tactical police units and militia to crush a five-day protest. In December the same year, armed police quashed protests in the fishing village of Wukan in southern China, as another 2,000 villagers marched in demonstration against forced land acquisitions.[119] Such incidents are viewed with disquiet within China's ruling Communist Party, and although they are far from coalescing into a nationwide movement, such incidents nonetheless indicate the growing dissatisfaction towards the government.[120]

In India, according to the National Commission on Farmers, in 1991/92 the bottom half of rural households owned only 3% of total land holdings, while the top 10% owned as much as 54%.[121] Since then, the competition for land between industry, urban development and agriculture has been intensifying, putting small farmers and marginalised communities at an even greater disadvantage.[122] Under the Land Acquisition Act, 1894, Indian farmers have been evicted from their lands for decades in the name of 'public purpose', often with little or no consultation and without adequate compensation.[123] Across India, poor indigenous communities have been forced off ancestral land that has provided them with livelihoods and food for generations. Implementation remains weak of a landmark Forest Rights Act passed in 2006 to legally recognise the rights of traditional forest-dwelling communities and give them a say in conservation policies.[124]

Attempts to take rural land for housing and industry have increasingly led to violence.[125] The establishment of Special Economic Zones (SEZs) – designed to incentivise foreign investment – on agricultural land and along coastlines without consultation with local communities has met heavy resistance.[126] In 2007, for example, the state government of West Bengal tried to forcibly acquire land in the area of Nandigram to set up an SEZ for the development of a chemical hub. However, local villagers refused to give up their land, blocking roads and destroying bridges to prevent government forces from entering the areas concerned. Repeated clashes between villagers, government supporters and police caused many fatalities and injuries.[127] In a widely condemned episode on 14 March, the government authorised 3,000 police officers to enter one of the areas earmarked for acquisition. They then opened fire on protesters, killing at least 14 and injuring more than 70.[128] The West Bengal government was finally forced to abandon its plans.

Several other SEZ projects across India have since been cancelled, delayed or downsized.[129] For example, in June 2013, Reliance Industries pulled out of a massive SEZ in Haryana state. The company was only able to buy around 3,379ha of the roughly 10,117ha it was supposed to acquire.[130] A US$12bn, 1,600ha SEZ being developed by South Korean steel giant Posco in Odisha (formerly Orissa) state has been bogged down by land and environmental challenges since 2006.[131]

Forced land acquisitions without adequate compensation, resettlement and rehabilitation have further fuelled the Maoist 'Naxalite' insurgency raging across many of India's eastern states,[132] described by Prime Minister Singh as the single-largest internal threat to the country's security. A recent study showed that shocks to agricultural land and forestlands supporting local livelihoods were strongly linked with upsurges in violence in certain districts affected by the insurgency.[133] Maoists also became involved in the land-acquisition related conflict in Nandigram in 2007.[134]

In the Philippines, where corruption and inefficiency have delayed agrarian reforms (see Chapter Five), local communities have also faced the loss of land and livelihoods via government deals wooing large agribusinesses under the multi-agency National Convergence Initiative (NCI). In the Indonesian province of West Papua, the Merauke Integrated Food and Energy Estate (MIFEE) Project launched in 2010 provides another demonstration of how land acquisitions can be damaging to local food security. Although the government first promoted the MIFEE as a way to create jobs and improve food security,[135] it transpired that most of the 1.28m ha of tropical forestland to be cleared was earmarked for industrial timber plantations (around 970,000ha) and oil palm (more than 300,000ha), with food crops comprising the smallest share (69,000ha).[136] West Papua has a long history of military oppression, and some investigations have found that indigenous communities, who derive sustenance from the region's rich forestlands, were being manipulated by the private companies involved and intimidated by the armed forces and police.[137] After reports of villagers being cheated into signing over their lands, disputes among clans and villages, and conflicts between communities and the agribusiness companies investing in the project,[138] the Indonesian government scaled it back in 2012.[139]

Vietnam has not been immune to land-rights disputes, either, with hundreds of farmers clashing with police in 2012 over the appropriation of land for a satellite city called EcoPark near Hanoi,[140] and one fish farmer even deploying shotguns and homemade mines in an effort to prevent police seizing his land.[141]

It is in Cambodia, however, that the land-rights problem appears particularly grim. This is one of the world's poorest and least-developed countries, where most rural households are engaged in subsistence-level rice farming, with forestry and fisheries the other major sources of food and livelihoods.[142] After three decades of brutality and genocide ended with the fall of the Khmer Rouge regime in the late 1970s, the country's move towards democracy included a focus on privatisation. In the early 1990s, the government identified trade and investment liberalisation as ways of reducing poverty and bringing about inclusive socio-economic growth. Reforms were implemented to facilitate an investment-friendly environment including 'changes in land tenure, tax and marketing policies, a new investment law designed to attract foreign capital, and a separation of the state from production through the reduction of subsidies and the privatisation of state-owned businesses'.[143]

The agricultural sector was also opened up to private investment, and as early as the mid-1990s Cambodia began leasing out agricultural land to private investors for logging and plantations (such as rubber, oil palm, pine and coconut) and agro-industrial production of cash crops (such as sugar cane, soybean, cassava and corn). Since 2007, there has been even greater interest from private investors in Cambodia's agricultural sector.[144]

Meanwhile, most of the population lacks access to land and faces tenure insecurity. In 2004, around 20–30% of Cambodian landowners – mainly businessmen, senior government and military officials – owned about 70% of the land, while around 10% belonged to the poorest 40%.[145] One-fifth of all rural households are landless, and one-quarter own plots of less than 0.5ha.[146] Only around one-fifth of Cambodians hold official title to the land they live and work on. Under the 2001 Land Law, Cambodians can apply for title if they have proof of occupation and use of their land for at least five years before 2001. However, the process is slow and relatively expensive, meaning not everyone can afford it.[147] Without land title, the poor and marginalised find it particularly difficult to prove ownership when the government and private companies attempt to acquire land.[148]

Under a Sub-Decree on Economic Land Concessions (ELCs), the Cambodian government can lease up to 10,000ha of state-owned land to a private company for agricultural or industrial-agricultural exploitation for up to 99 years.[149] ELCs can be acquired for as little as nothing (for 'threadbare' or 'deteriorated' land) or as much as US$5–10 per ha per year for land more highly valued.[150] The processes by which ELCs are granted and monitored by the Ministry of Agriculture, Forestry and Fisheries (MAFF) remain opaque and information on ELCs is limited.

In April 2010, MAFF announced that 87 ELCs had been granted between 1995 and 2009, covering nearly 1.1m ha. According to the Cambodian League for the Promotion and Defense of Human Rights, however, private firms now control a total area of 3.9m ha, amounting to more than 22% of the country's land.[151] Just over half of the listed ELCs belong to Cambodian nationals, most of them with connections to influential political elites. The rest are leased by foreign companies from China, India, Vietnam, South Korea, Thailand, Malaysia, Taiwan, the United States and other countries.[152]

Before they are granted, ELCs in theory need to comply with environmental and social-impact assessments, so as not to violate land ownership and land-use rights of peasants; they must also be undertaken by public consultation. The reality is rather different. For example, in a June 2007 report, the UN special representative of the secretary-general for human rights in Cambodia said that in the allocation of ELCs:

> Essential pre-conditions to the grant of concessions, such as the registration of land as state private land and conduct of public consultations and environmental and social impact assessments, have not been met. Likewise, restrictions on the size and ownership of economic land concessions have not been properly enforced. Individuals have used different companies to acquire interests in multiple concessions, contrary to the Land Law, and to obtain adjacent concessions for the same purposes, circumventing the 10,000 hectare size limit. Concessions have been granted over forested areas and former forest concessions, contrary to the Forestry Law and forestry regulations. Despite these breaches of the law, there has been no systematic review of concessions, as required by the Sub-Decree on [ELCs]. Further, the judicial system has failed to uphold the rights of affected communities and respect for the law, and to hold companies accountable for their actions.[153]

Land-related disputes and conflicts are more likely in areas where there is no clear legal ownership of land and resources – that is, forest areas or in places where land titling has yet to be implemented.[154] As it happens, around 40% of all ELCs in Cambodia are in northeastern provinces populated mainly by indigenous communities whose household incomes mainly rely on agricultural activities and non-timber forest products (NTFPs).[155] These communities have come under growing pressure in recent years to give up their lands in illegal or coercive land deals.[156] Companies usually offer to buy the land from villagers for around US$200 per ha, or give them the option to cultivate cash crops on their lands and partake in the ELC venture, whereby the company takes a cut of the harvest and charges the villagers operating costs and interest for cultivating the land. [157] Resettlement is the third option, usually to land that is far away and inadequate for cultivation. Often, under pressure from company representatives and officials, villagers are forced to relinquish their land rights and lose their source of livelihood.[158]

Despite the 2001 Land Law providing for strong protection of indigenous communities, illegal and forced eviction of such communities has been widespread. In Ratanakiri province, for example, ELCs have endangered the way of life of thousands of indigenous families and have also caused environmental damage. The province is home to some of the most biodiverse tropical forest and montane forest ecosystems in Southeast Asia.[159] More than 70% of the population belongs to eight different indigenous tribes that have traditionally practised long-fallow swidden (or slash-and-burn) subsistence agriculture, 'thus ensuring the continued regeneration of forests as part of their rotational systems'. This is supplemented heavily by hunting, fishing and the collection of NTFPs from communal forest resources.[160]

Since the 1990s, the government has been granting large tracts of land for logging and plantation agriculture to foreign companies in the province, upsetting the system of communal resource management, and disenfranchising local communities. Vietnamese companies, for example, hold as many as seven ELCs in the area, and in most cases villagers have been forced to sell their land under coercion and with false information.[161] Between 1991 and 2004, there were more than 1,500 land-related disputes and conflicts in Cambodia, affecting more than 160,000 farming families over 380,000ha. In 2006, two-thirds of these remained unresolved.[162]

In many instances, local communities have taken matters into their own hands as their complaints have fallen on deaf ears. They have mounted protests by physically blocking highways, commandeering bulldozers, detaining company officials or workers, and more.[163] Human-rights lawyers, civil-society groups and prominent individuals who have helped these communities have been threatened by the police and armed forces.[164] Often matters have turned violent. In January 2012, for example, villagers in Ratanakiri's Ka Nat Thum village were shot at by a military officer guarding a Vietnamese rubber company with a 2,361-ha ELC nearby. The villagers were returning home after attempting to prevent the company from clearing land. The shooting incident was reported to the district governor, but no immediate action was taken against the company.[165]

The shooting was one of at least five incidents across Cambodia in November–December 2011 in which armed forces opened fire on people protesting against ELCs – injuring 19 people, seven from gunfire.[166] There were many more such incidents in 2012 in a wave of violence against activists and protesters. In April 2012, for example, prominent environmental activist Chut Wutty was shot dead by military police while investigating illegal logging with two journalists.[167] In May, a teenager was killed when hundreds of heavily armed security forces personnel opened fire on villagers in Kratie province during a forced eviction.[168] In a separate incident, two people were injured and five others were arrested in clashes between armed forces and the residents of Prama village in Chhlong district, some of whom were armed with crossbows or axes.[169]

Few cases have been reported where ELCs have clearly resulted in benefits for local communities.[170] Nonetheless, the potential for increasing agricultural productivity for rice and other food crops in Cambodia is significant, and private investments could go a long way towards achieving this potential for the benefit of not just local smallholders, but also for investing parties. As a recent study evaluating the potential for Cambodia to serve as a long-term supplier of food for the Gulf Co-operation Council (GCC) member states suggests, investors would be better off putting their money in agricultural projects that are smallholder-focused and aimed at empowering and creating profit for local communities, rather than those which dispossess them of their most valuable natural resources, and potentially lead to conflict and instability. This is because the former is far more likely to be a reliable, sustainable and fair approach to raising productivity and producing surpluses for export, while ensuring that local communities also see an improvement in their livelihoods, food security and overall living standards.[171]

The government has a vital role in ensuring that private investments follow existing regulations concerning local communities, so that the latter's rights are protected. To this end, the completion of land titling remains a most urgent task for the Cambodian government, as well as the clarification of existing ambiguities in the country's land laws, thus minimising the potential for local communities to be treated in an illegal and unjust manner by either investors or corrupt government officials.

Conclusion

Asian governments face many challenges in seeking to ensure their national and regional food security. Much progress has been made in lifting millions out of poverty and hunger, but the region remains home to the largest number of the poor and hungry globally. Income inequalities continue to expand across developing countries in Asia, and rural areas are facing economic stagnation.

For small farming households, dwindling public spending on agricultural infrastructure and R&D has come at the same time as the benefits brought by the Green Revolution have begun to fade. Together with widespread environmental degradation, this has negatively affected productivity and farm incomes. Insecure access to land has added to the woes of poor farming households in the region.

In the face of growing constraints on natural resources and expanding populations, Asia's two most populous countries, China and India, are increasingly relying on imports to meet the demand for different food crops at home. China, in particular, has also purchased agricultural land abroad in order to safeguard future food and feed supplies (see

Chapter Three), raising concerns around the impact of such land deals on local food security and political stability in host countries. In Southeast Asia, such foreign investments in agricultural land have been at the heart of numerous protests and violent conflicts between local communities on the one hand and government and private companies on the other.

There is still plenty of scope to improve agricultural productivity in developing Asia, through better deployment of existing resources and technologies, stronger land rights, enhanced public investment in agriculture, accelerated rural development and similar measures. As rural farming households currently produce the vast majority of Asia's food, it is vital to sustainably improve small farm productivity. This involves, among other things, providing smallholder farmers with better access to the inputs they frequently lack, such as seeds and fertiliser, promoting agro-ecological farming methods that minimise damage to the environment, refurbishing or building local agricultural infrastructure to reduce waste and enhance efficiency, and improving small farmers' access to markets. Such an emphasis on sustainable local agriculture would help to improve food security not only by raising farm incomes and helping to regenerate rural economies, but also by increasing the amount of food available.

In recent years, governments in Asia have become increasingly aware of the need to focus on food security as a distinct national policy goal. Some policies have been designed and implemented, but as discussed in the following chapter, most countries continue to view food security in relatively narrow terms. Food and agricultural policies remain largely fragmented, uncoordinated and limited in the face of challenges to regional food systems.

Notes

1. Jikun Huang and Scott Rozelle, 'Agricultural Development and Nutrition: the Policies behind China's Success', World Food Programme Occasional Paper No. 19, November 2009, p. 11, http://home.wfp.org/stellent/groups/public/documents/newsroom/wfp213339.pdf.
2. Marites M. Tiongco and Kris A. Francisco, 'Philippines: Food Security versus Agricultural Exports?', Philippine Institute for Development Studies, Discussion Paper Series No. 2011–35, and Arsenio M. Balisacan, Mercedita A. Sombilla and Rowell C. Dikitanan, 'Rice Crisis in the Philippines: Why did it Occur and What are its Policy Implications?', in David Dawe (ed.), *The Rice Crisis: Markets, Policies and Food Security* (London and Washington DC: Earthscan and FAO, 2010), pp. 135–37.
3. Government of India (GoI), *Economic Survey 2011-12* (New Delhi: Ministry of Finance, 2012), pp. 181–82, http://indiabudget.nic.in/es2011-12/echap-08.pdf. See also Angus Deaton and Jean Drèze, 'Food and Nutrition in India: Facts and interpretation', *Economic and Political Weekly*, vol. XLIV, no. 7, 14 February 2009.
4. GoI, *Economic Survey 2013* (New Delhi: Ministry of Finance 2013), p. 174, http://indiabudget.nic.in/es2012-13/echap-08.pdf.
5. Raghbendra Jha, 'Investment and Subsidies in Indian Agriculture', Working Paper 2007/03, Australia South Asia Research Centre, Australian National University, https://crawford.anu.edu.au/acde/asarc/pdf/papers/2007/WP2007_03.pdf.
6. Shenggen Fan, Ashok Gulati and Sukhadeo Thorat, 'Investment, subsidies, and pro-poor growth in rural India', *Agricultural Economics*, vol. 38, no. 2 (September 2008), pp. 162–70.
7. GoI, 'Report of the Working Group for the Eleventh Five Year Plan (2007–12) on Crop Husbandry, Agricultural Inputs, Demand and Supply Projections and Agricultural Statistics', Planning Commission, December 2006, http://planningcommission.nic.in/aboutus/committee/wrkgrp11/wg11_rpcrop.pdf.
8. People's Republic of China, China Statistical Yearbook 2011.
9. Shuhao Tan, 'Impacts of Cultivated Land Conversion on Environmental Sustainability and Grain Self-sufficiency in China', *China & World Economy*, vol. 16, no. 3, May–June 2008, p. 79.
10. *Ibid*, pp. 78–79.
11. Liming Ye and Eric Van Ranst, 'Production scenarios and the

effect of soil degradation on long-term food security in China', *Global Environmental Change*, vol. 9, no. 4, October 2009, p. 465.

[12] Jingzhu Zhao et al., 'Opportunities and challenges of sustainable agricultural development in China', *Philosophical Transactions of the Royal Society B*, vol. 363, 2008, pp. 893–904.

[13] *Ibid.*, p. 475. It should be noted, however, that projections of the amount of grain China would require to remain self-sufficient in 2030 do vary. Bernard Gillard, for example, suggests that this amount could be as low as around 605m tonnes. See Bernard Gillard, 'World population and food supply: Can food production keep pace with population growth in the next half-century?', *Food Policy*, vol. 27, no. 1, February 2002, p. 60.

[14] World Bank World Development Indicators (WDIs), 2013. According to government sources, India's agricultural land availability is 0.32ha per capita, compared to the global average availability of 2.19ha per capita. See GoI, *State of Indian Agriculture 2011-12* (New Delhi: Ministry of Agriculture, 2012), p. 2, http://agricoop.nic.in/SIA111213312.pdf.

[15] GoI, *State of Indian Agriculture 2011-12*, p. 26.

[16] *Ibid.*

[17] Jian Xie, *Addressing China's Water Scarcity: Recommendations for Selected Water Resource Management Issues* (Washington DC: World Bank, 2009), p. 1.

[18] Jianguo Liu and Wu Yang, 'Water Sustainability for China and Beyond', *Science*, vol. 337, 10 August 2012, p. 649.

[19] Australian Government, Department of Agriculture, Fisheries and Forestry, 'Drought in China: Context, Policy and Management', March 2012, http://www.daff.gov.au/__data/assets/pdf_file/0007/2148919/drought-in-china-2012.doc.pdf.

[20] *Ibid.*, p. 7.

[21] See, for example, Yang Fangyi and Zhou Jiading, 'Why has water-rich Yunnan become a drought hotspot?', *China Dialogue*, 29 April 2013, https://www.chinadialogue.net/article/show/single/en/5940-Why-has-water-rich-Yunnan-become-a-drought-hotspot; and 'Drought affects 24m in China', *Deccan Herald*, 29 March 2013, http://www.deccanherald.com/content/322415/drought-affects-24-million-china.html.

[22] *Ibid.*, pp. 9–10.

[23] G.Q. Wang et al., 'Assessing water resources in China using PRECIS projections and VIC model', *Hydrology and Earth System Sciences Discussions*, vol. 8, no. 4, July 2011, p. 7,301.

[24] Ye and Van Ranst, 'Production scenarios and the effect of soil degradation'; and Jinxia Wanga et

al., 'Agriculture and groundwater development in northern China: trends, institutional responses, and policy options', *Water Policy*, vol. 9, supplement 1, 2007, p. 62.

[25] *Ibid.*

[26] Xie, *Addressing China's Water Scarcity*, pp. 11–13.

[27] Mindi Schneider, 'China's Pigs: Implications for the Environment, China's Smallholder Farmers and Food Security', Institute for Agriculture and Trade Policy, May 2011, p. 18, http://faculty.washington.edu/stevehar/Pigs--Schneider.pdf.

[28] Since 2004, China has been releasing annual 'No. 1' documents outlining the government's priorities for the following year. In the past, these documents have focused on issues such as rural and urban development and improvements in agriculture and farmer incomes. For more, see 'China targets rural issues in central document', Xinhua, 31 January 2013, http://www.chinadaily.com.cn/china/2013-01/31/content_16191918.htm.

[29] These usage limitations set out in the 2011 'No. 1' document – that China's total water usage should not exceed 670bn cubic metres in 2020, or 700 bn cubic metres in 2030 – will be a challenge to enforce, especially given that mainland China's water consumption was 600bn cubic metres in 2009. See Toh Han Shih, 'Beijing's water plan doesn't go far enough', *South China Morning Post*, 21 February 2011, http://www.scmp.com/article/738791/beijings-water-plan-doesnt-go-far-enough-critics-say.

[30] *Ibid.*

[31] Liu and Yang, 'Water Sustainability for China and Beyond'.

[32] *Ibid.* See also 'More than 40,000 Chinese dams at risk of breach', *Daily Telegraph*, 26 August 2011, http://www.telegraph.co.uk/news/worldnews/asia/china/8723964/More-than-40000-Chinese-dams-at-risk-of-breach.html.

[33] Keith Schneider et al., 'Choke Point China: Confronting water scarcity and energy demand in the world's largest country', *Vermont Journal of Environmental Law*, vol. 12, no. 3, Spring 2011, pp. 713–34, http://vjel.vermontlaw.edu/files/2013/06/Volume-12-Issue-31.pdf.

[34] Ministry of Agriculture, 'National Mission For Sustainable Agriculture: Strategies for Meeting the Challenges of Climate Change', Department of Agriculture and Cooperation, New Delhi, August 2010, p. 8, http://agricoop.nic.in/Climatechange/ccr/National%20Mission%20For%20Sustainable%20Agriculture-DRAFT-Sept-2010.pdf.

[35] Arathy Menon, Anders Levermann, and Jacob Schewe,

'Enhanced future variability during India's rainy season', *Geophysical Research Letters*, vol. 40, no. 12, June 2013, p. 3,242.

[36] GoI, *State of Indian Agriculture 2011–12*.

[37] GoI, 'Report of the Steering Committee on Agriculture and Allied Sectors for Formulation of the Eleventh Five Year Plan (2007-2012)', Planning Commission, 15 April 2007, p. 10, http://planningcommission.nic.in/aboutus/committee/strgrp11/str11_agriall.pdf.

[38] David Seckler, Randolph Barker and Upali Amarasinghe, 'Water Scarcity in the Twenty-first Century', *International Journal of Water Resources Development*, vol. 15, nos. 1–2, 2009, p. 40.

[39] *Ibid*.

[40] *Ibid*.

[41] International Rivers, 'South-North Water Transfer Project', http://www.internationalrivers.org/campaigns/south-north-water-transfer-project.

[42] Vijay P. Singh, Nayan Sharma and C. Shekhar P. Ojha (eds), *The Brahmaputra Basin Water Resources* (Berlin: Springer, 2004) quoted in Brahma Chellany, *Water: Asia's New Battleground* (Washington DC: Georgetown University Press, 2011), p. 191.

[43] See, for example, Amit Ranjan, 'Beijing's Threat to India's Water Security', *Asia Sentinel*, 10 November 2010, http://www.asiasentinel.com/politics/beijings-threat-to-indias-water-security; and Brahma Chellany, 'The Sino-Indian Water Divide', Project Syndicate, 9 August 2009, http://www.project-syndicate.org/commentary/the-sino-indian-water-divide. See also Chellany, *Water: Asia's New Battleground*.

[44] Chellany, 'The Sino-Indian Water Divide'.

[45] Chellany, *Water: Asia's New Battleground*, p. 144.

[46] Namrata Goswami, 'China's "Aggressive" Territorial Claim on India's Arunachal Pradesh: A Response to Changing Power Dynamics in Asia', *Strategic Analysis*, vol. 35, no. 5, 2011, pp. 781–92.

[47] Indrani Baghchee, 'Relief for India as China says no Brahmaputra diversion', *Times of India*, 14 October 2011, http://articles.timesofindia.indiatimes.com/2011-10-14/india/30278545_1_brahmaputra-yarlung-tsangpo-india-and-china.

[48] *Ibid*.

[49] Simon Denyer, 'Chinese dams in Tibet raise hackles in India', *Washington Post*, 7 February 2013, http://www.washingtonpost.com/world/asia_pacific/chinese-dams-in-tibet-raise-hackles-in-india/2013/02/07/ee39fc7a-7133-11e2-ac36-3d8d9dcaa2e2_story.html.

[50] Pau Khan Khup Hangzo, 'Transboundary rivers in the Hindu Kush-Himalaya (HKH) region: Beyond the "water as weapon" rhetoric', *NTS Insight*, September 2012, RSIS Centre for Non-Traditional Security (NTS) Studies, Singapore, http://www.rsis.edu.sg/nts/HTML-Newsletter/Insight/NTS-Insight-sep-1201.html.

[51] Sunil Khilnani et al., 'Nonalignment 2.0: A Foreign and Strategic Policy for India in the Twenty First Century', National Defence College and the Centre for Policy Research 2012, p. 40, http://www.cprindia.org/sites/default/files/NonAlignment%202.0_1.pdf.

[52] United Nations Development Programme (UNDP), 'One Planet to Share: Sustaining Human Progress in a Changing Climate', Asia-Pacific Human Development Report, April 2012, p. 27.

[53] Himanshu Pathak et al., 'Trends of climatic potential and on-farm yields of rice and wheat in the Indo-Gangetic Plains', *Field Crops Research*, vol. 80, no. 3, 30 January 2003, p. 224.

[54] Shilong Piao et al., 'The impacts of climate change on water resources and agriculture in China', *Nature*, vol. 467, no. 7,311, 2 September 2010, p. 48.

[55] Intergovernmental Panel on Climate Change (IPCC), *Climate Change 2001: Working Group II: Impacts, Adaptation and Vulnerability* (Cambridge: Cambridge University Press, 2001).

[56] IPCC, *Climate Change 2007: Working Group II: Impacts, Adaptation and Vulnerability* (Cambridge, United Kingdom, and New York: Cambridge University Press, 2007), pp. 472–506.

[57] Reiner Wassmann et al., 'Regional Vulnerability of Climate Change Impacts on Asian Rice Production and Scope for Adaptation', *Advances in Agronomy*, vol. 102, no. 9, 2009, p. 103.

[58] Piao et al., 'The impacts of climate change on water resources and agriculture in China', p. 43–51.

[59] *Ibid.*

[60] Gerald C. Nelson et al., 'Climate Change: Impact on Agriculture and Costs of Adaptation', IFPRI Food Policy Report, October 2009, p. 4, http://www.ifpri.org/sites/default/files/publications/pr21.pdf.

[61] *Ibid.*, and IPCC, *Climate Change 2007*, p. 483.

[62] IPCC, *Climate Change 2007.*

[63] Gayathri Sriskanthan and Simon Funge-Smith, 'The potential impact of climate change on fisheries and aquaculture in the Asian region', FAO RAP Publication 2011/16, Bangkok 2011, http://www.fao.org/docrep/015/ba0083e/ba0083e00.pdf.

[64] The El Niño–Southern Oscillation cycle refers to the fluctuations in

temperature between the ocean and atmosphere in the east-central Equatorial Pacific, consisting of two particular phenomena: El Niño (involving the above-average warming of sea surface temperatures) and La Niña (characterised by below-average sea surface temperatures). As surface temperatures deviate from normal averages, they can have major impacts on ocean processes as well as on global weather and climate. El Niño, for example, may lead to 'increased rainfall across the southern tier of the US and in Peru', causing destructive flooding, and 'drought in the West Pacific, sometimes associated with devastating bush fires in Australia'. La Niña is known to have the opposite effects to El Niño in many places, especially in the tropics. For more, see 'What are El Niño and La Niña?', National Oceanic and Atmospheric Administration, US Department of Commerce, http://oceanservice.noaa.gov/facts/ninonina.html.

[65] Caesar B. Cororaton and Erwin L. Corong, 'Philippine Agricultural and Food Policies: Implications on Poverty and Income Distribution', IFPRI Draft Research Report, Annual Meeting of International Agricultural Trade Research Consortium, 7–9 December 2008, Scottsdale, Arizona, p. 23.

[66] Erniel B. Barrios and Angela D. Nalica, 'Convergence of Growth in Rice Production in the Philippines', 10th National Convention on Statistics (NCS), EDSA Shangri-La Hotel, 1–2 October 2007, http://www.nscb.gov.ph/ncs/10thNCS/papers/invited%20papers/ips-23/ips23-01.pdf.

[67] 'Damage by Typhoon Ketsana to Philippine agriculture rises to $115 mln', Xinhua, 3 October 2009, http://news.xinhuanet.com/english/2009-10/03/content_12176542.htm.

[68] Barbara Mae Dacanay, 'Tropical storms hit production of rice in Philippines', Gulf News, 22 January 2011, http://gulfnews.com/news/world/philippines/tropical-storms-hit-production-of-rice-in-philippines-1.750123.

[69] Huu Ninh Nguyen, 'Flooding in Mekong River Delta, Viet Nam', UNDP Occasional Paper 2007/53, p. 3.

[70] Pamela McElwee et al., 'The Social Dimensions of Adaptation to Climate Change in Vietnam', World Bank Discussion Paper No. 12, December 2010, p. xiv, http://climatechange.worldbank.org/sites/default/files/documents/Vietnam-EACC-Social.pdf.

[71] World Bank, 'Vulnerability, Risk Reduction, and Adaptation to Climate Change', Climate Risk and Adaptation Country Profile,

April 2011, p. 9, http://sdwebx.worldbank.org/climateportalb/doc/GFDRRCountryProfiles/wb_gfdrr_climate_change_country_profile_for_VNM.pdf.

[72] Peter Chaudhry and Greet Ruysschaert, 'Climate Change and Human Development in Vietnam, UNDP Human Development Report', UNDP Occasional Paper 2007/46, p. 5, http://hdr.undp.org/en/reports/global/hdr2007-8/papers/Chaudhry_Peter%20and%20Ruysschaert_Greet.pdf.

[73] *Ibid.*

[74] *Ibid.*

[75] McElwee, 'The Social Dimensions of Adaptation to Climate Change in Vietnam', p. xiv.

[76] *Ibid.*

[77] Fiona Harvey, 'More than 30 million climate migrants in Asia in 2010, report finds', *Guardian*, 19 September 2011, http://www.theguardian.com/environment/2011/sep/19/climate-migrants-asia-2010.

[78] David Wheeler, 'Quantifying Vulnerability to Climate Change: Implications for Adaptation Assistance', Centre for Global Development, Working Paper 240, January 2011, p. 22, http://international.cgdev.org/files/1424759_file_Wheeler_Quantifying_Vulnerability_FINAL.pdf.

[79] Nelson et al., 'Climate Change: Impact on Agriculture and Costs of Adaptation', p. 6.

[80] Zhang Hongzhou, 'China's Evolving Fishing Industry: Implications for Regional and Global Maritime Security', RSIS Working Paper, S. Rajaratnam School of International Studies, Singapore, 16 August 2012.

[81] See, for example, Jane Perlez, 'Dispute Between China and Philippines Over Island Becomes More Heated', *New York Times*, 10 May 2012, http://www.nytimes.com/2012/05/11/world/asia/china-philippines-dispute-over-island-gets-more-heated.html?_r=0.

[82] Beijing News quoted in Hongzhou, 'China's Evolving Fishing Industry: Implications for Regional and Global Maritime Security'.

[83] 'Philippine warship "in stand-off" with Chinese vessels', BBC News, 11 April 2012, http://www.bbc.co.uk/news/world-asia-17673426; Jane Perlez, 'Philippines and China Ease Tensions in Rift at Sea', *New York Times*, 18 June 2012, http://www.nytimes.com/2012/06/19/world/asia/beijing-and-manila-ease-tensions-in-south-china-sea.html?_r=0.

[84] Teddy Ng, 'Beijing caught in crossfire over killing of Taiwanese fisherman', *South China Morning Post*, 16 May 2013, http://www.scmp.com/news/china/article/1238547/killing-taiwanese-fisherman-beijing-caught-crossfire.

[85] Zhang Hongzhou, 'China's Evolving Fishing Industry: Implications for Regional and Global Maritime Security'.

[86] *Ibid.*

[87] Sarah Raine and Christian Le Mière, *Regional Disorder: The South China Sea Disputes* (Abingdon: Routledge for IISS, 2013), p. 76.

[88] Michael Richardson, 'China's Gunboat Diplomacy', *Japan Times*, 30 July 2012. The original comment was made in an article by He Jianbin in *Global Times* on 28 June 2012.

[89] Scott Snyder, Brad Glosserman and Ralph A. Cossa, *Confidence Building Measures in the South China Sea, Issues and Insights*, no. 2-01, Pacific Forum CSIS, 2001, p. xxii, https://csis.org/files/publication/issuesinsightsv01n02.pdf.

[90] Raine and Le Mière, *Regional Disorder: The South China Sea Disputes*.

[91] See official government figures and 'Report sought on India farm suicides', BBC News, 11 December 2011, http://www.bbc.co.uk/news/world-asia-india-16281063.

[92] GoI, *Towards Faster and More Inclusive Growth: An Approach to the 11th Five Year Plan 2007–2012* (New Delhi: Planning Commission of India, December 2006), p. 71, http://planningcommission.nic.in/plans/planrel/app11_16jan.pdf.

[93] *Ibid.* See also Sok Siphana, Chap Sotharith and Chheang Vannarith, 'Cambodia's Agriculture: Challenges and Prospects', Cambodian Institute for Cooperation and Peace (CICP) Working Paper No. 37, January 2011, p. 8, http://www.cicp.org.kh/download/CICP%20Working%20series/CICP%20Working%20paper%20No.%2037.pdf; and Ganesh Thapa and Raghav Gaiha, 'Smallholder Farming in Asia and the Pacific: Challenges and Opportunities', paper presented at the International Fund for Agricultural Development (IFAD) conference on 'New Directions for Smallholder Agriculture', 24–25 January, 2011, p. 10, http://www.ifad.org/events/agriculture/doc/papers/ganesh.pdf.

[94] See Ben Shepherd, 'GCC States' Land Investments Abroad: The case of Cambodia', Summary Report No. 5, Center for International and Regional Studies, Georgetown University School of Foreign Service in Qatar, 2012, p. 8, http://www12.georgetown.edu/sfs/qatar/cirs/CambodiaSummaryReport.pdf; Rick Hodges, Jean C. Buzby and Ben Bennett, 'Postharvest losses and waste in developed and less developed countries: opportunities to improve resource use', *Journal of Agricultural Science*, vol. 149, supplement 1, February 2011, pp. 37–45; and Margarita Escaler and Paul Teng, 'Mind

the Gap': Reducing Waste and Losses in the Food Supply Chain', *NTS Insight*, June 2011, http://www.rsis.edu.sg/nts/HTML-Newsletter/Insight/NTS-Insight-jun-1101.html.

[95] See, for example, 'Analysis: The trouble with Nepal's agriculture', IRIN, 23 January 2013, http://www.irinnews.org/report/97321/analysis-the-trouble-with-nepal-s-agriculture; Valentine M. Moghadam, 'The "Feminization of Poverty" and Women's Human Rights', SHS Papers in Women's Studies/Gender Research, UNESCO, July 2005, http://www.cpahq.org/cpahq/cpadocs/Feminization_of_Poverty.pdf; and IFAD, 'Asia: The role of women's workload in passing on poverty the next generation', http://www.ifad.org/gender/learning/role/workload/in_generation.htm.

[96] GoI, *Towards Faster and More Inclusive Growth*, p. 5.

[97] *Ibid*.

[98] World Bank WDIs, 2013.

[99] The decline has been more prominent in rural areas, where food consumption has dropped from around 2,150kcal in 1993–94 to 2,028kcal in 2009–10. For more, see Deaton and Drèze, 'Food and Nutrition in India: Facts and interpretation', pp. 42–65; and Deepankar Basu and Amit Basole, 'The Calorie Consumption Puzzle in India: An Empirical Investigation', Working Paper No. 285, Political Economy Research Institute, University of Massachusetts Amherst, 12 July 2012, http://www.peri.umass.edu/fileadmin/pdf/working_papers/working_papers_251-300/WP285.pdf.

[100] Naandi Foundation, *HUNGaMA: Fighting Hunger and Malnutrition* (Hyderabad: Naandi Foundation, 2011), p. 4, http://hungamaforchange.org/HungamaBKDec11LR.pdf.

[101] GoI, 'PM's speech at the release of HUNGaMA (Hunger and Malnutrition) Report', 10 January 2012, New Delhi, http://pmindia.nic.in/speech-details.php?nodeid=1125.

[102] Kaushik Basu and Annemie Maertens, 'The pattern and causes of economic growth in India', *Oxford Review of Economic Policy*, vol. 23, no. 2, 2007, pp. 143–67. Agriculture's contribution to total GDP dropped from 40% in 1980/81 to 13.9% in 2011/12.

[103] PRC, China Statistical Yearbook 2011. See also Jikun Huang, Jun Yang and Scott Rozelle, 'Changing Food Consumption Pattern and Demand for Agri-based Industrial Products in China: Implications for Southeast Asia's Agricultural Trade', in Ponciano S. Intal Jr, Sothea Oum and Mercy J.O. Simorangkir (eds), *Agricultural*

Development, Trade and Regional Cooperation in Developing East Asia (Jakarta: Economic Research Institute for ASEAN and East Asia, 2011), pp. 164–65, http://www.eria.org/Chapter%204%20China.pdf.

[104] World Bank WDIs, 2013. All figures are for 2011.

[105] Huang, Yang and Rozelle, 'Changing Food Consumption Pattern and Demand for Agri-based Industrial Products in China', p. 195.

[106] FAO, 'To prevent a new food price crisis experts urge policy changes', Regional Office for Asia and the Pacific, 2 October 2012, http://www.fao.org/asiapacific/rap/home/news/detail/en/?news_uid=161451.

[107] IFAD, 'Rural Poverty Report 2011 - New realities, new challenges: new opportunities for tomorrow's generation', Rome, November 2010, p. 33, http://www.ifad.org/rpr2011/report/e/rpr2011.pdf.

[108] IFAD, 'Improving access to land and tenure security', Policy Brief, December 2008, p. 5, http://www.ifad.org/pub/policy/land/e.pdf.

[109] *Ibid.*

[110] Roel R. Ravanera and Vanessa Gorra, 'Commercial pressures on land in Asia: An overview', IFAD, ILC and CIRAD Agricultural Research and Development, January 2011, p. 5, http://www.landcoalition.org/sites/default/files/publication/909/RAVANERA_Asia_web_11.03.11.pdf.

[111] For example, see Oliver D. Schutter, 'Mission to the People's Republic of China from 15 to 23 December 2010 Beijing: Preliminary Observations and Conclusions', Report of the UN Special Rapporteur on the Right to Food, 23 December 2010, pp. 3–4.

[112] Yu Gao, 'China: One fire may be out, but tensions over rural land rights are still smoldering', Landesa Rural Development Institute, 6 February 2012, http://www.landesa.org/china-fire-out-tensions-rural-land-rights-smoldering/.

[113] *Ibid.*

[114] 'Research Report: Summary of the 2011 17-Province Survey's Findings', Landesa Rural Development Institute, 26 April 2012, http://www.landesa.org/wp-content/uploads/Landesa_China_Survey_Report_2011.pdf. See also Gao, 'China: One fire may be out but tensions over rural land rights are still smoldering'.

[115] *Ibid.*

[116] Songqing Jin, Jikun Huang and Scott Rozelle, 'Agricultural Productivity in China', in Julian M. Alston, Bruce A. Babcock, and Philip G. Pardey (eds), *The Shifting Patterns of Agricultural Production and Productivity Worldwide* (Ames, Iowa: Iowa State University, 2010), p. 237–38.

[117] As found in a study by researchers at Nankai University in China. Christina Larson, 'The New Epicenter of China's Discontent', *Foreign Policy*, 23 August 2011, http://www.foreignpolicy.com/articles/2011/08/23/the_new_epicenter_of_china_s_discontent?page=full.

[118] Brian Spegele, 'Chinese Police Quash Protest over Land Rights', *Wall Street Journal*, 1 April 2011, http://online.wsj.com/news/articles/SB10001424052748704530204576234491628881466?mg=reno64-wsj&url=http%3A%2F%2Fonline.wsj.com%2Farticle%2FSB10001424052748704530204576234491628881466.html.

[119] Daniel Bardsley, 'China tries to quell farmer protests over land seizures', *The National*, 16 December 2011, http://www.thenational.ae/news/world/asia-pacific/china-tries-to-quell-farmer-protests-over-land-seizures.

[120] 'Hundreds of Chinese pensioners protest over payments – report', Reuters, 22 February 2012, http://www.reuters.com/article/2012/02/22/china-protest-idUSL4E8DM67L20120222.

[121] In 'Swaminathan Committee on Farmers Report Summary', PRS Legislative Research, p. 1, http://www.prsindia.org/administrator/uploads/general/1242360972~~final%20summary_pdf.pdf.

[122] A later report says that the proportion of rural households without access to land for cultivation grew by 10.6% between 1993/94 and 2004/05; see Aparajita Bakshi, 'Social Inequality in Land Ownership in India: A Study with Particular Reference to West Bengal', *Social Scientist*, vol. 39, nos. 9–10, September–October 2008, pp. 95–116, http://www.fas.org.in/userfiles/file/1bakshi_social_inequality_in_land_ownership_in_india.pdf.

[123] For more, see Mihir Desai, 'Land Acquisition law and the Proposed Changes', *Economic and Political Weekly*, vol. 46, nos. 26–27, 25 June 2011, pp. 95–100.

[124] Asian Indigenous & Tribal Peoples Network, *The State of the Forest Rights Act: Undoing of historical injustice withered* (New Delhi: AITPN, 2012). For more, see 'The Forest Rights Act', http://www.forestrightsact.com/what-is-this-act-about.

[125] See, for example, 'Land acquisition conflicts ripple across India', *Kuwait Times*, 28 July 2011; and C. J. Kuncheria, 'Q+A: India confronts land grabs in industrialization push', Reuters, 19 August 2010, http://in.reuters.com/article/2010/08/19/idINIndia-50942720100819.

[126] Chigurupati Ramachandraiah and Ramasamy Srinivasan, 'Special Economic Zones as New Forms of Corporate Land Grab: Experiences from India', *Development*, vol. 54, no. 1, 2011, pp. 59–64.

[127] See, for example, 'Nandigram incident unfortunate: CM', *Times of India*, 7 January 2007, http://articles.timesofindia.indiatimes.com/2007-01-07/india/27877885_1_nandigram-issue-of-land-acquisition-sez-by-salim-group.

[128] Tushar Dhara, 'Nandigram Revisited: The scars of battle', Infochangeindia.org, April 2008, http://infochangeindia.org/agenda/battles-over-land/nandigram-revisited-the-scars-of-battle.html.

[129] Michael Levien, 'The Land Question: Special Economic Zones and the Political Economy of Disposession in India', *Journal of Peasant Studies*, vol. 39, nos. 3–4, 2012, p. 934, http://www.tandfonline.com/doi/abs/10.1080/03066150.2012.656268#.UupioT1_uSh.

[130] *Ibid.* See also 'Export objective hit as Reliance fails to set up SEZ in Gurgaon, Jhajjar, says CAG', *Press Trust of India*, 12 March 2013, http://archive.indianexpress.com/news/export-objective-hit-as-reliance-fails-to-set-up-sez-in-gurgaon-jhajjar-says-cag/1086783/.

[131] Although the company sought and received a government extension in late 2013 to complete the project, it continues to face stiff resistance from locals who refuse to give up their lands. See Amiti Sen, 'Posco gets more time to complete Odisha SEZ', *The Hindu Business Line*, 12 November 2013, http://www.thehindubusinessline.com/industry-and-economy/posco-gets-more-time-to-complete-odisha-sez/article5344243.ece; Sampat Mahapatra, 'POSCO stalled again: Green clearance cancelled', NDTV, 30 March 2012, http://www.ndtv.com/article/india/posco-stalled-again-green-clearance-cancelled-191908; and Prashant Mehra, 'Orissa's industrial dream mired in delays, protests', Reuters, 29 October 2012, http://in.reuters.com/article/2012/10/29/india-odisha-jindal-orissa-posco-idINDEE89S00C20121029.

[132] See, for example, Megha Bahree, 'The Forever War: Inside India's Maoist Conflict', *World Policy Journal*, 2010, pp. 83–9, http://www.firstpeoplesfirst.in/admin/pdf/53_The%20Forever%20War.pdf.

[133] Devesh Kapur, Kishore Gawande and Shanker Satyanath, 'Renewable Resource Shocks and Conflict in India's Maoist Belt', CASI Working Paper Series No. 12–02, July 2012, http://casi.sas.upenn.

edu/system/files/Renewable+Resource+Shocks+and+Conflict+in+India's+Maoist+Belt.pdf.

[134] Bidyut Roy, 'In Nandigram, Maoist newcomers take over "resistance movement"', *Indian Express*, 5 December 2007, http://archive.indianexpress.com/news/in-nandigram-maoist-newcomers-take-over-re/235369/.

[135] 'The global land-grab phenomenon', Down To Earth, Special Papua Edition, November 2011, http://www.down-toearth-indonesia.org/story/global-land-grab-phenomenon.

[136] *Ibid.*

[137] See, for example, 'An Agribusiness Attack in West Papua: Unravelling the Merauke Integrated Food and Energy Estate' by UK-based independent activist group Awas MIFEE, April 2012, https://awasmifee.potager.org/uploads/2012/03/mifee_en.pdf. The report provides an overview of the MIFEE project, its investors and news from villages on project-related developments and their impact on local communities.

[138] *Ibid.*

[139] Hatta Rajasa, 'Merauke food estate land likely to shrink by 80%', *Jakarta Post*, 12 July 2012, http://www.thejakartapost.com/news/2012/07/12/merauke-food-estate-land-likely-shrink-80.html.

[140] 'Vietnam police break up land protest', AFP, 24 April 2012, http://www.google.com/hostednews/afp/article/ALeqM5hP--LIhnP654U4wrpq402W5Yn_Cw; 'Vietnam land clash: Arrests after police evict hundreds', BBC News, 25 April 2012, http://www.bbc.co.uk/news/world-asia-17844198.

[141] 'Pitched battle over Vietnam farmland', BBC News, 17 January 2012, http://www.bbc.co.uk/news/world-asia-16571102.

[142] National Statistical Institute, *General Population Census of Cambodia 2008* (Ministry of Planning, Royal Government of Cambodia: Phnom Penh, 2008), http://nis.gov.kh/nis/census2008/Census.pdf. See also Ministry of Planning and UNDP Cambodia, 'Cambodia Human Development Report 2007', p. 66.

[143] Simon Springer, 'The neoliberalization of security and violence in Cambodia', in Sorpong Peou (ed.), *Human Security in East Asia: Challenges for collaborative action* (Abingdon: Routledge, 2009), pp. 125–41.

[144] Sothath Ngo and Sophal Chan, *Does Large Scale Agricultural Investment Benefit the Poor?* (Phnom Penh: Cambodian Economic Association, 2010), p. 7.

[145] World Bank, *A Fair Share for Women: Cambodia Gender Assessment* (New York and Phnom Penh: World Bank, 2004), http://www-wds.worldbank.org/external/default/WDSContentServer/WDSP/IB/20

05/08/11/000160016_20050811133611/Rendered/PDF/332760KH0FairoshareoforowomenIpdf.

[146] *Ibid.*

[147] Mu Sochua and Cecelia Wikstrom, 'Land grabs in Cambodia', *New York Times*, 18 July 2012, http://www.nytimes.com/2012/07/19/opinion/land-grabs-in-cambodia.html.

[148] *Ibid.*

[149] Ngo and Chan, *Does Large Scale Agricultural Investment Benefit the Poor?*, p. 6.

[150] Ministry of Agriculture, Forestry and Fisheries, Royal Government of Cambodia, 'The Fixation of Concession Land Rental Fee', 31 May 2001, http://www.elc.maff.gov.kh/index.php/laws/12-the-fixation-of-concession-land-rental-fee.

[151] Paul Vrieze and Kuch Naren, 'Carving up Cambodia', *Cambodian Daily Weekend*, no. 730, 10–11 March 2012, p. 6, http://www.camnet.com.kh/cambodia.daily/selected_features/Carving%20Up%20Cambodia.pdf.

[152] Ngo and Chan, *Does Large Scale Agricultural Investment Benefit the Poor?*, p. 8.

[153] 'Economic land concessions in Cambodia: A human rights perspective', UN Cambodia Office of the High Commissioner for Human Rights, Phnom Penh, June 2007, p. 1, http://cambodia.ohchr.org/WebDOCs/DocReports/2-Thematic-Reports/Thematic_CMB12062007E.pdf.

[154] Land Information Centre, 'Statistical Analysis on Land Dispute Occurring in Cambodia 2008', The NGO Forum on Cambodia, Land and Livelihoods Programme 2009, http://en.cisa.org.kh/index.php?option=com_content&task=view&id=1485&Itemid=62.

[155] Men Prachvuthy and Guus van Westen, 'Land acquisition by non-local actors', in 'Focus: Food Security and Land Grabbing', *The Newsletter*, International Institute for Asian Studies, vol. 58, Autumn/Winter 2011, p. 26.

[156] *Ibid.* See also UN Cambodia OHCHR, 'Economic land concessions in Cambodia', p. 16.

[157] Prachvuthy and van Westen, 'Land acquisition by non-local actors', p. 26.

[158] *Ibid.*

[159] Graeme Brown, *Forest Stewardship in Ratanakiri: Linking Communities and Government* (Phnom Penh: Community Forest International, 2006), p. iv.

[160] Ian G. Baird, 'Reflecting on changes in Ratanakiri province, northeastern Cambodia', *Watershed*, vol. 12, no. 3, November 2008, p. 68.

[161] Cambodian League for the Promotion and Defense of Human Rights (LICADHO), 'Reclamation of the indigenous land illegally

taken in Rattanakiri', Press Release, 23 January 2007, http://www.licadho-cambodia.org/pressrelease.php?perm=139, and Welthungerhilfe, 'Large-scale land investments: A danger or a development opportunity?', In Brief No. 23, November 2011.

[162] Land Watch Asia, 'Overcoming a Failure of Law and Political Will', Cambodia Country Paper, 2009, http://www.angoc.org/dmdocuments/SRL_Cambodia.pdf.

[163] Cambodian Center for Human Rights, 'Desperate measures in Ratanakiri land dispute', CCHR Case Study Series, vol. 4, April 2012, https://www.greenleft.org.au/node/51279.

[164] LICADHO, 'Attacks and Threats Against Human Rights Defenders in Cambodia', Briefing Paper, August 2008, pp. 20–21, http://www.licadho-cambodia.org/reports/files/126LICADHOHumanRightsDefendersReport2007Eng.pdf.

[165] LICADHO, 'Five Shooting Incidents at Land Dispute Protests in the Past Two Months Show Alarming Increase in Use of Lethal Force', Press Release, 26 January 2012, http://www.licadho-cambodia.org/pressrelease.php?perm=269.

[166] *Ibid.*

[167] 'Cambodian environmental campaigner shot dead by police', BBC News, 26 April 2012, http://www.bbc.co.uk/news/world-asia-pacific-17859016.

[168] May Titthara and David Boyle, 'Teenage girl gunned down by security forces in eviction', *Phnom Penh Post*, 17 May 2012, http://www.phnompenhpost.com/national/teenage-girl-gunned-down-security-forces-eviction.

[169] *Ibid.*

[170] See, for example, Ngo and Chan, *Does Large Scale Agricultural Investment Benefit the Poor?*, pp. 44–49, and Shepherd, 'GCC States' Land Investments Abroad: The case of Cambodia', pp. 19–20.

[171] Shepherd, 'GCC States' Land Investments Abroad: The case of Cambodia', p. 27.

CHAPTER FIVE

Where policies fail

Despite looming food-security challenges, many national policymakers remain preoccupied with other pressing objectives, such as attracting foreign investment and ensuring energy security. When governments do turn to food considerations, unfortunately their approach too often remains limited in scope and vision. Food security in developing Asia continues to be understood largely in terms of supply and demand, and of production and consumption, without fully recognising that other policy goals, such as foreign investment and energy requirements, are not entirely divorced from the quest for food security.

Most countries have yet to undertake concrete efforts to link the goal of food security to underlying issues. Where policies related to food security are being designed and implemented, their focus often remains fragmented and even contradictory. This is particularly true in the case of agricultural policies to increase production and accelerate economic growth, which may actually undermine the livelihoods of small farmers and marginalised communities at the expense of national food security. Such policies also fail to consider the connections between food security, human security and local peace and stability. Food insecurity and the factors driving it – such as high food prices and lack of access to productive resources – not only affect health, education and livelihoods, but have also been known to fuel social unrest and violent demonstrations throughout history.

Even where countries, such as India, the Philippines and Indonesia, have been operating subsidised food-distribution programmes, the poor implementation of such schemes, and high levels of mismanagement and corruption associated with them, frequently serve to undermine their central goal of providing welfare to those most in need. The lack of adequate and effective design, implementation, monitoring and evaluation of food-security related policies – whether focused on agriculture, energy, foreign investment or socio-economic welfare – remains a serious challenge in developing Asia.

China and Indonesia: biofuels and foreign investments

Global biofuel production has been led by the United States, Europe and Brazil, while Asian countries have remained relatively far behind. Nonetheless, China has a nascent bioethanol industry and Indonesia has increasingly been using palm oil (as the largest global producer of the resource) to produce biodiesel[1] as well as cooking oil.

With economic growth, China's energy needs have soared. It is the largest producer and consumer of coal and relies on imports for more than half of its domestic fuel-oil consumption. This reliance on imports is projected to increase to around 76% by 2020.[2] To reduce the country's overwhelming dependence on fossil fuels, increase energy efficiency and reduce carbon emissions, the government has emphasised the need to roughly double primary energy consumption from renewable resources to 15% by 2020.[3] According to one study, China will need to produce 11 million tonnes of bioethanol and 2m tonnes of biodiesel to meet this target.[4]

Bioethanol production is the present focus of China's biofuel industry. This relies on maize (accounting for around 80% of fuel ethanol) and, to a lesser extent, on crops such cassava, sweet potato, sweet sorghum and sugar cane.[5] Government policies currently prevent the further expansion of grain-fed bioethanol. However, the effectiveness of these policies is questionable as several facilities for producing grain-fed bioethanol have already been developed and, with limited supplies of non-grain feedstock such as cassava and sweet sorghum, 'many existing biofuel plants have continued to make ethanol from maize.'[6]

As China strives to meet its biofuel target for 2020, it is estimated that the task, using both grain and non-grain feed crops, may require anything between 5% and 10% of China's current 121.7m ha of cultivated land, and as much water as there is in the total discharge of the Yellow River in 2020 (31.9–71.7 trillion litres).[7] Moreover, with droughts and floods becoming more frequent in certain parts of China, the diversion of food crops for biofuels in times of intermittent supply shortages (because of failed harvests or destroyed crops) may intensify upward pressure on domestic food prices, undermining the food security of China's hundreds of millions of poor, with implications for social and political stability.

Currently, however, the biggest biofuels story in Asia is in Indonesia. Jakarta's cultivation of oil palm, from which crude palm oil (CPO) is produced, has been increasing since the late 1960s, when the World Bank assisted President Suharto's New Order regime in investing in CPO production through state-owned companies.[8] As international CPO prices began to rise in this century, the government saw oil-palm plantations as a way of promoting socio-economic development in rural areas, by raising incomes, creating jobs and financing critical infrastructure development. By early 2011, oil-palm plantations covered around 7.8m ha of land[9] in Indonesia, much of it in Sumatra and Kalimantan, and to a lesser extent on the islands of Java, Papua and Sulawesi.[10] Between 2000 and 2010, CPO production in Indonesia grew almost threefold, from 7m tonnes to 19.7m tonnes (see Figure 1). Around one-quarter of total production is consumed at home, mainly as cooking oil, and the rest is exported.[11] In 2010, export earnings from CPO and derivatives exceeded US$11 billion.[12] India is the largest importer of Indonesian CPO, followed by China and the EU.

The EU's biofuel target[13] has been a particular stimulus for increasing CPO production in Indonesia, leading to the consolidation of crops into large plantations. In 2006, Jakarta also underlined biofuels as an alternative to importing energy to meet its growing needs. Presidential Instruction No. 5/2006 relating to the country's national energy policy requires that, by 2025, up to 5% of the national energy mix come from biofuels. There is also a mandatory transport fuel-blending target rising from 5% in 2006 to 25% in 2025.[14] The government has introduced several financial incentives to encourage private and foreign agribusinesses to invest in

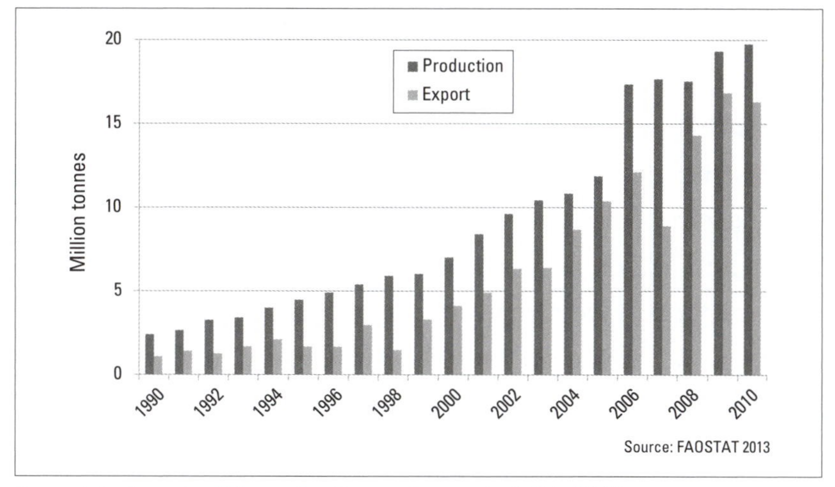

Figure 1. **Indonesia CPO production and exports, 1990–2010**

oil-palm production and biodiesel plants. Biodiesel production picked up in 2009 and has grown strongly since then.[15] In 2011, Indonesia produced 1.5bn litres of biodiesel and exports increased by 177% from the previous year, to 1.2bn litres.[16] Experts suggest that by 2020 an extra 3–7m ha of oil palm may be planted to respond to the burgeoning global demand for palm oil for food and fuel.[17]

As these plantations have spread rapidly, they have resulted in a significant loss of forest cover and redirected land away from use in food (including rice) production. These developments have alarmed environmentalists and other experts, who argue that the benefits of oil-palm production are far outweighed by the ecological and socio-economic costs for Indonesia's forests, local communities and food systems. Widespread deforestation,[18] with accompanying peat-land degradation[19] and forest fires, has turned Indonesia into the world's largest emitter of greenhouse gases.[20] In May 2011, in a bid to curb deforestation-induced carbon emissions, Norway signed a US$1bn climate pact with Indonesia which included a two-year moratorium on clearing forests.[21] However, this has proved difficult to implement at the local level, where governors allocate land concessions. Moreover, the agreement does not require the Indonesian government to revoke existing forestry concessions and it remains unclear how much land provincial governments have already allocated to plantations – which will have a bearing on overall emissions. In mid-2013, forest fires in Indonesia spread choking smoke across the region,[22] in a stark demonstration of the environmental damage that oil-palm cultivation is causing.

As well as being environmentally damaging, large oil-palm plantations are also of questionable benefit to local communities. Various models have existed for smallholder ownership and participation in plantations and, while direct government financing for these programmes has declined since the late 1990s,[23] the World Bank still found in 2010 that small farmers managed around 40% of the oil-palm plantation area in Indonesia, and up to 1m small farmers were likely to have benefitted directly from the crop.[24] However, another study published in 2010 on the impact of oil-palm plantations on local communities in the Jambi province in Central Sumatra found that, under the New Order regime's internal migration programme to promote oil-palm planting by smallholders in remote areas, local indigenous communities benefitted much less from oil-palm related development than did the new arrivals from other parts of Indonesia.[25] Indigenous communities were traditionally reliant on forestry activities and were used to growing food sustainably using shifting cultivation practices. The development of large plantations disrupted both these activities, causing a decline in income from forest products and reduced access to sources of food.[26]

Production involves expensive start-up costs and is input intensive. Plantations only become productive after three to four years and generally only start making profits a few years after that. Without government support, independent small farmers who lack the money for agrochemicals and the technical know-how to cultivate oil palm are not only far less likely to be successful than wealthier farmers with access to technical services[27] but are also highly vulnerable to price fluctuations and more likely to default on loans taken out to fund start-up costs – so the risks they undertake in cultivating oil palm are relatively quite high. This helps explain why 'smallholders tend to be tied to large palm oil concerns, limiting their ability to negotiate fair prices or manage their lands according to their own inclinations.'[28]

For many local communities, the most damaging aspect of oil-palm production has been the way in which land has been acquired by agribusinesses, usually with government involvement. In many cases, local communities have been forced to give up their land without consideration for their customary land rights, land-use practices or food-security needs. A 'complex web' of national laws with 'little provision for community rights and interests' makes these land acquisitions possible.[29] Land that in practice belongs to indigenous communities is commonly considered as belonging to the state and allocated to companies for conversion into plantations.[30] Although government agencies stress the need to obtain prior consent from relevant communities, they usually withdraw after issuing concession permits to let the investing company conduct negotiations on compensation.[31]

This has caused growing resentment against the government and conflicts have erupted between local communities and government forces, private companies and plantation workers, who have arrived from elsewhere in Indonesia. There have also been disputes within communities about the sale of land.[32] In Central Kalimantan, for instance, repeated communal violence between local Dayak communities and plantation workers, originally from the island of Madura, has resulted in hundreds of deaths.[33] Protests against unfair land deals are often met with violence from private security forces, police and military personnel. There is little recourse to justice for those affected, as local rights groups report that the military and police are directly involved in company activities or stand to benefit from working in their favour.[34]

Global awareness has been growing about the damaging effects of oil-palm production. Industry efforts have been made to promote sustainable oil-palm cultivation with, for example, the Roundtable on Sustainable Palm Oil which promotes better production and management practices. However these guidelines remain voluntary, so positive action has been limited. Some activists argue that the onus of ensuring sustainability should be on countries buying CPO from Indonesia. The EU already has a Renewable Energy Directive (RED) that sets the sustainability standards for all biofuels being consumed within its jurisdiction, though there are concerns about the impact of RED on smallholders and issues relating to 'social sustainability'.[35] Greenpeace suggests that India and China, as large importers, could play an important role by adopting a 'zero deforestation' policy when engaging with suppliers and shunning those who continue to use unsustainable methods of production.[36] For its part, the Indonesian government needs to take appropriate measures to ensure that its drive for biofuels does not come at the cost of the future sustainability of its local food systems.[37]

Vietnam and the Philippines: over-emphasis on rice self-sufficiency?

Rice is central to Vietnamese diets, livelihoods and traditions. Around 80% of the country's rural population is involved in rice farming, with almost half growing a surplus to sell in the market.[38] Vietnam turned itself from a rice importer in the 1980s to the world's second-largest exporter of rice behind Thailand through privatisation, liberalisation and agricultural investment, including the use of high-yielding rice varieties (see Chapter Three). In 2012, it exported nearly 8m tonnes, or one-third of its rice output, with enough

Figure 2. **Vietnam rice exports quantity (milled) and value, 1990–2012**

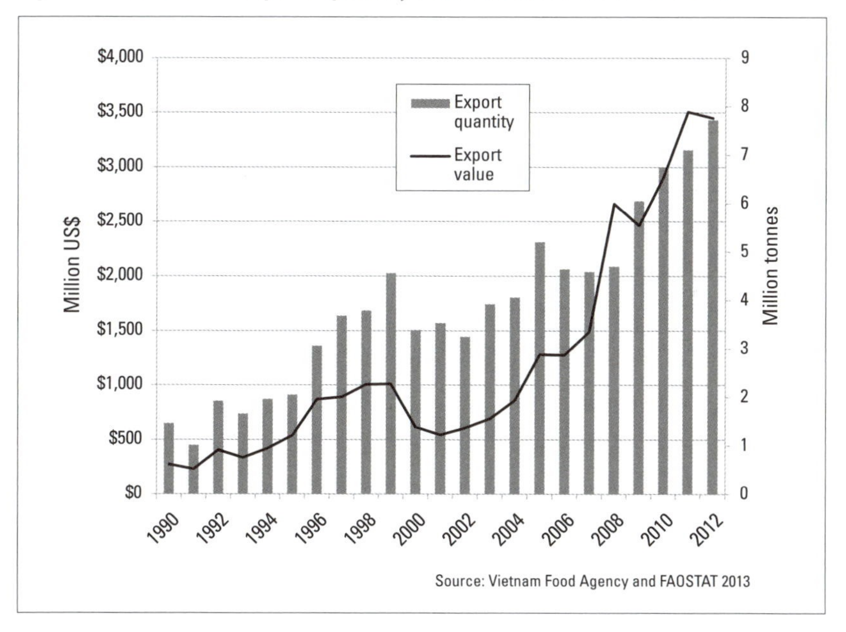

remaining for domestic consumption and other uses, such as livestock feed, seed and industrial use. Still, the emphasis on self-sufficiency runs deep, and rice production continues to be the main driver of Hanoi's food-security policies. Rice exports are also a significant foreign-exchange earner, bringing in more than US$3bn in 2012 (see Figure 2).

In August 2008, Resolution No. 26-NQ/TW on Agriculture, Farmers and Rural Areas committed the government to continuing to enhance the intensive cultivation of rice, particularly in the Mekong Delta and the Red River Delta, to ensure national food safety for immediate and long-term demands and other front-row priorities in agriculture development.[39] In December 2009, the government launched Resolution No. 63/NQ-CP on National Food Security, aiming: 'by 2020 with a vision towards 2030, to ensure adequate food supply sources with an output higher than the population growth rate; to put an end to food shortage and hunger and raise meal quality; to ensure that rice producers earn profits averagely [*sic*] more than 30% over production costs.'[40]

The resolution sets a target of 3.8m ha of land to be protected as 'rice land' to ensure 'an output of 41–43m tons of paddy to meet the total domestic consumption and export demand of around 4m tons of rice [per] year'.[41] While one of its objectives is to meet the population's nutritional needs and reduce child malnutrition, most of the resolution's 'major tasks and solutions' focus on boosting and supporting rice production.

For Asian and other countries relying on rice imports from Vietnam, the prospect of Hanoi further expanding its rice surplus further for export is positive news. During the 2007–08 global food crisis, Vietnam's export restrictions on rice helped fuel panic on the international market, further pushing up prices as supplies tightened. At the local level, however, the emphasis on increasing rice production and exports is problematic, notwithstanding government quotas to balance exports and quantities available for domestic sale.[42] Economic and social-welfare policies since 1989, when Vietnam became self-sufficient in rice, have helped to greatly reduce poverty and malnourishment. Nonetheless, despite more than two decades of relative abundance in rice and ever-increasing exports, roughly 11% of the population remains malnourished. Around 43% of Vietnamese live on less than US$2 a day, while 17% are extremely poor, surviving on under US$1.25 a day. Child malnourishment levels are especially high – almost one-third of under-fives are stunted and 20% are underweight for their age.[43]

Ethnic minorities[44] comprise less than 13% of Vietnam's population, but nearly half of its poor.[45] Poverty is also higher in rural areas, especially in the north and the central highlands,[46] where there is a relative lack of adequate healthcare, sanitation or educational facilities, poor infrastructure (including irrigation and transport) and few, if any, agricultural support services, as well as 'nutritional (im)balance, household income vulnerability, and consumer price volatility'.[47] These factors suggest that food insecurity in Vietnam is linked more to growing socio-economic inequalities than to national-level rice availability.

Rice production in Vietnam is mainly concentrated in the Mekong Delta region and the Red River Delta, where there is significant surplus production. More than half of Vietnam's national rice output and over 90% of its exports come from the Mekong Delta. More than half the rice growers in the Mekong farm 0.5–2ha plots and most of the region's nearly 1.5m rice farmers are net rice buyers. Most of the productivity gains achieved recently and the bulk of the marketed surplus are concentrated in the hands of 20% of rice growers in the region with larger farms of an average 2.7ha.[48] Moreover, as a recent World Bank study conducted with the Mekong Delta Development Institute points out, Vietnam's rice value chain – getting rice from the paddy field to the consumer – is in poor shape. It is:

> relatively fragmented and uncoordinated and features high levels of physical losses. Excessive use is made of seed, fertilizer, agro-chemicals, and water, ostensibly due to a widespread perception that more inputs translate into higher yields. These practices have weakened profitability while contributing to high (unmeasured) environmental costs. Prevailing incentives and support systems for quality management are weak. There are relatively few consumers, at home or abroad, who actually prefer Vietnamese rice over alternatives. Hence, the value chain adds little value and Vietnam 'competes' on the basis of selling a lower cost product than others.[49]

In short, Vietnam produces generally low-quality rice, which it exports at prices that are amongst the lowest in the world.[50] Consequently, rising exports have not benefitted small farming households, especially as they face escalating input costs. Some analysts even argue that the country has been 'exporting some of its consumer welfare and subsidising rice consumers in importing countries' with its cheap exports.[51] Indeed, it is the trading sector that has reaped most of the benefits of recent higher prices.[52]

Overall, small farming households have limited scope to raise farm incomes from rice cropping alone.[53] To boost their incomes, small rice farmers have increasingly been relying on other ways of supplementing their wages, for example by diversifying production to include livestock, fruits and vegetables or looking for non-farm employment.[54]

It is just as important for Vietnam to guard against the unsustainable conversion of agricultural land as it is for any other industrialising Asian country.[55] However, a recent study shows farmers can easily keep up with demand and produce substantial surpluses on less than the 3.8m ha mandated by the country's national food-security policy.[56] Reserving agricultural land for rice production alone denies small farmers the chance to increase their incomes by growing other crops, particularly in regions where environmental conditions are not best suited for rice farming.[57] And there is certainly a burgeoning market for such crops as the consumption of meat, fish, dairy, fruits and vegetables has been on the increase.

Therefore, it would make more sense for the Vietnamese government to focus on the development of infrastructure to strengthen rice value chains, address inefficiencies in the system (including unsustainable use of inputs and post-harvest losses), provide better access to extension services, knowledge and skills training, and encourage the diversification of crops to improve incomes and livelihoods. At the regional level, Hanoi could encourage rice-importing states to invest sustainably in rice production and rice value chains in the country. If done responsibly, for example as outlined by the FAO's Voluntary Guidelines on the Responsible Governance of Tenure of Land, Fisheries and Forests in the Context of National Food Security,[58] such investment could not only help boost the production of better quality rice, and improve the profitability and efficiency of small farmers in Vietnam, but also help import-dependent countries to guarantee rice supplies for domestic consumption in a sustainable and reliable manner.

In the Philippines, Manila also has a determined eye on rice self-sufficiency in the twenty-first century, although it has yet to achieve it. Policymakers began talking about the need to boost declining rice productivity about a decade ago, but the government really only returned to this goal after the 2007–08 food crisis. In 2008, it found itself, as the world's largest rice importer, buying in more than 2.4m tonnes at an inflated cost of nearly US$2bn.[59] For the two decades before that, it had suffered declining agricultural

Figure 3. **Philippines rice supply, 1990–2011**

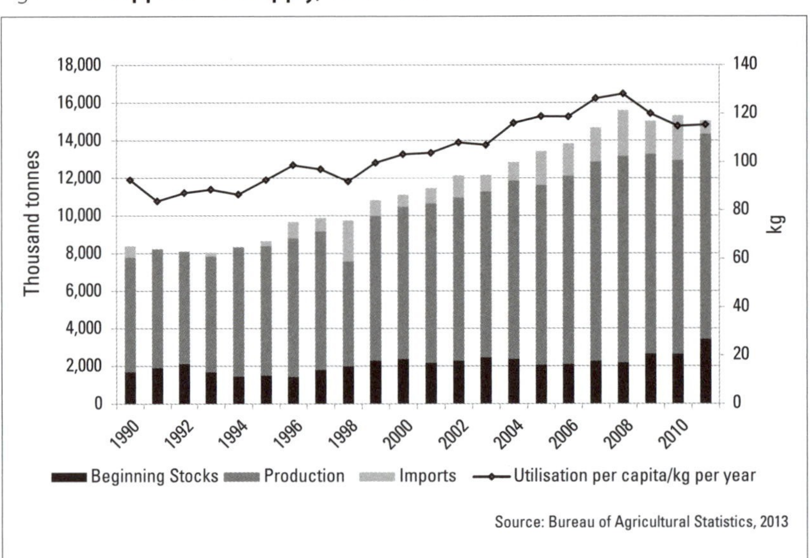

Source: Bureau of Agricultural Statistics, 2013

productivity and was relying significantly on rice imports (see Figure 3) to feed one of the fastest-growing populations in Asia, with a rising per capita rice intake.[60] However, much of its rice purchasing in 2008 was panic-buying in the face of rising global food prices and export restrictions by major rice suppliers in the region. Due to the excessive importation of (expensive) rice, in the first half of 2009, the Philippines' rice stock exceeded the 90-day optimum national inventory by more than 17 days.[61]

In April 2008, as the crisis was unfolding, the Arroyo administration launched the country's multibillion-dollar FIELDS (Fertiliser, Infrastructure and Irrigation, Extension and Education, Loans, Drying and other Post-harvest Facilities, and Seeds) Initiative to revitalise agriculture and increase rice production.[62] The Department of Agriculture also unveiled its Rice Self-Sufficiency Plan for 2009–10 at that time. In 2010, the new Aquino administration renewed calls for rice self-sufficiency and set a target to achieve this goal by 2013–14.[63]

The Philippines has been less successful than most Asian nations in reducing poverty.[64] Moreover, even when domestic rice production has been supplemented by substantial imports, lack of sufficient economic access to food has remained a key hurdle, as 49 out of the country's 77 provinces remain vulnerable to varying degrees of food insecurity.[65]

Agricultural production in the Philippines is dominated by rice. It uses almost one-third of the country's agricultural land and is grown by a significant majority of farmers, most of whom are net rice consumers. Other major crops include maize, coconut and sugar cane. Given that some 34% of the workforce remains employed in agriculture[66]

Thailand's flawed rice scheme

Thailand is the world's top rice producer,[68] but its exports plummeted from 10.7 million tonnes in 2011 to 6.9m tonnes in 2012,[69] after the government rolled out another 'rice mortgage scheme' in October 2011. Under this scheme, Bangkok pledged to buy white rice from Thai farmers at a guaranteed price of 15,000 baht (around US$500) per tonne – around 50% above the market price – and Thai jasmine rice at 20,000 baht per tonne.[70] The policy was designed to provide income support to Thailand's poor paddy farmers. The government also seemingly figured that restricting the international availability of Thai rice would put upwards pressure on global rice prices, creating a profitable environment for the government to release its domestic stocks of rice for export at an opportune time.

Given the significant price mark-up, the scheme proved hugely popular with Thailand's paddy farmers, and by August 2012 the government had stocks of a staggering 17m tonnes of rice.[71] At a time when other major rice producers India and Vietnam have been exporting more favourably priced rice, selling this costly stock has proved to be difficult.

The Thai government has also faced criticism for what is widely seen as an inefficient and populist policy that has been pushing up domestic rice prices, adding to taxpayers' burden and inflating government debt.[72] In its first year alone, the policy cost the government US$4.4 billion. The scheme has been dogged by allegations of corruption[73] and has encouraged rampant smuggling of rice into Thailand by farmers and traders from neighbouring Cambodia and Myanmar, seeking to sell their produce for a sizeable profit.[74]

Around 2.6m of Thailand's poorest rice-farming households do not grow a surplus for sale and therefore fail to benefit from the scheme.[75] Furthermore, since it was rolled out, the cost of growing rice for small farmers has risen substantially, as the costs of renting farmland, farm equipment, labour costs, fertilisers, pesticides and fuel have all increased.[76]

In Thailand's main rice-growing central region, most agricultural land is owned by landlords who rent out small plots of land (up to 1.6ha) to rice farmers.[77] Few small farmers own the land they work on and only 16% of poor farmers derive their entire income from farming.[78] Consequently, the scheme mainly benefits well-off landlords and rich farmers, as well as rice millers who may buy the rice at a lower price and yet receive the full procurement rate from the government.[79] Experts argue that other measures would better help small farmers directly address the challenges of agricultural production and boost productivity and efficiency, such as adequate irrigation infrastructure, assistance with agricultural diversification and a more efficient and affordable price-support policy.[80]

and that alternative rural employment is limited, increasing self-sufficiency in rice by boosting productivity is valuable insofar as it encourages desperately needed public investment in a cash-starved agricultural sector and promises to raise small farmers' incomes. Yet, the Philippines' declining agricultural productivity has been caused not just by lack of investment. It is also linked to incomplete land reforms; poor overall governance of the agricultural sector; rising input costs and relatively low farm-gate prices; and environmental degradation.[67]

Although the Philippines has been engaged in agrarian reform for decades, the pace of change has been glacial, with the programme plagued by bureaucracy and corruption. Therefore, it is vital that efforts to boost rice productivity are made within broader measures to strengthen the support base of small farming households. This includes providing the latter with greater access to land, bolstering tenure security and improving overall governance, among other things.

The Philippines, Indonesia and India: corruption, inefficiency and waste

In 1998, then-UN Secretary-General Kofi Annan identified good governance as 'perhaps the single most important factor in eradicating poverty and promoting development'.[81] In Asia, the persistence of widespread hunger and food insecurity is largely rooted in problems of state weakness and dysfunction,[82] increasing the prospects of political violence in reaction to rising food prices.[83] Violent protests in the wake of recent food-price spikes have predominantly occurred in lower-income countries with weak state institutions, high inequality, corruption, lack of accountability and little respect for the rule of law. In South and Southeast Asia, most developing countries rank poorly on Transparency International's Corruption Perceptions Index.[84] Almost all South Asian countries fare badly on the World Bank's Worldwide Governance Indicators for political stability and absence of violence.[85]

Problems of governance may affect the most basic factors underpinning food security at the local level. In countries with high levels of corruption, for example, bribery and political connections are often the only ways to gain access to goods and services to which citizens are entitled. Corruption, mismanagement and inefficiency can also seriously affect major government agencies involved in policymaking on food-related and agricultural issues. Take the Philippines as an example, where the National Food Authority is responsible for providing rice farmers with price support and for supplying rice to consumers at subsidised prices. It also manages buffer stocks and, until recently, had a monopoly over rice imports.[86] In 2011, an audit report of the agency showed that from 2008–10, the government's private-sector financed importation of rice was plagued with corruption that amounted to 'legalised smuggling'; the agency also made errors in estimating domestic consumption requirements and mismanaged stocks leading to huge imports of rice that not only ballooned the agency's debt (therefore imposing a significant burden on the taxpayer), but also hurt Filipino paddy farmers by lowering farm-gate prices.[87]

Millions have also been spent in the Philippines on irrigation projects that have barely materialised, according to Transparency International.[88] Between 1995 and 2005, around US$2.9m was spent on the 1,000ha Talibon Small

Reservoir Irrigation Project, for example, but 'the only progress was some excavations, a row of piping, a bridge-like structure, an office building and abandoned construction equipment.'[89]

The Philippines' agrarian reforms have also been affected by inefficiency and corruption. The redistribution of 8.2m ha of public and private agricultural land to around 5m farmers was to be completed by 1998 under the Comprehensive Agrarian Reform Law (1988), but the programme is still incomplete and the government has admitted that a new 2014 deadline is unachievable.[90] Most of the holdings still to be distributed are 24ha or larger and owned by the country's influential elites. According to Land Watch Asia (LWA), landlords have been blocking agrarian reform through the exploitation of legal loopholes and the harassment of agrarian reform beneficiaries (ARBs). LWA reports that, since 1998, almost 19,000 farmers and rural organisers have been victims of human-rights abuses.[91] Moreover, the success of agrarian reforms has been patchy.[92] Many ARBs who have been allocated land have not yet received promised support services like access to credit and post-harvest facilities; others have had to lease back their land or been forced to sell it.[93] In some cases, farmers who may have been officially allocated land have yet to get possession, while others awarded land have reportedly had the award revoked and the land redesignated for industrial purposes.[94]

The government has also been actively wooing large agribusinesses under the National Convergence Initiative aimed at developing almost 2m ha of 'idle' lands for agribusinesses, mainly for biofuel feed crops such as jatropha,[95] cassava and oil palm.[96] Such land deals with foreign investors often involve ARBs 'who are lured into leasing out their newly-awarded lands in exchange for cash and offers of employment'.[97] In some cases, local governments themselves facilitate the lease of larger private landholdings yet to be redistributed.[98] A recent report by Oxfam suggests that around 5.7m ha have been allocated for the production of biofuels and exports.[99] The resulting deals are often controversial; a series of agreements in early 2007 between the Philippines and China on agriculture and fisheries was suspended after a public outcry. Concerns revolved around the impact on local food security if 1m ha of land was leased to Chinese agribusinesses to grow hybrid rice, sorghum and corn, but allegations of corruption involving government officials stiffened public opposition.[100]

Government ineffectiveness and corruption also have direct implications for food safety-net programmes in place in Asia. In Indonesia, for example, it is estimated that up to 47% of the subsidised rice that is meant to be delivered to poor households, under the Raskin programme,[101] ends up going to households that are not entitled under the scheme to receive the subsidy.[102] As Benjamin Olken points out, the level of corruption involved is 'sufficiently large to turn an otherwise welfare-enhancing program into a program that may have been welfare-reducing on net'.[103] In the Philippines, administrative costs alone account for 87% of the total cost of the National Food Authority's universal subsidised-rice programme.[104] In 2009, more than half of the country's poor were unable to access government-subsidised rice, while the country's year-old conditional cash-transfer programme targeted at the poor had an inclusion error[105] of 24%.

In India, since 1997, the Targeted Public Distribution System (PDS) has been the main vehicle for providing subsidised food to the country's poor.[106] Under this system, the Food Corporation of India, a central government agency, has been buying food grains directly from farmers at established minimum support prices and transporting them to its storage depots across India. State governments then distribute this grain, through 'fair price shops', to targeted households with ration cards at heavily subsidised prices. Other key safety-net programmes for tackling poverty and hunger include the 1975 Integrated Child Development Services, focused on improving health and nutrition amongst young children and pregnant and nursing mothers; the Mid Day Meal Scheme (MDMS) that provides primary students with cooked midday meals in government and local authority schools; and the 2005 National Rural Employment Guarantee Act that guarantees 100 days of wage employment in a financial year to all rural households who volunteer to do unskilled manual work.

The PDS has long suffered problems of leakage through relatively high 'exclusion and inclusion errors' – namely, excluding the needy and including others – and through corruption all along the supply chain. The government claims that drastic improvements in recent years have reduced the leakage rate to 10–15% on average.[107] However, in most states, 60% and more of rural citizens end up being excluded from the scheme.[108] A 2005 government study found that only 57% of intended recipients were reached by the system. Fair-price shops selling subsidised food grains were largely financially unviable, and survived mainly through leakages and diversions of stock.[109]

Large amounts of government-procured food grains go to waste in India because of inadequate storage.[110] From the lack of enough jute bags for farmers to store and transport their produce to insufficient sheltered storage space in government warehouses, mismanagement has resulted in staggering wastage of stocks. Between 1997 and 2007, for example, 183,000 tonnes of wheat, 395,000 tonnes of rice, 22,000 tonnes of paddy rice and 110 tonnes of maize rotted away in government warehouses.[111]

The welfare costs of subsidies not reaching those being targeted, and pilfering along the supply chain, hit the poor the hardest. At the same time, governments bear the fiscal burden of relatively high numbers of unintended beneficiaries of subsidised food programmes. To better target those needing such schemes, relevant state institutions need to have the capacity and resources to re-evaluate policies and ensure adequate implementation. These include better identification and targeting mechanisms, improved delivery and storage facilities, better inter- and intra-agency communication and greater accountability at all levels. In general, reducing leakages 'requires political commitment and participation of the people in the delivery process'.[112] Unfortunately, in most developing countries in Asia political commitment and accountability are rare, and there is often little or no participation by poor and marginalised communities in the formulation and implementation of policies that affect them the most.

Conclusion

Food security is a complex challenge for policymakers in developing Asia. Providing 'physical, social and economic

India's food-security bill

India has taken a new approach to food security with the National Food Security Bill (NFSB) that came into effect in September 2013. The landmark bill, passed into law after a lengthy and rocky legislative process, makes food a legal right and holds the Indian state responsible for providing it. It proposes supplying some 800 million Indians living in poverty – or two-thirds of the population – with 5kg of subsidised rice, wheat and coarse cereals per month at nominal prices of 1–3 rupees. The poorest households are entitled to 35kg of food grains at these prices.[113]

The new bill will deliver this food through India's main food safety-net programme, the targeted public distribution system (PDS, see p. 174), and smaller safety-net schemes. Under the new law, the PDS will be expanded considerably and other safety-net provisions streamlined.

Rights activists who lobbied for universal coverage by the PDS have been disappointed by the bill,[114] although they have welcomed the shift towards a rights-based approach to food security.[115] The food bill's opponents say it is a populist scheme, presenting a huge expense the government can ill afford given the state of India's fiscal deficit.[116]

Under the NFSB, government expenditure on food subsidies will most likely increase, to just over US$20 billion or roughly 1.3% of GDP in the next fiscal year[117] – well below the 3% (approximately US$45bn) suggested by some critics.[118] Also, while the new law has increased the amount of food grains required for distribution through the PDS to 62m tonnes, the system already handles larger quantities.[119]

More concerning is that the PDS has suffered from major problems of corruption, targeting errors and leakages. If the NFSB is to be effective, these flaws must be addressed urgently. The bill also assumes that food insecurity is more about hunger rather than malnutrition. By focusing on cereals that are being eaten in shrinking quantities across India, the bill may not adequately address nutritional needs. Critics say that its exclusion so far of edible oils and pulses from the list of subsidised food items is a serious weakness.[120]

The NFSB also has nothing to say about the challenges of production and livelihood sustainability faced by India's farmers, who also constitute the bulk of India's food insecure.[121] Given growing water scarcity, declining productivity, shrinking agricultural land and climate change, activist Vandana Shiva says: 'The silence on production makes many people feel that the [NFSB] could increase India's dependence on food imports.'[122]

access to safe and nutritious food' to the hundreds of millions who are hungry and malnourished across the region is an urgent task. At the same time, policymakers must realise that food systems are being undermined by a host of factors – such as environmental degradation, declining agricultural productivity, lack of access to productive resources and tenure security, and the impacts of climate change – which cannot be adequately addressed in isolation.

Government policies need to be mindful of the links between food security and other goals. For example, policies to promote economic growth through foreign investment in agricultural resources (such as land) need to be designed and administered with the interests of local communities and the natural environment in mind. Otherwise, they can end up being detrimental to other food-security related goals of raising agricultural productivity and reducing hunger. In pursuing energy security, governments must be aware of the impact on food prices and availability of shifting food crops (such as cereals and edible oils) towards biofuel production, as well as the environmental fallouts of growing biofuel feedstock (such as deforestation, monocropping and loss of biodiversity) and the socio-economic costs (for example, land consolidation in the hands of richer farmers and agri-businesses at the expense of small farmers).

In countries such as Vietnam and the Philippines, focusing on rice self-sufficiency alone is a blinkered approach to food security, especially as food systems in both countries face challenges that will not be alleviated simply by boosting production. Investments in infrastructure, agricultural research and development and support services to farmers are much needed, yet they must be part of a more comprehensive, holistic and integrated national food-security strategy that places the needs of small farmers, and not rice production per se, at its heart. Such an approach becomes all the more important given that climate-change impacts pose a huge risk to agriculture and small farmers in these and other developing countries in Asia. Natural resources, such as land, fresh water and fisheries, are already under great stress from widespread degradation, growing populations and demand for food in these countries.

Decades of corruption, neglect and mismanagement have severely undermined local food systems in several countries in developing Asia and left the needs of those most vulnerable to the abuse of government authority and political power.[123] From India, Bangladesh, Nepal and Pakistan in South Asia to China in East Asia, and the Philippines, Cambodia and Laos in Southeast Asia, the rot of poor governance is deep set and requires urgent attention. Unless the stronghold of vested interests – particularly of powerful and land-owning elites – over leading governing institutions is broken, and good-governance practices become pervasive, even well-intended policies to raise productivity and improve overall food security are unlikely to be entirely successful.

Notes

1 Krystof Obidzinski et al., 'Environmental and Social Impacts of Oil Palm Plantations and their Implications for Biofuel Production in Indonesia', *Ecology and Society*, vol. 17, no. 1, March 2012. Bioethanol is ethanol produced from sugar or starch crops, such as sugar cane, wheat, maize or soybeans, among others, and used as a substitute for petrol. Biodiesel is produced from vegetable oils from crops such as oil palm and rapeseed, and is used as a substitute for diesel fuel.

2 Hong Yang, Yuan Zhou and Junguo Liu, 'Land and water requirements of biofuel and implications for food supply and the environment in China', *Energy Policy*, vol. 37, no. 5, May 2009, pp. 1,877–85.

3 V. Thavasi and S. Ramakrishna, 'Asia energy mixes from socio-economic and environmental perspectives', *Energy Policy*, vol. 37, no. 11, November 2009, p. 4,246.

4 L.S. Shi et al., 'Renewable energy', in G.B. Zhang (ed.), *Report on China's Energy Development for 2010* (Beijing: Economic Science Press, 2010, 1st edition), pp. 133–67 (in Chinese). Cited in Shiyan Chang et al., 'Biofuels development in China: Technology options and policies needed to meet the 2020 target', *Energy Policy*, vol. 51, December 2012, p. 65.

5 Yang, Zhou and Liu, 'Land and water requirements of biofuel', p. 1,878.

6 *Ibid.*

7 Hong Yang and Shaofeng Jia, 'Meeting the basin closure of the Yellow River in China', *International Journal on Water Resources Development*, vol. 24, no. 2, 2008, pp. 265–74. Quoted in Yang, Zhou and Liu, 'Land and water requirements of biofuel', p. 1,881.

8 Eye on Aceh, 'The Golden Crop? Oil palm in post-Tsunami Aceh', September 2007, p. 6, http://www.conflictrecovery.org/bin/The_golden_crop-Palm_oil_in_post-tsunami_Aceh.pdf.

9 Although only some 6.1m ha were productive plantations under harvest, see Obidzinski et al., 'Environmental and Social Impacts of Oil Palm Plantations'.

10 *Ibid.*

11 *Ibid.*

12 'Indonesia 2010 Palm Oil Export Value May Reach $14 Bln-15 Bln – Dep Trade Min', *Palm Oil HQ*, 2 December 2010, http://www.palmoilhq.com/PalmOilNews/indonesia-2010-palm-oil-export-value-may-reach-14-bln-15-bln-dep-trade-min/.

13 In 2003, the EU's Biofuel Directive (2003/30/EC) called for biofuels to comprise 2% of transport fuels used by member states by 2005, increasing to 5.75% by the end of 2010. In 2009, the EU's Renewable Energy Directive (2009/28/EC) set the share of transport fuels derived from renewable sources to reach 10% by 2020. In September 2013, following years of growing concerns around the impact of biofuel production on food prices, the displacement of food crops and greenhouse-gas emissions, the European Parliament voted to restrict the contribution of biofuels to the renewable energy use target for transports fuels to 6%. For more, see Karl Mathiesen, 'European biofuels vote delivers

'desperately weak compromise', *Guardian*, 12 September 2013, http://www.theguardian.com/environment/2013/sep/11/european-biofuels-vote.

14 'Indonesia 2010 Palm Oil Export Value May Reach $14 Bln-15 Bln – Dep Trade Min'.

15 *Ibid.*

16 USDA, 'Indonesia Biofuels Annual', GAIN Report No. ID1222, 14 August 2012, http://gain.fas.usda.gov/Recent%20GAIN%20Publications/Biofuels%20Annual_Jakarta_Indonesia_8-14-2012.pdf.

17 Obidzinski et al., 'Environmental and Social Impacts of Oil Palm Plantations'.

18 According to the Indonesia Forest Climate Alliance (IFCA), 70% of oil-palm plantations have been set up by replacing forestlands, where income generated from timber from the forests cleared is used to offset the costs of setting up the plantation. Quoted in Colin Hunt, 'The costs of reducing deforestation in Indonesia', *Bulletin of Indonesian Economic Studies*, vol. 46, no. 2, May 2010, pp.187–92.

19 Most licences granted for oil-palm plantations during 2000–05 involved peatlands, which need to be drained of water before they can become suitable for plantation, a process which results in huge GHG emissions from peat decomposition. See Paul Burgers and Ari Susanti, 'A new equation for palm oil', in 'Focus: Food Security and Land Grabbing', *The Newsletter*, International Institute for Asian Studies, vol. 58, Autumn/Winter 2011, p. 23.

20 Adhityani Arga, 'Indonesia world's No. 3 greenhouse gas emitter', Reuters, 4 June 2007, http://www.reuters.com/article/2007/06/04/environment-climate-indonesia-dc-idUSJAK26206220070604.

21 Hunt, 'The costs of reducing deforestation in Indonesia', p. 189.

22 'Singapore haze hits record high from Indonesia fires', BBC News, 21 June 2013, http://www.bbc.co.uk/news/world-asia-22998592.

23 Zahari Zen, John F. McCarthy and Piers Gillespie, 'Linking pro-poor policy and oil palm cultivation', Policy Brief, Crawford School of Economics and Government, ANU College of Asia and the Pacific, 2008, p. 2.

24 World Bank, 'Environmental, economic, and social impacts of oil palm in Indonesia: a synthesis of opportunities and challenges', Discussion Paper, May 2010.

25 John F. McCarthy, 'Processes of inclusion and adverse incorporation: oil palm and agrarian change in Sumatra, Indonesia', *The Journal of Peasant Studies*, vol. 37, no. 4, October 2010, pp. 828-30.

[26] *Ibid.*

[27] *Ibid.*

[28] Marcus Colchester et al., *Promised land: palm oil and land acquisition in Indonesia: implications for local communities and indigenous peoples* (Moreton-in-Marsh and Bogor: Forest Programme and Perkumpulan Sawit Watch, 2006), p. 9.

[29] *Ibid.*, p.14.

[30] *Ibid.*

[31] Obidzinski et al., 'Environmental and Social Impacts of Oil Palm Plantations'.

[32] *Ibid.*

[33] Serge Marti, *Losing ground: the human rights impacts of oil palm plantation expansion in Indonesia* (London: Friends of the Earth, Life Mosaic and Sawit Watch, 2008), p. 46, http://www.foei.org/en/resources/publications/pdfs/2008/losingground.pdf/view.

[34] Colchester et al., *Promised land*, p. 14.

[35] As Laura German and George Schoneveld point out, to ensure that they comply with the sustainability criteria set out under RED, member states need biofuel operators to provide proof of compliance, and one way of doing so is by obtaining certification under a European Commission-approved 'voluntary scheme'. However, some of these schemes 'take a minimum compliance approach with EU RED and are devoid of any commitment to social sustainability' including matters of labour rights, land and resource rights, local food security and the identification and mitigation of social impacts of biofuel production. For more, see Laura German and George Schoneveld, 'Social sustainability of EU-approved voluntary schemes for biofuels: Implications for rural livelihoods', Working Paper 75, Center for International Forestry Research (CIFOR), 2011, http://www.cifor.org/publications/pdf_files/WPapers/WP75German.pdf.

[36] Greenpeace, *Frying the Forest: How India's Use of Palm Oil is Having a Devastating Impact on Indonesia's Rainforests, Tigers and the Global Climate* (Bengaluru: Greenpeace, 2012).

[37] Nicola Colbran and Asbjørn Eide, 'Biofuel, the Environment, and Food Security: A Global Problem Explored Through a Case Study of Indonesia', *Sustainable Development Law & Policy*, vol. 9, no. 1, Fall 2008, p. 7. Such measures include 'full compliance with principles of good governance: adequate and representative legislative capacity' linking 'human rights principles to the concrete situations and needs of the country concerned, people's participation, accountability, transparency, rule of law, and an independent judiciary, well versed with human rights' (p. 10).

[38] Mercedita A. Sombilla, Arsenio M. Balisacan, Donato B. Antiporta and Rowell C. Dikitanan, 'Policy responses to the food price crisis and their implications: The case of four Greater Mekong Subregion countries', IFAD Occasional Paper no. 12, 2011, p. 73, http://www.ifad.org/operations/projects/regions/pi/paper/12.pdf.

[39] Government of Vietnam, 'Resolution of the 7th Congress issued by the Session X Central Executive Committee on Agriculture, Farmers and Rural Areas', http://www.isgmard.org.vn/VHDocs/NationalPrograms/Resolution%2026%20(NN-ND-NT)-EN.pdf.

[40] Government of Vietnam, 'Resolution on national food security', 23 December 2009, http://www.isgmard.org.vn/VHDocs/NationalPrograms/Resolution%2063_Food%20security_EN.pDF.

[41] *Ibid*. In Vietnam, the government holds the right to decide on the use of land for different purposes and regularly implements national and provincial level land-use plans that outline land acreage for agricultural (such as rice, annual and perennial crops, forestry and aquaculture) and non-agricultural purposes. Any change in land use needs to be approved by relevant authorities at the provincial or district level. As pointed out in James A. Giesecke et al., 'Rice Land Designation Policy in Vietnam and the Implications of Policy Reform for Food Security and Economic Welfare', p. 3, http://rse.anu.edu.au/news_events/vietnam_workshop_pdfs/paddy.pdf.

[42] Kazunari Tsukada, 'Vietnam: Food Security in a Rice-Exporting Country', in Shinichi Shigetomi, Kensuke Kubo and Kazunari Tsukada, 'The World Food Crisis and the Strategies of Asian Rice Exporters', Institute of Developing Economies, Japan External Trade Organization, *Spot Survey*, no. 32, February 2011, http://d-arch.ide.go.jp/idedp/SPT/SPT003200_005.pdf, p. 55.

[43] Figures for 2008, World Bank, Worldwide Development Indicators (WDIs), 2012.

[44] Around 86% of Vietnam's population are ethnic Kinh, while all remaining 53 ethnic groups are considered minority communities. The largest of these include the Tay, Thai, Muong, Khmer, Mong, Nung, Hoa, Dao and Gia Rai groups. For more, see United Nations Population Fund, 'Ethnic Groups in Vietnam: An analysis of key indicators from the 2009 Viet Nam Population and Housing Census', December 2011, http://unfpa.org/webdav/site/vietnam/shared/Publications%202011/Ethnic_Group_ENG.pdf.

[45] IFAD, 'Vietnam Country Results brief', Rome, June 2011, http://www.ifad.org/governance/replenishment/briefs/vietnam.pdf.

[46] Linh Vu and Paul Glewwe, 'Impacts of rising food prices on poverty and welfare in Vietnam', University of Minnesota, October 2008, http://bit.ly/QwgnAt. The poorest regions are the northwest (with more than 50% living in poverty), the central highlands, the north central coast and the northeast (with poverty rates of 25–30%).

[47] Giesecke et al., 'Rice Land Designation Policy in Vietnam', p. 31.

[48] Steven Jaffee et al., 'From Rice Bowl to Rural Development: Challenges and Opportunities Facing Vietnam's Mekong Delta Region', in Jaffee (ed.), *Vietnam Rice, Farmers and Rural Development: From Successful Growth to Sustainable Prosperity* (World Bank, 2012).

[49] *Ibid.*, p. 37.

[50] 'Vietnam rice exports subdued on lower demand, Thai resurgence', *Thanh Nien News*, 24 October 2013, http://www.thanhniennews.com/index/pages/20131024-vietnam-rice-exports-subdued-on-lower-demand-thai-resurgence.aspx.

[51] Pham Hoang Ngan, 'The Vietnamese rice industry during the global crisis', in Dave Dawe (ed.), *Rice crisis: Markets, policies and food security* (London: Earthscan, 2010), pp. 219–32, cited in IFAD, 'Policy responses to the food price crisis and their implications', Occasional Paper No. 12, December 2011, p. 14, http://www.ifad.org/operations/projects/regions/pi/paper/12.pdf.

[52] Jaffee et al., 'From Rice Bowl to Rural Development', pp. 30–31.

[53] IFAD, 'Interrelationships between labour outmigration, livelihoods, rice productivity and gender roles', Occasional Paper No. 11, December 2010, http://www.ifad.org/operations/projects/regions/pi/paper/11.pdf.

[54] See Roel H. Bosma et al., 'Agriculture Diversification in the Mekong Delta: Farmers' Motives and Contributions to Livelihoods', *Asian Journal of Agriculture and Development*, vol. 2, nos. 1–2, 2005, pp. 49–66.

[55] Bingxin Yu et al., 'Impacts of Climate Change on Agriculture and Policy Options for Adaptation: The Case of Vietnam', IFPRI Discussion Paper 01015, August 2010, http://www.ifpri.org/sites/default/files/publications/ifpridp01015.pdf. In 2000–07, the area under rice cultivation declined by 6%, mainly because of industrial and urban demands on agricultural land.

[56] Steven Jaffee et al., 'Moving the Goal Posts: Vietnam's Evolving

Rice Balance and Other Food Security Considerations', paper given at the Seventh Asian Society of Agricultural Economists (ASAE) International Conference on 'Meeting the Challenges Facing Asian Agriculture and Agricultural Economics Towards a Sustainable Future', held in Hanoi, 13–15 October 2011, p. 14.

57 Author interviews with agricultural experts at the Centre for Agricultural Policy, Institute for Policy and Strategy for Agriculture and Rural Development; Centre for Agrarian Systems Research and Development; World Bank and Oxfam America in Hanoi, November 2011.

58 See FAO, 'Voluntary Guidelines on the Responsible Governance of Tenure of Land, Fisheries and Forests in the Context of National Food Security', 11 May 2012, http://www.fao.org/fileadmin/user_upload/newsroom/docs/VGsennglish.pdf.

59 FAOSTAT 2013.

60 Between 1990 and 2011, the Philippines population grew at an average rate of just over 2% per year. Annual rice consumption per person has been rising in the Philippines since 1990. Analysts suggest this is due to the fact that for the large number of poor and low-income households in the country, rice remains the largest and cheapest source of calories.

61 'Rice overimported in last 3 years of Gloria Macapagal-Arroyo', *Philippine Daily Inquirer*, 18 May 2011, http://www.inquirer.net/specialfeatures/riceproblem/view.php?db=1&article=20110518-337105, and Roel Landingin, 'New administration pledged to make the Philippines self-sufficient in rice', *Financial Times*, 5 July 2010, http://blogs.ft.com/beyond-brics/2010/07/05/54006/?Authorised=false.

62 Arsenio M. Balisacan, Mercedita A. Sombilla and Rowell C. Dikitanan, 'Rice Crisis in the Philippines: Why did it Occur and What are its Policy Implications?', in David Dawe (ed.), *The Rice Crisis: Markets, Policies and Food Security* (FAO: Rome, 2010), p. 133.

63 Landingin, 'New administration pledged to make the Philippines self-sufficient in rice'.

64 According to the World Bank, in 2009 around 18% of Filipinos – roughly 17m – were living on less than US$1.25 a day, while 42% – around 40m – survived on less than US$2 a day. In March 2011, a national survey found that an estimated 4.1m families (20.5%) had experienced involuntary hunger in the three months leading up to the survey period, up two percentage points from the previous quarter.

65 In Marites M. Tiongco and Kris A. Francisco, 'Philippines: Food

Security versus Agricultural Exports?', Philippine Institute for Development Studies, Discussion Paper Series No. 2011–35. The statistic reflects the findings of the FAO's Food Insecurity and Vulnerability Information and Mapping Systems assessment in the Philippines in 2004. For more, see Philippines National Nutrition Council, 'Food Insecurity and Vulnerability Information and Mapping Systems (FIVIMS)', 15 March 2011, http://www.nnc.gov.ph/plans-and-programs/philippine-food-and-nutrition-surveillance-system/fivims/item/95-food-insecurity-and-vulnerability-information-and-mapping-systems-fivims.

[66] Bureau of Agricultural Statistics Philippines, 2013.

[67] Tiongco and Francisco, 'Philippines: Food Security versus Agricultural Exports?', and Balisacan et al., 'Rice Crisis in the Philippines', pp. 135–7.

[68] In 2012, Thai rice production was 37.8m tonnes, more than double 1990 output. See FAOSTAT 2013.

[69] 'Thailand's loses top rice exporter title', *The Nation*, 4 January 2013, http://www.nationmultimedia.com/national/Thailands-loses-top-rice-exporter-title-30197275.html.

[70] Royal Thai Government, 'Rice mortgage scheme to start 7 October', http://www.thaigov.go.th/en/news-room/item/61372-rice-mortgage-scheme-to-start-7-october.html.

[71] Warangkana Chomchuen, 'Thai Government's Tough Job: Selling Rice', *Wall Street Journal*, 21 August 2013, http://blogs.wsj.com/searealtime/2013/08/21/thai-governments-tough-job-selling-rice/.

[72] See, for example, Wichit Chaitrong, 'Scheme headed for disaster: academic', *The Nation*, 2 March 2012, http://www.nationmultimedia.com/business/Scheme-headed-for-disaster-academic-30177126.html; 'Thai rice: Less paddy power', *The Economist*, 14 July 2013, http://www.economist.com/node/21558633; Steve Finch, 'How Rice is Causing a Crisis in Thailand', *The Diplomat*, 10 November 2012, http://thediplomat.com/2012/11/rice-piles-how-thailand-lost-its-spot-as-worlds-top-rice-exporter/; and 'Thailand's rice price scheme: A policy too far?', BBC News, 29 August 2013, http://www.bbc.co.uk/news/business-23875084.

[73] Dan Kedmy, 'How Thailand's Botched Rice Scheme Blew a Big Hole in its Economy', *Time*, 12 July 2013, http://world.time.com/2013/07/12/how-thailands-botched-rice-scheme-blew-a-big-hole-in-its-economy/.

[74] See, for example, Apornrath Phoonphongphiphat and Naveen

Thukral, 'Insight: Smuggling rice to Thailand - like coals to Newcastle', Reuters, 14 July 2013, http://www.reuters.com/article/2013/07/14/us-thailand-rice-insight-idUSBRE96D0E520130714.

75 'Pledging scheme "aids rich"', *Bangkok Post*, 5 August 2013, http://www.bangkokpost.com/news/local/363001/rice-pledging-helps-rich-as-well-as-farmers.

76 Petchanet Pratruangkrai and Yossarin Boonwiwattanakarn, 'Farmers see only a part of rice scheme's rewards', *The Nation*, 15 July 2013, http://www.nationmultimedia.com/business/Farmers-see-only-a-part-of-rice-schemes-rewards-30210409.html.

77 *Ibid*. See also Petchanet Pratruangkrai and Achara Pongvutitham, 'Rice associations, farmers call for urgent review of pledging policy', *The Nation*, 7 August 2012, http://www.nationmultimedia.com/business/Rice-associations-farmers-call-for-urgent-review-0-30187778.html.

78 Paritta Wangkiat, 'Researchers call for an end to pledging', Thai Development Research Institute Press Release, 19 August 2013, http://tdri.or.th/en/tdri-insight/researchers-call-for-an-end-to-pledging/.

79 Vikram Nehru, 'Thailand's rice policy gets sticky', East Asia Forum, 13 June 2012, http://www.eastasiaforum.org/2012/06/13/thailand-s-rice-policy-gets-sticky/.

80 See, for example, Wangkiat, 'Researchers call for an end to pledging', and Samarendy Mohanty, 'Why does everyone hate the Thai rice mortgage scheme?', International Rice Research Institute, 5 November 2012, http://irri.org/blogs/item/why-does-everyone-hate-the-thai-rice-mortgage-scheme.

81 United Nations, 'Annual Report of the Secretary General on the Work of the Organization 1998', Document A/53/1, United Nations, New York, 1998, paragraph 114.

82 See, for example, Mahbub ul Haq Human Development Centre, *Human Development in South Asia 2010/2011: Food Security in South Asia* (Karachi, Pakistan: Oxford University Press, 2011), pp. 5–6, http://mhhdc.org/wp-content/themes/mhdc/reports/HDSA%20 2010-2011.pdf.

83 See, for example, Rabah Arezki and Markus Bruckner, 'Food prices and political instability', IMF Working Paper 11/62, March 2011, http://www.imf.org/external/pubs/ft/wp/2011/wp1162.pdf.

84 Transparency International, 'Corruption Perceptions Index 2012', http://www.transparency.org/cpi2012/results.

85 Afghanistan, Bangladesh, Nepal and Pakistan all appear in the

lowest tenth percentile. Developing Southeast Asian countries that ranked poorly for political stability and absence of violence included the Philippines, Myanmar, Thailand, Indonesia, Cambodia and Laos. See World Bank 'Worldwide Governance Indicators 2013', http://data.worldbank.org.

86 See Czeriza Valencia, 'Gov't urged to review rules on rice imports', *Philippine Star*, 3 August 2012, http://www.philstar.com/bansa/2012/08/02/833988/pasahero-ng-bus-pinag-iingat.

87 Kristine L. Alave, 'Rice overimported in last 3 years of Gloria Macapagal-Arroyo', *Philippine Daily Inquirer*, 18 May 2011, http://www.noypi.ph/index.php/nation/3859-nfa-audit-team-calls-arroyo-rice-imports-a-scam.html.

88 Transparency International, *Global Corruption Report 2008: Corruption in the Water Sector* (Cambridge: Cambridge University Press, 2008), p. 81.

89 *Ibid.*

90 Delon Porcalla, 'CARP deadline can't be met', *Philippine Star*, 23 January 2013, http://www.philstar.com/headlines/2013/01/23/900042/carp-deadline-cant-be-met.

91 Land Watch Asia, 'Defending the Gains of Tenurial Reform', Philippines Country Paper, p. 145, http://www.angoc.org/dmdocuments/SRL_Philippines.pdf.

92 Benjamin Shepherd, 'Redefining food security in the face of foreign land investors: The Philippine Case', NTS-Asia Research Paper No. 6, Singapore 2011, p. 16, http://www.rsis.edu.sg/nts/HTML-Newsletter/Report/pdf/NTS-Asia_Ben_Shepherd.pdf.

93 Land Watch Asia, 'Defending the Gains of Tenurial Reform', p. 140.

94 Thin Lei Wi, 'Activists sceptical about land reform under new Philippines President', ANGOC 2010, http://www.angoc.org/Angoc-News/activists-sceptical-about-land-reform-under-new-philippines-president.html.

95 Jatropha is a drought-resistant shrub or tree grown in various parts of the world including Southeast Asia and India. It is well suited to arid and semi-arid environments and wasteland, requires little irrigation or fertiliser, and is pest-resistant. Jatropha seeds have a very high (30–40%) oil content and there has been increasing interest in using this oil as a non-edible feedstock for biodiesel in Asia and elsewhere. For more, see Rakesh Sarin et al., 'Jatropha–Palm biodiesel blends: An optimum mix for Asia', *Fuel*, vol. 86, no. 10–11, July–August 2007, pp. 1,365–71.

96 Author interviews with food security and agricultural experts in

Manila, November 2011. See also 'National Convergence Initiative', Philippines Department of Agrarian Reform, http://www.dar.gov.ph/national-convergence-initiative; and ANGOC, 'Mindanao Lands for AgriInvestments or Agri-Colonialism?', 16 September 2009, http://www.angoc.org/portal/wp-content/uploads/2010/08/10/mindanao-lands-for-agri-investments-or-agri-colonialism-proceedings/Mindanao-Lands-for-Agri-Investments-or-Agri-Colonialism-Proceedings.pdf.

97 Antonio B. Quizon, 'The rush for Asia's farmland: Its impact on land rights and security of the rural poor', *Lokniti*, vol. 18, no. 1, March 2012, p. 14.

98 *Ibid*.

99 Jeanne Frances Illo and Dante Dalabajan, 'Weathering the Crisis, Feeding the Future: Philippine Food Justice Report', Oxfam, September 2011, p. 21, http://www.oxfam.org/sites/www.oxfam.org/files/cr-weathering-crises-feeding-future-philippines-261011.pdf.

100 Carlos H. Conde, 'Philippines suspends Chinese-funded projects in wake of scandal', *New York Times*, 25 September 2007, http://www.nytimes.com/2007/09/25/business/worldbusiness/25iht-peso.1.7629492.html?_r=1&.

101 Launched in 1998, Raskin is Indonesia's public rice-distribution programme, which provides subsidised rice to the poor. In 2012, the government allocated 15.7tr rupiah to subsidise 3.41m tonnes of rice to be distributed to 17.5m households. For more, see the International Labour Organization, 'Raskin: Rice Subsidy for the Poor', http://www.ilo.org/dyn/ilossi/ssimain.viewScheme?p_lang=en&p_geoaid=360&p_scheme_id=3153.

102 Hastuti et al., 'The Effectiveness of the Raskin Program', Research Report, SMERU Research Institute, 2008, p. 16, http://www.smeru.or.id/report/research/raskin2007/raskin2007_eng.pdf.

103 Benjamin A. Olken, 'Corruption and the costs of redistribution: Micro evidence from Indonesia', *Journal of Public Economics*, vol. 90, no. 4–5, May 2006, pp. 853–70, http://ideas.repec.org/a/eee/pubeco/v90y2006i4-5p853-870.html.

104 The Philippines' subsidised rice programme, in place since the 1960s, is administered by the government's National Food Authority (NFA) and provides rice at lower-than-market prices to general consumers through accredited retailers, government agencies and private institutions. For more, see Luisa Fernandez and Rashiel Velarde, 'Who Benefits from Social Assistance in the Philippines? Evidence from

the Latest National Household Surveys', The World Bank Group and Australian Government Aid Programme, Philippine Social Protection Note No. 4, March 2012, http://www-wds.worldbank.org/servlet/WDSContentServer/WDSP/IB/2012/06/08/000333038_20120608041740/Rendered/PDF/694160BRI0P1180PUBLIC00FINAL0PSPN04.pdf.

[105] When people benefit from a subsidy but were not originally meant to be its beneficiaries, this is referred to as an 'inclusion error'. Conversely, an exclusion error refers to intended beneficiaries (in this case, the poor) not receiving a subsidy.

[106] A targeted public distribution system (PDS) replaced a universal PDS that had existed until the early 1990s, and was dismantled as the country embraced economic reforms under the structural adjustment programmes of the IMF and World Bank. For more, see Madhura Swaminathan, 'Structural Adjustment, Food Security and System of Public Distribution of Food', *Economic and Political Weekly*, vol. 31, no. 26 (29 June 1996), pp. 1,665–72.

[107] 'Targeted PDS leakage dips to 10%-15%', *Times of India*, 13 December 2011, http://articles.timesofindia.indiatimes.com/2011-12-13/india/30511227_1_tomato-prices-leakage-public-distribution.

[108] Madhura Swaminathan, 'Programmes to Protect the Hungry: Lessons from India', UN Department of Economic and Social Affairs Working Paper No. 70, ST/ESA/2008/DWP/70, October 2008, http://www.un.org/esa/desa/papers/2008/wp70_2008.pdf.

[109] GoI, 'Performance Evaluation of Targeted Public Distribution System (TPDS)', Programme Evaluation Organisation, Planning Commission, New Delhi, March 2005, http://planningcommission.nic.in/reports/peoreport/peo/peo_tpds.pdf.

[110] See, for example, 'Foodgrains rot in India's godown with no space to store', *India Today*, 22 June 2011, http://indiatoday.intoday.in/story/foodgrains-rot-in-india-godown-no-space-to-store-bumper-crop/1/142399.html.

[111] Amitabha Bhattasali, 'India food grain waste revealed', BBC News, 4 July 2008, http://news.bbc.co.uk/1/hi/business/7489816.stm.

[112] Swaminathan, 'Programmes to Protect the Hungry'.

[113] See GoI, 'National Food Security Bill 2013', http://www.thehindu.com/multimedia/archive/01404/National_Food_Secu_1404268a.pdf.

[114] See, for example, Reetika Khera and Jean Drèze, 'A bill that asks too much of the poor', *The Hindu*, 5 September 2012, http://www.thehindu.com/opinion/lead/article3859455.ece.

[115] See, for example, Revati Laul, 'The Food Security Bill Can Help To Protect The People From Poverty And Insecurity', *Tehelka*, 7 September 2013, http://www.tehelka.com/the-food-security-bill-can-help-to-protect-the-people-from-poverty-and-insecurity/.

[116] See, for example, William Thomson, 'India's Food Security Problem', *The Diplomat*, 2 April 2012, http://thediplomat.com/2012/04/indias-food-security-problem/.

[117] Bharat Ramaswami, Milind Murugkar and Ashok Kotwal, 'Correct costs of the Food Security Bill', *Financial Express*, 23 September 2013, http://www.financialexpress.com/news/correct-costs-of-the-food-security-bill/1156251/0.

[118] See, for example, Surjit S. Bhalla, 'Manmonia's FSB: 3% of GDP', *Indian Express*, 6 July 2013, http://archive.indianexpress.com/news/manmonias-fsb-3--of-gdp/1138195/. GDP calculations are based on Reserve Bank of India figures at factor cost, base year 2004–05, http://www.rbi.org.in/scripts/PublicationsView.aspx?id=15121.

[119] In 2011/12 India's food-grain procurement exceeded 63m tonnes; in 2012/13 it reached 72m tonnes. See Anil Padmanabhan, 'Five myths about the food security bill', LiveMint.com, 1 September 2013, http://www.livemint.com/Opinion/xZJcbnt9CPPz9nSaEU-WRkO/Five-myths-about-the-Food-Security-Bill.html.

[120] See, for example, 'Traders urge govt to club pulses with Food Security Act', *Business Standard*, 27 August 2013, http://www.business-standard.com/article/specials/traders-urge-govt-to-club-pulses-with-food-security-act-113082700409_1.html; and Sachin Kumar Jain, 'India's National Food Security Act: Entitlement of Hunger', *Ethics in Action*, vol. 4, no. 2, April 2010, http://www.humanrights.asia/resources/journals-magazines/eia/eiav4n2/indias-national-food-security-act-entitlement-of-hunger.

[121] Vandana Shiva, 'India's food security Act: Myths and reality', Al Jazeera, 21 September 2013, http://www.aljazeera.com/indepth/opinion/2013/09/201398122228705617.html.

[122] *Ibid.*

[123] Illo and Dalabajan, 'Weathering the Crisis, Feeding the Future', p. 5.

CONCLUSION

The geopolitical impact of Asia's astounding economic growth over the last two decades has been such that this is already being called the 'Asian Century'. China and India have enjoyed spectacular rises as global economic heavy-weights, while other countries such as Indonesia, Vietnam, the Philippines, Cambodia, Malaysia and Thailand have grown rapidly. However, this is only one side of the story. An equally important aspect is that, as home to the largest number of poor and malnourished people in the world, Asia also lies at the centre of global food-security concerns.

National agricultural systems have so far kept heavily populated Asian countries largely self-sufficient in the most important crops. However, domestic agriculture is operating under increasingly widespread environmental degradation and pollution, looming water shortages and the unpredictable effects of climate change. As it becomes ever more difficult to meet rising demand for food using national resources, the reliance on imports is accordingly increasing.

Within Asia, the livelihoods of many communities relying on agriculture are under threat, and strains are already beginning to show in the social fabric as community land and smallholder farms have been expropriated for urban, industrial or agribusiness use. Clashes between the authorities and dispossessed farmers or communities have become more frequent – sometimes deadly – in China, Cambodia, the Philippines and Vietnam. At times, in countries such as Bangladesh and India, people have also rioted over the high consumer cost of food. A related risk of water wars on the continent is increasing as neighbouring nations – particularly China and India – tussle over the use of cross-border rivers in agriculture and industry. Access to fisheries, among other resources, underpins some of the territorial disputes between China and several Southeast Asian countries in the South China Sea.

Combined, food insecurity within Asia and a larger reliance on imports would mean a greater drain on international food stocks and higher food prices on the world market, with all the consequences that might result for consumers and producers.

China and India: food security, conflict and geopolitics

Over the past few decades, the fact that China and India have managed to remain largely self-sufficient in staple cereal crops has greatly helped the relative stability of international food markets. For major food-importing countries, it has helped keep additional pressure off global food stocks and therefore prices. Current trends suggest, however, that in coming years these countries may need to rely more on food imports of cereals and other essential items (such as oil seeds, edible oils, sugar and pulses). The extent to which such imports will be necessary will depend partly on domestic achievements in raising agricultural productivity. This requires direct efforts to: increase spending on agricultural research and development (R&D); expand irrigation infrastructure, sustainable water use and conservation; curb the use of agricultural land for non-food purposes; improve extension (that is, training and advisory) services, financial-support services and the efficient and sustainable use of new technologies; increase multi-cropping; and strengthen local capacity to deal with natural disasters and climate change. At the same time, there is a strong role for wider policy goals of poverty reduction and improvements in other human-development indicators (such as health and education).

Although efforts to boost productivity have been renewed in recent years in both China and India, these often clash with other relevant policies, such as those concerning the use of agricultural resources. The encroachment of industrial and urban-development projects on agricultural land, facilitated by investor-friendly policies and poor governance, including corrupt and apathetic government officials, is a particular case in point. China's 'new wave of urbanisation' has been described as 'at times a violent struggle between the state and farmers'.[1] In a growing number of instances where rural households have been evicted from their lands using force or on unfair terms, it has led to violent confrontations between civilian actors and others such as government authorities, private-security forces and armed law-enforcement agencies. Social unrest and violence related to forced or unfair land evictions have been on the rise in recent years; such events serve to undermine the legitimacy of the Chinese government and heighten the risk of political instability and violent conflict at the local level.

In India too, the issue of land acquisition for industrial development has become a flashpoint between rural communities and government authorities across the country. There have been numerous incidents of violent clashes between local villagers and armed forces, with fatalities and serious injuries becoming common. In general, India has recently seen a huge wave of civic activism, with issues relating to government ineffectiveness such as corruption, poor law enforcement and what is overall seen as government apathy towards the wider sufferings of ordinary Indians. Within this context, the continuation of forced land evictions without adequate consent or compensation is likely to fuel further conflict and political instability in India.

One reason the two Asian giants seem likely to rely more on imports is that there is still tremendous scope for incomes to expand in both countries and, as the ranks of their middle classes swell, demand will continue to surge for food overall and for higher-value agricultural products such as animal products, sugar, edible oils, fruits and vegetables in particular. Given the constraints they face on natural resources, as well as the adverse impacts of climate change, ongoing urbanisation and industrialisation, the Chinese and Indian governments may decide that resorting to greater imports of certain water- and land-intensive crops is a more efficient way of meeting their rising demand at home than trying to grow these crops domestically. That would, however, pit them against other food-importing countries in Asia and elsewhere on the international food market, exerting serious upwards pressure on global food prices. This, in turn, would damage human security and risk exposing to food insecurity those food-importing countries where large sections of the population are poor and vulnerable.

As Chinese and Indian policymakers weigh their choices, their decisions will have real geopolitical implications. In addition to opening up access to agricultural markets in other countries, more Chinese and Indian agribusinesses have been investing in agricultural land overseas. In many reported cases, this is being done mainly, if not solely, to produce crops to supply domestic markets at home rather than in the host countries. The leasing of large tracts of agricultural land in Asia, Africa and South America is intended to provide China and India with not just the agricultural land required to grow the food and feed the crops they need, but also to save water at home. Although the data on such deals remains unclear, Chinese investments, both private and state-led, in agricultural production and land deals in Southeast Asia (in, for example, Indonesia, the Philippines, Cambodia, Malaysia, Laos and Myanmar), Africa and South America have been expanding. A growing number of Indian companies, supported by their government, have also been investing in agricultural land and food production in countries such as Indonesia, Ethiopia, Uganda, Rwanda, the Democratic Republic of the Congo (DRC), Gabon, Madagascar, Argentina and Brazil.

Unfortunately, these deals often seem to be occurring in developing countries where there are already relatively high levels of food insecurity, and where poor and marginalised communities lack adequate access to productive resources. Host governments have often been leasing out land without adequate consultation with local communities that live and work on the land in question. In cases where compensation has been offered, it is usually unsatisfactory from the farmer's perspective, and evicted communities are left without access to their traditional source of livelihood and food security. In many cases, local agricultural systems are being adversely affected by large-scale industrial, plantation-style agricultural production driven not by local food-security needs, but by the preferences of investing companies. Again, the implications of these developments for local food security, and the potential for violent conflict and political instability at the local level, are substantial. Several countries have experienced a serious public backlash against foreign investments in agricultural land, which are seen as a form of neo-imperialism or neocolonialism. Both Brazil and Argentina, for example, have passed laws restricting foreign ownership of land and the purchase of land by local companies controlled by foreigners – laws mainly intended to curb rapidly growing Chinese investments.

Arguably, if done in a socially responsible and sustainable manner, China and India's respective overseas agricultural investments may be able to bring long-term benefits to local communities. The Voluntary Guidelines on the Responsible Governance of Tenure of Land, Fisheries and Forests in the Context of National Food Security,[2] endorsed by the FAO Committee on World Food Security in May 2012, outline how investment in agriculture could be undertaken for the benefit of local communities and the sustainability of agricultural resources. They include, for example, the principle that responsible investments should be conducted transparently and align with the broader objectives of socio-economic growth and sustainable development of smallholders in host countries. Agricultural investments 'should do no harm, safeguard against dispossession of legitimate tenure right holders and environmental damage, and should respect human rights'.[3] The guidelines also stress the need for investors to work together with host governments and local communities who hold tenure, and:

> contribute to … poverty eradication; food security and sustainable use of land, fisheries and forests; support local communities [and] rural development; promote and secure local food production systems; enhance social and economic sustainable development; create employment; diversify livelihoods [and] provide benefits to the country and its people, including the poor and most vulnerable.[4]

Unfortunately, these guidelines are voluntary and are unlikely to be embraced by governments and investors without a mechanism to enforce them.

Meanwhile, China's growing demand for fish and declining fisheries are increasingly coinciding with its strategic interests in the Western Pacific. As the country's distant-water fishing fleet is venturing increasingly farther offshore in search of catch, it is sailing into disputed waters. Other than being of great strategic importance in the region and potentially rich in oil and gas, the disputed South China Sea, for example, also offers bountiful fishing grounds. It has been attracting more Chinese fishing vessels, which often find themselves competing with other fishing vessels from countries that also have territorial claims over the sea, including the Philippines and Vietnam. This has seen the number of incidents in the South China Sea escalate, often resulting in major diplomatic tensions that tend to spill over into the different multilateral forums involving the claimant states.[5] Southeast Asian countries like the Philippines and Vietnam rely on fish in far greater measure than China for their food security – as fish is the main source of protein for people in Southeast Asia – and for their overall economic development.[6] China's quest for more fish and its increasingly aggressive stance over its territorial claims in the South China Sea, therefore, heighten the risk of conflict in the region. The situation calls, among other things, for policymakers and others to realise that adhering to international norms with respect to the sustainable use and management of fisheries is vital for 'the long-term sustainability of fisheries resources, regional peace and stability and food security and livelihoods for millions of Asians'.[7] In addition, there is a strong need for improved fisheries' management in the region, with enhanced licensing and monitoring, including 'better compliance, stock assessments and cooperation enacted in bilateral and multilateral fishing agreements'.[8]

Finally, tensions between China and India over the disputed Arunachal Pradesh border underline the need for an overarching and permanent framework for cooperation on shared cross-border water resources, particularly the Yarlung Tsangpo/Brahmaputra River. Given the existing tensions, it is important for these countries to be engaged in permanent institutional frameworks for cooperation that involve: collecting and disseminating trusted data on shared resources; transparency on development projects that may have cross-border implications; and measures that facilitate the development of shared norms around the protection, conservation and efficient use of precious resources by all relevant parties.[9] These efforts should be accompanied by wider measures towards building an integrated, holistic and comprehensive approach to water security in both China and India, cutting across 'regional, national, provincial and local levels so as to put the accent on water efficiency, conservation, environmental protection, rainwater capture and water recycling'.[10]

Small farmers and food security across Asia

To effectively deal with the challenge of mitigating food insecurity and ensuring the long-term sustainability of food systems in Asia, policymakers need to design integrated national food-security strategies. In doing so, they also must ensure that proposed solutions to counter one aspect of food insecurity do not undermine goals related to others. To begin with, such strategies could include sound and efficient social safety-net programmes that help to protect vulnerable communities – in rural as well as urban areas – against shocks to food prices and supplies, and help such communities to emerge from multidimensional poverty. More broadly, policymakers in Asia would do well to place smallholders at the heart of their concern.[11]

Small farmers already produce around 80% of all the food Asia consumes. As urban areas expand across the region, adding to the growing demand for more and different food, small farmers' role in food production becomes even more important in terms of sustainably increasing agricultural yields from shrinking resources. Data shows that relatively smaller farmers tend to produce much higher levels of agricultural output per unit area than larger farms, and are more efficient in terms of total factor productivity (the average product of an aggregate of different inputs such as land, labour and capital).[12] This is because, amongst other things, they use complex farming systems 'highly adapted to local conditions, allowing them to sustainably manage production in harsh environments'.[13] They also employ high-quality labour, in terms of the personal commitment of family members involved, and use mixed inputs, such as manure and compost, rather than relying only on chemical fertilisers and pesticides.[14]

It is, however, only when small farmers have secure access to productive resources such as agricultural land, fresh water, fisheries and forestland that they are assured of gaining from them in the long-term and therefore fully motivated to invest in the sustainable use and management of these resources, with knock-on positive effects for the environment and agricultural productivity.[15]

In developing countries in Asia, the process of land reform has been excruciatingly slow and, in many countries, the existence of land-reform laws has not translated into widespread equitable distribution of land or greater security of tenure. Small farming households would benefit from the process of land redistribution and titling – for example, in the Philippines – being speeded up and properly implemented. Land titles and tenure certificates including the names of both male and female heads of households would ensure greater equity of access. Rural communities in countries such as Cambodia require greater protection from forced evictions and, where such communities consent to being relocated, adequate compensation, resettlement and rehabilitation (including suitable job opportunities) should be ensured, with provisions for legal recourse to those who might need it.

As Vietnam's export-driven performance underlines, agricultural land-use policies better address domestic food-security needs when they take into consideration the livelihood strategies of local communities, rather than being driven by trade-related goals. Given the growing scarcity of land in Asia, it would be prudent for governments in the region to reconsider plans for large-scale conversion of agricultural land for non-agricultural purposes in light of future food-security requirements. If governments follow Indonesia's lead in producing more biofuels, they risk ensuring their energy security at the expense of rural farmers' security and the future sustainability of local food systems.[16] There might also be a role for the international promotion of sustainable oil-palm cultivation. Such efforts include the Roundtable on Sustainable Palm Oil,[17] which has a certification system encouraging better practices for the production and management of oil palm. There have also been suggestions that large importing countries such as India and China adopt a 'zero deforestation' policy when choosing suppliers, avoiding those who do not use sustainable production methods.[18] A problem is that such guidelines remain voluntary and difficult to monitor. As mentioned earlier, the EU does have a mandatory Renewable Energy Directive that lays out the sustainability standards for all biofuels that are consumed within its jurisdiction, but serious concerns have emerged around the directive's impact on smallholders and their livelihoods.

Forestlands are a significant source of livelihoods and food security for indigenous communities in South and Southeast

Asia. Yet, their customs of ownership remain widely unacknowledged and relatively little effort has been made to identify and provide land-use rights and titles to such communities. Doing this would help vulnerable communities legally protect themselves against unwanted private-investment projects as well as government-initiated development that threaten to uproot them from their traditional sources of livelihoods and way of life, without consent or guarantees of adequate compensation or rehabilitation. Governments would also do well to provide recourse to fair conflict resolution when disputes over land rights and tenure do occur.

In a region where agriculture remains largely at the mercy of timely and adequate rainfall, irrigation has a serious role to play in raising agricultural productivity. At the same time, unsustainable irrigation practices and the use of dilapidated infrastructure have worsened the problem of water shortages, scarcity and degradation in parts of Asia. Equitable access to water resources needs to be coupled with the widespread adoption of sustainable irrigation practices such as drip-feed irrigation and rainwater harvesting, and improvements in existing irrigation infrastructure. In countries such as India, Bangladesh and Nepal, drip-irrigation kits have been successfully adopted by many small farmers, and such technology could help decelerate water over-exploitation rates and improve water-use efficiency.

Public investment in agriculture and rural development

Farm incomes are dependent on productivity, and raising productivity requires improvements in agricultural infrastructure such as irrigation, transport, communication, markets and storage facilities. It depends on access to support services such as extension services, credit facilities and insurance cover, education and skills training, timely weather and market updates, and more. As climate change raises the unpredictability of conditions which agricultural production relies on, the need for greater agricultural R&D to increase the capacity of small farmers to rise to these challenges becomes all the more important. Private companies could potentially play a more significant role in agricultural R&D in Asia, given their capacity to develop and deliver new technologies for boosting productivity. Private-sector investment, however, tends to focus mainly on 'high value and market-oriented production systems'.[19] The improvement of natural-resource management and biodiversity maintenance 'typically fall outside the scope of purely private innovations'.[20] Moreover, as a 2012 inter-agency report to the G20 Mexico Presidency on sustainable agricultural-productivity growth for small farms points out:

> Greater protection of intellectual property, rapid progress in molecular biology and the integration of global output and input markets have generated strong incentives for the private sector to invest in [agricultural] R&D. The adoption of such possibly scale-biased technologies requires management skills and effective learning which could limit access by smallholders, in particular women, to innovative inputs in developing countries. At the same time, the record of private research in natural resource management and in maintaining biodiversity is limited, with the exception of a few public-private initiatives.[21]

This makes public investment in agriculture in Asia all the more important, particularly in infrastructure development, R&D and extension services. Unfortunately, the general trend over the past two decades in developing countries in the region has been one of declining or relatively low levels of agricultural investment, both in real terms and as a proportion of total agricultural GDP. This trend needs to be forcefully reversed; agricultural R&D, in particular, requires serious attention. At the same time, governments need to acknowledge that agricultural-growth policies are most effective when they are part of wider rural development projects that help alleviate poverty, malnourishment and illiteracy, and also focus on goals such as providing reliable and stable access to electricity, sanitation, clean drinking water, education and healthcare services, amongst others. In all such projects, a focus on women and improvements in their overall social and economic conditions is particularly important. Despite comprising nearly half of the agricultural workforce in the region, women continue to lack sufficient access to resources that would allow them to raise their productivity and incomes.

Environmental sustainability and climate change

Declining productivity in developing Asian countries is in many ways a fallout of input-intensive, industrial agricultural practices. The overuse of agrochemicals, such as fertilisers and pesticides, expansion of monocultures and intensive farming in ecologically delicate environments have caused widespread land and water degradation and loss of biodiversity. This has had serious consequences for farm productivity and incomes. Climate change will challenge food production and productivity even further.

In 2008, the report of the International Assessment of Agricultural Knowledge, Science and Technology for Development (IAASTD)[22] suggested ways for governments to improve environmental sustainability. These included ending subsidies on pesticides and fertiliser and replacing them with incentives to use ecologically sound agricultural practices such as 'integrated pest management'.[23] (This combines the use of pest-resistant crops with different planting or harvesting times, crop rotation, the disruption of pest mating and the destruction of pest habitats, depending on local conditions.) Other policies put forth included payments to farmers and local communities for 'ecosystem services' – essentially paying them for, among other things, keeping land farmed, looking after the land around it, keeping waterways clean, treating any farm animals well and maintaining the social structure of rural areas.[24] The strengthening of local markets and the creation of alternative consumer markets for certified organic and sustainably produced food were also recommended,[25] as were the development of resource-conservation technologies, the breeding of crop varieties for tolerance to climatic variations and pests, and biological substitutes for agrochemicals.[26]

Today, there are serious challenges associated with both the use of genetically modified (GM) crops and the current emphasis on biotechnological R&D (often to the exclusion of other agricultural research). As it is undertaken mainly by private firms, innovation in agricultural biotechnology is driven by profit rather than the need to increase agricultural productivity and efficiency in developing countries.[27]

Monsanto, for example, has genetically engineered soybean seeds to be resistant to its own 'Roundup' herbicide (thus allowing farmers to spray weeds without killing the crop around them). However, these seeds are patented, so they cannot be stored, shared, reproduced or replanted by farmers who have chosen to purchase them. Consequently, these farmers find themselves repeatedly buying the company's expensive seed and chemical packages.[28] In the US, the near-ubiquitous use of Roundup in GM soybean-planted fields has been accompanied by the evolution of resistant 'super weeds' that require increasing quantities of Roundup, other herbicides or manual labour to be killed, pushing up on-farm costs.[29] In 2009, Monsanto scientists detected and subsequently admitted pink-bollworm resistance to its first-generation Bt Cotton variety (designed to produce its own insecticide) used in four districts in Gujurat, India.[30] Critics claim that GM crops containing pest-resistant proteins accelerate resistance in pests and may eventually render useless traditional biological insecticides widely used by farmers in the past.[31]

As a solution, the IAASTD report underlined the need to take a 'problem-oriented approach' to the use of biotechnology in pursuing food security and environmental sustainability, whereby the priorities of local farmers and agricultural systems are the main focus of investment.

The IAASTD argues that the utility of biotechnologies is best assessed in the context of how they impact on the abilities of local communities to collectively own expertise and germplasm (plant genetic resources such as seed and trees in nurseries), and the capacity to undertake further agricultural research independently. In this light, R&D emphasising participatory breeding projects and agro-ecology becomes all the more pertinent.[32]

As the impacts of climate change begin to bear down on agriculture in highly vulnerable Asian countries, there is a critical need for bottom-up approaches to climate-change adaptation. Comprehensive adaptation and mitigation policies are required not just at the national level, but also at the local level, where emphasis is placed on both 'hard' adaptive measures – for example, the creation of infrastructure such as sea dykes and reinforced and more durable buildings – as well as 'soft' adaptive measures 'like community mobilisation plans, social-safety nets, insurance schemes, livelihood diversification, increasing institutional capacity' and so on.[33] Such an approach views climate-change adaptation 'as a complex set of responses to existing climatic and non-climatic factors that contribute to people's vulnerability', rather than something that requires a mainly technical response to lessen the impact of climate change.[34]

Regional policies: ASEAN and SAARC

In South and Southeast Asia, regional responses to dealing with food insecurity have come from within SAARC and ASEAN respectively. The latter has been engaging with the problem for some time now, establishing 'a labyrinth of food security authorities and arrangements' through 'declarations, programmes, frameworks and plans'.[35] The ASEAN Integrated Food Security Framework and the Strategic Plan of Action on ASEAN Food Security were endorsed in October 2008 and adopted in 2009, with the main goal of ensuring long-term food security and improving the livelihoods of farmers in the ASEAN region. In November 2009, the ASEAN Ministerial Meeting on Agriculture and Forestry endorsed the ASEAN Multi-Sectoral Framework on Climate Change: Agriculture, Fisheries and Forestry towards Food Security, a comprehensive framework covering sectors such as agriculture, fisheries, livestock, forestry, environment, health and energy. Also, the ASEAN Plus Three (China, Japan and Korea) signed an agreement on 7 October 2011 to establish an emergency rice reserve; the Emergency Rice Reserve Accord initially establishes a stockpile of 787,000 tons of rice that countries in need can draw on if natural disasters cause sudden instabilities in supply and production.[36]

However, more needs to be done. While there have been a growing number of initiatives on food security in ASEAN in the past decade, it remains unclear how much they actually alleviate related concerns around human and national security. This is mainly because there is little agreement on how the success of these initiatives could be evaluated.[37] Moreover, the design of such policies is not necessarily based on the question of what small rural farmers in the region need to be able to lift themselves out of poverty and food insecurity. Rather, it remains focused on national food production and availability, responding to food shortages in times of disaster, and an overall calorie-counting approach that neglects, amongst other things, challenges of malnutrition and related socio-economic, environmental and governance issues.[38] This is a very limited approach to an extremely broad and complex problem, and by not adopting a multi-sectoral approach, governments are setting themselves up for failure when it comes to tackling the challenges food systems face in the region.

SAARC member states, meanwhile, signed an agreement on establishing a SAARC Food Bank in 2007. With a few modifications, the initiative essentially revives a 1988 agreement to establish a SAARC Food Security Reserve (SFSR). This was a dismal failure due to the lack of any real effort to implement it. Recent experience shows that the SAARC Food Bank is suffering similar problems, 'i.e. a lack of necessary storage infrastructure and the failure of member nations to produce accessible agricultural surpluses'.[39] South Asia is home to more poor and malnourished people than any other part of the world. This means states in the region have a particular responsibility to step up efforts to provide safety nets for their vulnerable populations to deal with lack of adequate access to food, as well as more long-term measures to revitalise agricultural productivity through sustainable measures such as those discussed above.

As regional organisations try to help mitigate food insecurity in member countries through a collective regional approach, their policies will also need to be informed by a holistic view of food systems, and the understanding that these are shaped by a complex set of interrelated issues. Therefore, regional approaches to food security need to be in sync with national policies, both requiring an appreciation of the different factors shaping food systems at the local level and a consideration of how regional governance mechanisms may be relevant to resolve them. These mechanisms, either new or improved, must allow for effective implementation, monitoring and evaluation of policies in a clear and transparent manner.[40]

Effective governance

Ultimately, effective governance is essential to dealing with food insecurity in developing countries in Asia. The mismanagement of agricultural resources discussed in this book often stems not only from poorly designed policies, but also from the poor implementation of potentially sound policies and government ineffectiveness – usually rooted in weak institutional capacity, lack of accountability and transparency, and corruption within state institutions. These factors play a role, for example, in the vast quantities of foodstuffs wasted, misdirected, siphoned off onto the black market or otherwise lost via subsidised food programmes such as India's PDS. The mere presence of well-meaning laws and policies is futile without the will and capacity to implement them properly, or to re-evaluate and adjust policies on the advice of the communities at which they are aimed.

Efforts to improve governance are under way to varying degrees in developing countries across the region. Civil-society groups, NGOs, international institutions and media personalities have been playing an important role here, for example, in pushing governments to be accountable and transparent in their dealings with respect to natural resources and emphasising the rights of communities that rely on them. However, such efforts need to be amplified at local, national and regional levels.

Some national governments within Asia have already taken steps towards improving agricultural productivity, saving water or mitigating against climate change. The Philippines has been promoting renewed agricultural investment, China has recently put water-conservation measures in place and India has a National Action Plan on Climate Change. However, these measures alone are insufficient. Food security is a complex challenge, demanding complex integrated solutions to prevent unintended consequences or negative feedback loops.

All of these issues highlight the need for food security to be understood and tackled in a far more joined-up manner than is currently the case. Food and agricultural policies are not pursued in a vacuum, but need to take account of the wider socio-economic, environmental and political contexts within which they are embedded. And, as this book shows, the stakes are high. Failure to meet the challenge of food security in Asia poses a real threat to the most populous continent's economic and political stability – and in doing so, could affect us all.

Notes

1 'China's farmers choose death over eviction', *Straits Times*, 10 September 2013, in Reuters picture caption, http://www.stasiareport.com/the-big-story/asia-report/china/story/chinas-farmers-pick-death-over-eviction-20130910.

2 FAO, 'Voluntary Guidelines on the Responsible Governance of Tenure of Land, Fisheries and Forests in the Context of National Food Security', 11 May 2012, http://www.fao.org/fileadmin/user_upload/newsroom/docs/VGsennglish.pdf. These guidelines were developed through a partnership of international, regional and national organisations of different types interested in achieving global changes in governance of tenure. Ten regional, one private-sector and four civil-society consultation meetings were organised between September 2009 and November 2010. These meetings brought together almost 1,000 people from more than 130 countries. The participants represented government institutions, civil society, private sector, academia and UN agencies.

3 *Ibid.*

4 *Ibid.*

5 Centre for International Security Studies, 'Food Security in Asia: A report for policymakers', March 2013, p. 27, http://sydney.edu.au/arts/ciss/downloads/CISS_Food_Security_Policy_Report.pdf.

6 *Ibid.*, p. 28.

7 *Ibid.*

[8] *Ibid.*

[9] Brahma Chellany, *Water: Asia's New Battleground* (Washington DC: Georgetown University Press, 2011), p. 305.

[10] *Ibid*, pp. 306–07.

[11] Leonardo Q. Montemayor, 'Right to food in Asia and the Pacific – The worm's point-of-view', keynote address, World Food Day, 16 October 2007, ftp://ftp.fao.org/docrep/fao/010/ai385e/ai385e00.pdf.

[12] Peter Rossett, 'The Multiple Functions and Benefits of Small Farm Agriculture: In the Context of Global Trade Negotiations', Policy Brief No. 4, *Food First*, The Institute for Food and Development Policy, September 1999, pp. 6–7, http://www.foodfirst.org/sites/www.foodfirst.org/files/pdf/pb4.pdf. See also Robert Eastwood, Michael Lipton and Andrew Newell, 'Farm size', in Prabhu Pingali and Robert Evenson (eds), *Handbook of Agricultural Economics, Volume 4* (Oxford: Elsevier, 2010), pp. 3,323–93 and Peter Hazell, 'Five Big Questions about Five Hundred Million Small Farms', paper presented at the IFAD Conference on 'New Directions for Smallholder Agriculture', 24–25 January, 2011, http://www.ifad.org/events/agriculture/doc/papers/hazell.pdf.

[13] *Ibid.*

[14] *Ibid.*, p. 14.

[15] IFAD, 'Empowering the rural poor through access to land', http://www.ifad.org/events/icarrd/factsheet_eng.pdf.

[16] Nicola Colbran and Asbjørn Eide, 'Biofuel, the Environment, and Food Security: A Global Problem Explored Through a Case Study of Indonesia', *Sustainable Development Law & Policy*, vol. 9, no. 1, Fall 2008, p. 7.

[17] See http://www.rspo.org/.

[18] Greenpeace, *Frying the Forest: How India's Use of Palm Oil is Having a Devastating Impact on Indonesia's Rainforests, Tigers and the Global Climate* (Bengaluru: Greenpeace, 2012).

[19] *Ibid.*

[20] 'Sustainable Agricultural Productivity Growth and Bridging the Gap for Small Family Farms', Interagency Report to the Mexican G20 Presidency Final Draft, 27 April 2012, p. 27, http://ictsd.org/downloads/2012/05/g20-2012-27-april-2.pdf.

[21] *Ibid.*

[22] International Assessment of Agricultural Knowledge, Science and Technology for Development (IAASTD), *Agriculture at a Crossroads: Executive Summary of the Synthesis Report* (Washington DC: Island Press, 2009), http://www.unep.org/dewa/agassessment/reports/IAASTD/EN/Agriculture%20at%20a%20

Crossroads_Executive%20 Summary%20of%20the%20 Synthesis%20Report%20 (English).pdf.

23 Mary L. Flint, *IPM In Practice: Principles and Methods of Integrated Pest Management* (Richmond, CA: University of California Division of Agriculture and Natural Resources, 2012), 2nd edition, p. 2.

24 For a formal definition of ecosystem services, see UNEP, *Ecosystems and Human Well-being: A Framework for Assessment* (Washington DC: Island Press, 2003), p. 49, in which they are referred to as the benefits gained from ecosystems, including 'provisioning services such as food and water; regulating services such as flood and disease control; cultural services such as spiritual, recreational, and cultural benefits; and supporting services, such as nutrient cycling, that maintain the conditions for life on Earth'.

25 IAASTD, *Agriculture at a Crossroads: Executive Summary of the Synthesis Report*.

26 *Ibid.*

27 See, for example, Miguel A. Altieri and Peter Rosset, 'Ten Reasons Why Biotechnology Will Not Ensure Food Security, Protect the Environment and Reduce Poverty in the Developing World', AgBio Forum, *The Journal of Agrobiotechnology Management and Economics*, vol. 2, nos. 3 and 4, 1999, p. 156, http://agbioforum.org/v2n34/v2n34a03-altieri.pdf.

28 *Ibid.*

29 See, for example, William Neuman and Andrew Pollack, 'Farmers Cope With Roundup-Resistant Weeds', *New York Times*, 3 May 2010, http://nyti.ms/1jkbJpf; Matt McGrath, 'Agent Orange chemical in GM war on resistant weeds', BBC News, 19 September 2012, http://bbc.in/1eQWAax; and Tom Philpott, 'Meet the weeds that Monsanto can't beat', for *Mother Jones* as part of the Guardian Environment Network, 21 December 2012, http://www.theguardian.com/environment/2012/dec/21/weeds-monsato-cant-beat.

30 Monsanto, 'Pink Bollworm Resistance to GM Cotton in India', http://www.monsanto.com/newsviews/Pages/india-pink-bollworm.aspx. Monsanto noted that it then 'worked closely with farmers to contain the resistance and implement effective insect resistance management programs'. See also 'Monsanto accepts its Bt cotton failed pest-control tests', *The Times of India*, 7 March 2010, http://articles.timesofindia.indiatimes.com/2010-03-07/india/28117555_1_bollworm-bt-cotton-cry1ac; Dinesh C. Sharma, 'Bt cotton has failed admist Monsanto', *India Today*, 6 March 2010,

http://indiatoday.intoday.in/story/Bt+cotton+has+failed+admits+Monsanto/1/86939.html; and Priscilla Jebaraj, 'Bt cotton ineffective against pest in parts of Gujarat, admits Monsanto', *The Hindu*, 6 March 2010.

31 Altieri and Rosset, 'Ten Reasons Why Biotechnology Will Not Ensure Food Security, Protect the Environment and Reduce Poverty in the Developing World'.

32 *Ibid.*

33 Pamela McElwee, 'The Social Dimensions of Adaptation to Climate Change in Vietnam', World Bank Discussion Paper No. 12, December 2010, p. 31, http://climatechange.worldbank.org/sites/default/files/documents/Vietnam-EACC-Social.pdf.

34 Bernadette P. Resurreccion, Edsel E. Sajor and Elizabeth Fajber, *Climate Adaptation in Asia: Knowledge Gaps and Research Issues in Southeast Asia* (London: ISET-International and DFID, 2008), p. 3.

35 Lorraine Elliot, 'Securitizing Food Futures in the Asia-Pacific: Human Securitizing Regional Frameworks', *Asia Security Initiative*, Policy Series No. 15, RSIS Centre for Non-Traditional Security Studies, Singapore 2011, p. 9, http://www.rsis.edu.sg/NTS/resources/research_papers/MacArthur_Working_Paper_Lorraine%20Elliott2.pdf.

36 'Southeast Asia to start emergency rice reserve', *Japan Times*, 9 October 2011, http://grainmarketnews.com/2011/10/rice-market-news/southeast-asia-to-start-emergency-rice-reserve. Although the agreement is said to be the 'first permanent mechanism for establishing an emergency rice reserve in the region', it follows a 1979 ASEAN Emergency Rice Reserve that proved ineffective. An East Asian Emergency Rice Reserve was also piloted between 2003 and 2010. For more, see Roehlano M. Briones, 'Regional Cooperation for Food Security: The Case of Emergency Rice Reserves in the ASEAN Plus Three', ADB Sustainable Development Working Paper Series No. 18, November 2011, http://www.adb.org/sites/default/files/adb-wp18-regional-cooperation-food-security.pdf.

37 Elliot, 'Securitizing Food Futures in the Asia-Pacific'.

38 *Ibid.*

39 Matthew J.D. Robinson, *Regional Grain Banking for Food Security: Past and Present Realities from SAARC Initiatives* (Jaipur: CUTS International, 2011), p. 11.

40 Elliot, 'Securitizing Food Futures in the Asia-Pacific'.

INDEX

I

J

K

L

M

N

O

V

W

Y

Z

Adelphi books are published eight times a year by Routledge Journals, an imprint of Taylor & Francis, 4 Park Square, Milton Park, Abingdon, Oxfordshire OX14 4RN, UK.

A subscription to the institution print edition, ISSN 1944-5571, includes free access for any number of concurrent users across a local area network to the online edition, ISSN 1944-558X. Taylor & Francis has a flexible approach to subscriptions enabling us to match individual libraries' requirements. This journal is available via a traditional institutional subscription (either print with free online access, or online-only at a discount) or as part of the Strategic, Defence and Security Studies subject package or Strategic, Defence and Security Studies full text package. For more information on our sales packages please visit www.tandfonline.com/librarians_pricinginfo_journals.

2014 Annual Adelphi Subscription Rates			
Institution	£585	$1,028 USD	€865
Individual	£207	$353 USD	€282
Online only	£512	$899 USD	€758

Dollar rates apply to subscribers outside Europe. Euro rates apply to all subscribers in Europe except the UK and the Republic of Ireland where the pound sterling price applies. All subscriptions are payable in advance and all rates include postage. Journals are sent by air to the USA, Canada, Mexico, India, Japan and Australasia. Subscriptions are entered on an annual basis, i.e. January to December. Payment may be made by sterling cheque, dollar cheque, international money order, National Giro, or credit card (Amex, Visa, Mastercard).

For a complete and up-to-date guide to Taylor & Francis journals and books publishing programmes, and details of advertising in our journals, visit our website: **http://www.tandfonline.com.**

Ordering information:
USA/Canada: Taylor & Francis Inc., Journals Department, 325 Chestnut Street, 8th Floor, Philadelphia, PA 19106, USA. **UK/Europe/Rest of World:** Routledge Journals, T&F Customer Services, T&F Informa UK Ltd., Sheepen Place, Colchester, Essex, CO3 3LP, UK.

Advertising enquiries to:
USA/Canada: The Advertising Manager, Taylor & Francis Inc., 325 Chestnut Street, 8th Floor, Philadelphia, PA 19106, USA. Tel: +1 (800) 354 1420. Fax: +1 (215) 625 2940. **UK/Europe/Rest of World**: The Advertising Manager, Routledge Journals, Taylor & Francis, 4 Park Square, Milton Park, Abingdon, Oxfordshire OX14 4RN, UK. Tel: +44 (0) 20 7017 6000. Fax: +44 (0) 20 7017 6336.

The print edition of this journal is printed on ANSI conforming acid-free paper by Bell & Bain, Glasgow, UK.